Collins
French
Grammar

HarperCollins Publishers
Westerhill Road
Bishopbriggs
Glasgow
G64 2QT
Great Britain

Second Edition 2011

Reprint 10 9 8 7 6 5 4 3 2 1

© HarperCollins Publishers 2004, 2011

ISBN 978-0-00-736782-5

Collins® is a registered trademark of
HarperCollins Publishers Limited

www.collinslanguage.com

A catalogue record for this book is available
from the British Library

Typeset by Davidson Publishing Solutions,
Glasgow

Printed in India by
Gopsons Papers Ltd

Acknowledgements
We would like to thank those authors and
publishers who kindly gave permission for
copyright material to be used in the Collins
Word Web. We would also like to thank
Times Newspapers Ltd for providing
valuable data.

SERIES EDITOR
Rob Scriven

MANAGING EDITOR
Gaëlle Amiot-Cadey

EDITORIAL COORDINATION
Susanne Reichert
Rachel Smith

CONTRIBUTORS
Wendy Lee
Di Larkin

We would like to give special thanks to
Di Larkin, Foreign Languages Consultant,
and Irene Muir, Faculty Head, Belmont
House School, for all their advice on
teaching practice in today's classroom.
Their contributions have been invaluable
in the writing of this book.

CONTENTS

Note on trademarks
Entered words which we have reason to believe constitute trademarks have been designated as such. However, neither the presence nor the absence of such designation should be regarded as affecting the legal status of any trademark.

FOREWORD FOR LANGUAGE TEACHERS

The *Easy Learning French Grammar* is designed to be used with both young and adult learners, as a group reference book to complement your course book during classes, or as a recommended text for self-study and homework/coursework.

The text specifically targets learners from *ab initio* to intermediate or GCSE level, and therefore its structural content and vocabulary have been matched to the relevant specifications up to and including Higher GCSE.

The approach aims to develop knowledge and understanding of grammar and to improve the ability of learners to apply it by:

- defining parts of speech at the start of each major section, with examples in English to clarify concepts
- minimizing the use of grammar terminology and providing clear explanations of terms both within the text and in the Glossary
- illustrating all points with examples (and their translations) based on topics and contexts which are relevant to beginner and intermediate course content

The text helps you develop positive attitudes to grammar learning in your classes by:

- giving clear, easy-to-follow explanations
- prioritizing content according to relevant specifications for the levels
- sequencing points to reflect course content, e.g. verb tenses
- highlighting useful Tips to deal with common difficulties
- summarizing Key points at the end of sections to consolidate learning

In addition to fostering success and building a thorough foundation in French grammar, the optional Grammar Extra sections will encourage and challenge your learners to further their studies to higher and advanced levels.

INTRODUCTION FOR STUDENTS

Whether you are starting to learn French for the very first time, brushing up on topics you have studied in class, or revising for your GCSE exams, the *Easy Learning French Grammar* is here to help. This easy-to-use guide takes you through all the basics you will need to speak and understand modern, everyday French.

Newcomers can sometimes struggle with the technical terms they come across when they start to explore the grammar of a new language. The *Easy Learning French Grammar* explains how to get to grips with all the parts of speech you will need to know, using simple language and cutting out jargon.

The text is divided into sections, each dealing with a particular area of grammar. Each section can be studied individually, as numerous cross-references in the text point you to relevant points in other sections of the book for further information.

Every major section begins with an explanation of the area of grammar covered on the following pages. For quick reference, these definitions are also collected together on pages viii–xii in a glossary of essential grammar terms.

> **What is a verb?**
> A **verb** is a 'doing' word which describes what someone or something does, what someone or something is, or what happens to them, for example, *be*, *sing*, *live*.

Each grammar point in the text is followed by simple examples of real French, complete with English translations, to help you understand the rules. Underlining has been used in examples throughout the text to highlight the grammatical point being explained.

➤ If you are talking about a part of your body, you usually use a word like *my* or *his* in English, but in French you usually use the definite article.

Tourne <u>la</u> tête à gauche.	Turn your head to the left.
Il s'est cassé <u>le</u> bras.	He's broken his arm.
J'ai mal à <u>la</u> gorge.	My throat hurts.

In French, as with any foreign language, there are certain pitfalls which have to be avoided. **Tips** and **Information** notes throughout the text are useful reminders of the things that often trip learners up.

Key points sum up all the important facts about a particular area of grammar, to save you time when you are revising and help you focus on the main grammatical points.

Key points

✔ With masculine singular nouns → use **un**.

✔ With feminine singular nouns → use **une**.

✔ With plural nouns → use **des**.

✔ **un**, **une** and **des** → change to **de** or **d'** in negative sentences.

✔ The indefinite article is not usually used when you say what jobs people do, or in exclamations with **quel**.

If you think you would like to continue with your French studies to a higher level, check out the **Grammar Extra** sections. These are intended for advanced students who are interested in knowing a little more about the structures they will come across beyond GCSE.

Grammar Extra!

If you want to use an adjective after **quelque chose, rien, quelqu'un** and **personne**, you link the words with **de**.

quelqu'un **d'**important	someone important
quelque chose **d'**intéressant	something interesting
rien **d'**amusant	nothing funny

Finally, the supplement at the end of the book contains **Verb Tables**, where 93 important French verbs (both regular and irregular) are declined in full. Examples show you how to use these verbs in your own work. If you are unsure of how a verb conjugates in French, you can look up the **Verb Index** on pages 95–105 to find either the conjugation of the verb itself, or a cross-reference to a model verb, which will show you the pattern that verb follows.

We hope that you will enjoy using the *Easy Learning French Grammar* and find it useful in the course of your studies.

GLOSSARY OF GRAMMAR TERMS

ABSTRACT NOUN a word used to refer to a quality, idea, feeling or experience, rather than a physical object, for example, *size, reason, happiness*. Compare with concrete noun.

ADJECTIVE a 'describing' word that tells you more about a person or thing, such as their appearance, colour, size or other qualities, for example, *pretty, blue, big*.

ADVERB a word usually used with verbs, adjectives or other adverbs that gives more information about when, where, how or in what circumstances something happens, for example, *quickly, happily, now*.

AGREE (to) to change word endings according to whether you are referring to masculine, feminine, singular or plural people or things.

AGREEMENT changing word endings according to whether you are referring to masculine, feminine, singular or plural people or things.

APOSTROPHE S an ending ('s) added to a noun to show who or what someone or something belongs to, for example, *Danielle's dog, the doctor's wife, the book's cover*.

ARTICLE a word like *the, a* and *an*, which is used in front of a noun. See also definite article, indefinite article and partitive article.

AUXILIARY VERB a verb such as *be, have* and *do* when it is used with a main verb to form tenses and questions.

BASE FORM the form of the verb without any endings added to it, for example, *walk, have, be, go*. Compare with infinitive.

CARDINAL NUMBER a number used in counting, for example, *one, seven, ninety*. Compare with ordinal number.

CLAUSE a group of words containing a verb.

COMPARATIVE an adjective or adverb with *-er* on the end of it, or *more* or *less* in front of it, that is used to compare people, things or actions, for example, *slower, less important, more carefully*.

COMPOUND NOUN a word for a living being, thing or idea, which is made up of two or more words, for example, *tin-opener, railway station*.

CONCRETE NOUN a word that refers to an object you can touch with your hand, rather than to a quality or idea, for example, *ball, map, apples*. Compare with abstract noun.

CONDITIONAL a verb form used to talk about things that would happen or would be true under certain conditions, for example, *I would help you if I could*. It is also used to say what you would like or need, for example, *Could you give me the bill?*

CONJUGATE (to) to give a verb different endings according to whether you are referring to *I, you, they* and so on, and according to whether you are referring to past, present or future, for example, *I have, she has, he had*.

CONJUGATION a group of verbs which have the same endings as each other or change according to the same pattern.

CONJUNCTION a word such as *and*, *because* or *but* that links two words or phrases of a similar type, or two parts of a sentence, for example, *Diane and I have been friends for years.; I left because I was bored.*

CONSONANT a letter of the alphabet which is not a vowel, for example, *b, f, m, s, v.* Compare with vowel.

CONSTRUCTION an arrangement of words together in a phrase or sentence.

DEFINITE ARTICLE the word *the.* Compare with indefinite article.

DEMONSTRATIVE ADJECTIVE one of the words *this, that, these* and *those* used with a noun to point out a particular person or thing, for example, *this woman, that dog.*

DEMONSTRATIVE PRONOUN one of the words *this, that, these* and *those* used instead of a noun to point out people or things, for example, *That looks fun.*

DIRECT OBJECT a noun referring to the person or thing affected by the action described by a verb, for example, *She wrote her name; I shut the window.* Compare with indirect object.

DIRECT OBJECT PRONOUN a word such as *me, him, us* and *them* which is used instead of a noun to stand in for the person or thing directly affected by the action described by the verb. Compare with indirect object pronoun.

EMPHATIC PRONOUN a word used instead of a noun when you want to emphasize something, for example, *Is this for me?; 'Who broke the window?' – 'He did.'* Also called stressed pronoun.

ENDING a form added to a verb, for example, *go —> goes,* and to adjectives, nouns and pronouns depending on whether they refer to masculine, feminine, singular or plural things or persons.

EXCLAMATION a word, phrase or sentence that you use to show you are surprised, shocked, angry and so on, for example, *Wow!; How dare you!; What a surprise!*

FEMININE a form of noun, pronoun or adjective that is used to refer to a living being, thing or idea that is not classed as masculine.

FUTURE a verb tense used to talk about something that will happen or will be true.

GENDER whether a noun, pronoun or adjective is feminine or masculine.

IMPERATIVE the form of a verb used when giving orders and instructions, for example, *Shut the door!; Sit down!; Don't go!*

IMPERFECT one of the verb tenses used to talk about the past, especially in descriptions, and to say what was happening or used to happen, for example, *I used to walk to school; It was sunny at the weekend.* Compare with perfect.

IMPERSONAL VERB one which does not refer to a real person or thing, and where the subject is represented by *it,* for example, *It's going to rain; It's 10 o'clock.*

INDEFINITE ADJECTIVE one of a small group of adjectives used to talk about people or things in a general way, without saying who or what they are, for example, *several, all, every.*

INDEFINITE ARTICLE the words *a* and *an*. Compare with **definite article**.

INDEFINITE PRONOUN a small group of pronouns such as *everything, nobody* and *something*, which are used to refer to people or things in a general way, without saying exactly who or what they are.

INDIRECT OBJECT a noun used with verbs that take two objects. For example, in *I gave the carrot to the rabbit, the rabbit* is the indirect object and *carrot* is the direct object. Compare with **direct object**.

INDIRECT OBJECT PRONOUN when a verb has two objects (a direct one and an indirect one), the indirect object pronoun is used instead of a noun to show the person or the thing the action is intended to benefit or harm, for example, *me* in *He gave me a book* and *Can you get me a towel?* Compare with **direct object pronoun**.

INDIRECT QUESTION used to tell someone else about a question and introduced by a verb such as *ask, tell* or *wonder*, for example, *He asked me what the time was; I wonder who he is.*

INFINITIVE the form of the verb with *to* in front of it and without any endings added, for example, *to walk, to have, to be, to go.* Compare with **base form**.

INTERROGATIVE ADJECTIVE a question word used with a noun to ask *who?, what?* or *which?*, for example, *What instruments do you play?; Which shoes do you like?*

INTERROGATIVE PRONOUN one of the words *who, whose, whom, what* and *which* when they are used instead of a noun to ask questions, for example, *What's happening?; Who's coming?*

INVARIABLE used to describe a form which does not change.

IRREGULAR VERB a verb whose forms do not follow a general pattern or the normal rules. Compare with **regular verb**.

MASCULINE a form of noun, pronoun or adjective that is used to refer to a living being, thing or idea that is not classed as feminine.

NEGATIVE a question or statement which contains a word such as *not, never* or *nothing*, and is used to say that something is not happening, is not true or is absent, for example, *I never eat meat; Don't you love me?*

NOUN a 'naming' word for a living being, thing or idea, for example, *woman, desk, happiness, Andrew.*

NUMBER used to say how many things you are referring to or where something comes in a sequence. See also **ordinal number** and **cardinal number**.

OBJECT a noun or pronoun which refers to a person or thing that is affected by the action described by the verb. Compare with **direct object, indirect object** and **subject**.

OBJECT PRONOUN one of the set of pronouns including *me, him* and *them*, which are used instead of the noun as the object of a verb or preposition. Compare with **subject pronoun**.

ORDINAL NUMBER a number used to indicate where something comes in an order or sequence, for example, *first, fifth, sixteenth.* Compare with **cardinal number**.

PART OF SPEECH a word class, for example, *noun, verb, adjective, preposition, pronoun*.

PARTITIVE ARTICLE the words *some* or *any*, used to refer to part of a thing but not all of it, for example, *Have you got any money?*; *I'm going to buy some bread*.

PASSIVE a form of the verb that is used when the subject of the verb is the person or thing that is affected by the action, for example, *we were told*.

PAST PARTICIPLE a verb form which is used to form perfect and pluperfect tenses and passives, for example, *watched, swum*. Some past participles are also used as adjectives, for example, *a broken watch*.

PERFECT one of the verb tenses used to talk about the past, especially about actions that took place and were completed in the past. Compare with imperfect.

PERSON one of three classes: the first person (*I, we*), the second person (*you* singular and *you* plural), and the third person (*he, she, it* and *they*).

PERSONAL PRONOUN one of the group of words including *I, you* and *they* which are used to refer to yourself, the people you are talking to, or the people or things you are talking about.

PLUPERFECT one of the verb tenses used to describe something that had happened or had been true at a point in the past, for example, *I had forgotten to finish my homework*.

PLURAL the form of a word which is used to refer to more than one person or thing. Compare with singular.

POSSESSIVE ADJECTIVE one of the words *my, your, his, her, its, our* or *their*, used with a noun to show that one person or thing belongs to another.

POSSESSIVE PRONOUN one of the words *mine, yours, hers, his, ours* or *theirs*, used instead of a noun to show that one person or thing belongs to another.

PREPOSITION a word such as *at, for, with, into* or *from*, which is usually followed by a noun, pronoun or, in English, a word ending in *-ing*. Prepositions show how people and things relate to the rest of the sentence, for example, *She's at home; a tool for cutting grass; It's from David*.

PRESENT a verb form used to talk about what is true at the moment, what happens regularly, and what is happening now, for example, *I'm a student; I travel to college by train; I'm studying languages*.

PRESENT PARTICIPLE a verb form ending in *-ing* which is used in English to form verb tenses, and which may be used as an adjective or a noun, for example, *What are you doing?; the setting sun; Swimming is easy!*

PRONOUN a word which you use instead of a noun, when you do not need or want to name someone or something directly, for example, *it, you, none*.

PROPER NOUN the name of a person, place, organization or thing. Proper nouns are always written with a capital letter, for example, *Kevin, Glasgow, Europe, London Eye*.

QUESTION WORD a word such as *why, where, who, which* or *how* which is used to ask a question.

REFLEXIVE PRONOUN a word ending in *-self* or *-selves*, such as *myself* or *themselves*, which refers back to the subject, for example, *He hurt himself.; Take care of yourself.*

REFLEXIVE VERB a verb where the subject and object are the same, and where the action 'reflects back' on the subject. A reflexive verb is used with a reflexive pronoun such as *myself, yourself, herself,* for example, *I washed myself.; He hurt himself.*

REGULAR VERB a verb whose forms follow a general pattern or the normal rules. Compare with irregular verb.

RELATIVE PRONOUN a word such as *that, who* or *which,* when it is used to link two parts of a sentence together.

SENTENCE a group of words which usually has a verb and a subject. In writing, a sentence has a capital letter at the beginning and a full stop, question mark or exclamation mark at the end.

SINGULAR the form of a word which is used to refer to one person or thing. Compare with plural.

STEM the main part of a verb to which endings are added.

STRESSED PRONOUN a word used instead of a noun when you want to emphasize something, for example, *Is this for me?; 'Who broke the window?' – 'He did.'* Also called emphatic pronoun.

SUBJECT the noun in a sentence or phrase that refers to the person or thing that does the action described by the verb or is in the state described by the verb, for example, *My cat doesn't drink milk.* Compare with object.

SUBJECT PRONOUN a word such as *I, he, she* and *they* which carries out the action described by the verb. Pronouns stand in for nouns when it is clear who is being talked about, for example, *My brother isn't here at the moment. He'll be back in an hour.* Compare with object pronoun.

SUBJUNCTIVE a verb form used in certain circumstances to express some sort of feeling, or to show doubt about whether something will happen or whether something is true. It is only used occasionally in modern English, for example, *If I were you, I wouldn't bother.; So be it.*

SUPERLATIVE an adjective or adverb with *-est* on the end of it or *most* or *least* in front of it, that is used to compare people, things or actions, for example, *thinnest, most quickly, least interesting.*

SYLLABLE a consonant+vowel unit that makes up all or part of a word, for example, *ca-the-dral (3 syllables), im-po-ssi-ble (4 syllables).*

TENSE the form of a verb which shows whether you are referring to the past, present or future.

VERB a 'doing' word which describes what someone or something does, what someone or something is, or what happens to them, for example, *be, sing, live.*

VOWEL one of the letters *a, e, i, o* or *u.* Compare with consonant.

NOUNS

What is a noun?
A **noun** is a 'naming' word for a living being, thing or idea, for example, *woman, happiness, Andrew.*

Using nouns

➤ In French, all nouns are either <u>masculine</u> or <u>feminine</u>. This is called their <u>gender</u>. Even words for things have a gender.

➤ Whenever you are using a noun, you need to know whether it is masculine or feminine as this affects the form of other words used with it, such as:

- adjectives that describe it
- articles (such as le or une) that go before it
- pronouns (such as il or elle) that replace it

➡ *For more information on **Adjectives, Articles** or **Pronouns**, see pages 25, 12 and 42.*

➤ You can find information about gender by looking the word up in a dictionary. When you come across a new noun, always learn the word for *the* or *a* that goes with it to help you remember its gender.

- le or un before a noun tells you it is masculine
- la or une before a noun tells you it is feminine

➤ We refer to something as <u>singular</u> when we are talking about just one of them, and as <u>plural</u> when we are talking about more than one. The singular is the form of the noun you will usually find when you look a noun up in the dictionary. As in English, nouns in French change their form in the plural.

➤ Adjectives, articles and pronouns are also affected by whether a noun is singular or plural.

Tip

Remember that you have to use the right word for *the* and *a* according to the gender of the French noun.

Gender

1 Nouns referring to people

➤ Most nouns referring to men and boys are <u>masculine</u>.

un homme	a man
un roi	a king

➤ Most nouns referring to women and girls are <u>feminine</u>.

une fille	a girl
une reine	a queen

➤ When the same word is used to refer to either men/boys or women/girls, its gender usually changes depending on the sex of the person it refers to.

un camarade	a (male) friend
une camarade	a (female) friend
un Belge	a Belgian (man)
une Belge	a Belgian (woman)

Grammar Extra!

Some words for people have only <u>one</u> possible gender, whether they refer to a male or a female.

un bébé	a (male or female) baby
un guide	a (male or female) guide
une personne	a (male or female) person
une vedette	a (male or female) star

➤ In English, we can sometimes make a word masculine or feminine by changing the ending, for example, *Englishman* and *Englishwoman,* or *prince* and *princess*. In French, very often the ending of a noun changes depending on whether it refers to a man or a woman.

un Anglais	an Englishman
une Anglaise	an Englishwoman
un prince	a prince
une princesse	a princess
un employé	a (male) employee
une employée	a (female) employee

➡ *For more information on **Masculine and feminine forms of words**, see page 7.*

For further explanation of grammatical terms, please see pages viii-xii.

2 Nouns referring to animals

➤ In English we can choose between words like *bull* or *cow*, depending on the sex of the animal we are referring to. In French too there are sometimes separate words for male and female animals.

| **un** taureau | a bull |
| **une** vache | a cow |

➤ Sometimes, the same word with different endings is used for male and female animals.

| **un** chien | a (male) dog |
| **une** chienne | a (female) dog, a bitch |

> ### Tip
> When you do not know or care what sex the animal is, you can usually use the masculine form as a general word.

➤ Words for other animals do not change according to the sex of the animal. Just learn the French word with its gender, which is always the same.

| **un** poisson | a fish |
| **une** souris | a mouse |

3 Nouns referring to things

➤ In English, we call all things – for example, *table, car, book, apple* – '*it*'. In French, however, things are either <u>masculine</u> or <u>feminine</u>. As things do not divide into sexes the way humans and animals do, there are no physical clues to help you with their gender in French. Try to learn the gender as you learn the word.

➤ There are lots of rules to help you:

- words ending in -e are generally <u>feminine</u> (**une boulangerie** a baker's; **une banque** a bank)

- words ending in a consonant (any letter except *a, e, i, o* or *u*) are generally <u>masculine</u> (**un aéroport** an airport; **un film** a film)

➤ There are some exceptions to these rules, so it is best to check in a dictionary if you are unsure.

4 NOUNS

➤ These endings are often found on <u>masculine nouns</u>.

Masculine ending	Examples
-age	<u>un</u> vill<u>age</u> a village <u>un</u> voy<u>age</u> a journey <u>un</u> ét<u>age</u> a floor <u>le</u> from<u>age</u> cheese BUT: <u>une</u> image a picture <u>une</u> page a page <u>la</u> plage the beach
-ment	<u>un</u> apparte<u>ment</u> a flat <u>un</u> bâti<u>ment</u> a building <u>le</u> ci<u>ment</u> cement <u>un</u> vête<u>ment</u> a garment
-oir	<u>un</u> mir<u>oir</u> a mirror <u>un</u> coul<u>oir</u> a corridor <u>le</u> s<u>oir</u> the evening <u>un</u> mouch<u>oir</u> a handkerchief
-sme	<u>le</u> touri<u>sme</u> tourism <u>le</u> raci<u>sme</u> racism
-eau	<u>un</u> cad<u>eau</u> a present <u>un</u> chap<u>eau</u> a hat <u>un</u> gât<u>eau</u> a cake <u>le</u> rid<u>eau</u> the curtain BUT: <u>la</u> peau skin <u>l'</u>eau water
-eu	<u>un</u> j<u>eu</u> a game
-ou	<u>un</u> ch<u>ou</u> a cabbage <u>le</u> gen<u>ou</u> the knee
-ier	<u>le</u> cah<u>ier</u> the exercise book <u>un</u> quart<u>ier</u> an area <u>un</u> escal<u>ier</u> a staircase
-in	<u>un</u> magas<u>in</u> a shop <u>un</u> jard<u>in</u> a garden <u>un</u> dess<u>in</u> a drawing <u>le</u> v<u>in</u> the wine BUT: <u>la</u> fin the end <u>une</u> main a hand

For further explanation of grammatical terms, please see pages viii-xii.

-on	un champign**on** a mushroom un ball**on** a ball **le** citr**on** the lemon BUT: **une** mais**on** a house **la** sais**on** the season

➤ The following types of word are also masculine:

- names of the days of the week, and the months and seasons of the year

le lundi	Monday
septembre prochain	next September
le printemps	Spring

- the names of languages

le français	French
le portugais	Portuguese
Tu apprends le français depuis combien de temps?	How long have you been learning French?

- most metric weights and measures

un gramme	a gramme
un mètre	a metre
un kilomètre	a kilometre

- English nouns used in French

le football	football
un tee-shirt	a tee-shirt
un sandwich	a sandwich

➤ These endings are often found on <u>feminine nouns</u>.

Feminine ending	Examples
-ance -anse -ence -ense	**la** ch**ance** luck, chance **une** d**anse** a dance **la** pati**ence** patience **la** déf**ense** defence BUT: **le** sil**ence** silence
-ion	**une** rég**ion** a region **une** addit**ion** a bill **une** réun**ion** a meeting **la** circulat**ion** traffic BUT: **un** av**ion** a plane
-té -tié	**une** spéciali**té** a speciality **la** moi**tié** half BUT: **un** é**té** a summer **le** pâ**té** pâté

Grammar Extra!

A few words have different meanings depending on whether they are masculine or feminine. These are the most common:

Masculine	Meaning	Example	Feminine	Meaning	Example
<u>un</u> livre	a book	un livre de poche a paperback	<u>une</u> livre	a pound	une livre sterling a pound sterling
<u>un</u> mode	a method	le mode d'emploi the directions for use	<u>la</u> mode	fashion	à la mode in fashion
<u>un</u> poste	a set (*TV/radio*); a post (*job*); an extension (*phone*)	un poste de professeur a teaching job	<u>la</u> poste	post the post office	mettre quelque chose à la poste to post something
<u>un</u> tour	a turn; a walk	faire un tour to go for a walk	<u>une</u> tour	tower	la tour Eiffel the Eiffel Tower

Key points
✔ Most nouns referring to men, boys and male animals are <u>masculine</u>; most nouns referring to women, girls and female animals are <u>feminine</u>. The ending of a French noun often changes depending on whether it refers to a male or a female.

✔ Generally, words ending in -e are feminine and words ending in a consonant are masculine, though there are many exceptions to this rule.

✔ These endings are often found on masculine nouns: -age, -ment, -oir, -sme, -eau, -eu, -ou, -ier, -in and -on.

✔ These endings are often found on feminine nouns: -ance, -anse, -ence, -ense, -ion, -té, -tié.

✔ Days of the week, months and seasons of the year are masculine. So are languages, most metric weights and measures, and English nouns used in French.

4 **Masculine and feminine forms of words**

➤ In French there are sometimes very different words for men and women, and for male and female animals, just as in English.

un homme	a man
une femme	a woman
un taureau	a bull
une vache	a cow
un neveu	a nephew
une nièce	a niece

➤ Many masculine French nouns can be made feminine simply by changing the ending. This is usually done by adding an -e to the masculine noun to form the feminine.

un ami	a (male) friend
une amie	a (female) friend
un employé	a (male) employee
une employée	a (female) employee
un Français	a Frenchman
une Française	a Frenchwoman

➤ If the masculine singular form already ends in -e, no further e is added.

un élève	a (male) pupil
une élève	a (female) pupil
un camarade	a (male) friend
une camarade	a (female) friend
un collègue	a (male) colleague
une collègue	a (female) colleague

Tip

If a masculine noun ends in a vowel, its pronunciation does not change when an -e is added to form the feminine. For example, ami and amie (meaning *friend*) are both pronounced the same.

If a masculine noun ends with a consonant that is not pronounced, for example, -d, -s, -r or -t, you DO pronounce that consonant when an -e is added in the feminine. For example, in étudiant (meaning *student*), you cannot hear the t; in étudiante, you can hear the t.

> *Tip*
> Some masculine nouns, such as voisin (meaning *neighbour*), end
> in what is called a <u>nasal vowel</u> and an -n. With these words, you pronounce
> the vowel 'through your nose' but DO NOT say the n. When an -e is
> added in the feminine – for example, voisine – the vowel becomes a
> normal one instead of a nasal vowel and you DO pronounce the n.

5 Some other patterns

➤ Some changes to endings from masculine to feminine are a little more
complicated but still fall into a regular pattern.

Masculine ending	Feminine ending	Example	Meaning
-f	-ve	un veuf/une veuve	a widower/a widow
-x	-se	un époux/une épouse	a husband/a wife
-eur	-euse	un danseur/ une danseuse	a (male) dancer/ a (female) dancer
-teur	-teuse -trice	un chanteur/ une chanteuse un acteur/une actrice	a (male) singer/ a (female) singer an actor/an actress
-an	-anne	un paysan/ une paysanne	a (male) farmer/ a (female) farmer
-ien	-ienne	un Parisien/ une Parisienne	a (male) Parisian/ a (female) Parisian
-on	-onne	un lion/une lionne	a lion/a lioness
-er	-ère	un étranger/ une étrangère	a (male) foreigner/ a (female) foreigner
-et	-ette	le cadet/la cadette	the youngest (male) child the youngest (female) child
-el	-elle	un professionnel/ une professionnelle	a (male) professional/ a (female) professional

Key points
✔ Many masculine French nouns can be made to refer to females
 by adding an -e. If the masculine singular form already ends in
 -e, no further e is added.
✔ The pronunciation of feminine nouns is sometimes different from
 that of the corresponding masculine nouns.
✔ Other patterns include:

-f → -ve	-teur → -teuse or -trice	-er → -ère
-x → -se	-an, -ien and -on → -anne,	-et → -ette
-eur → -euse	-ienne and -onne	-el → -elle

For further explanation of grammatical terms, please see pages viii-xii.

Forming plurals

1 Plurals ending in -s

➤ In English we usually make nouns plural by adding an -s to the end (*garden* → *gardens*; *house* → *houses*), although we do have some nouns which are <u>irregular</u> and do not follow this pattern (*mouse* → *mice*; *child* → *children*).

> ### Tip
> Remember that **les** is the plural form of **le**, **la** and **l'**.
> Any adjective that goes with a plural noun has to agree with it, as does any pronoun that replaces it.
>
> ⟹ *For more information on **Adjectives**, **Articles** and **Pronouns**, see pages 25, 12 and 42.*

➤ Most French nouns also form their plural by adding an -s to their singular form.

un jardin	a garden
des jardin<u>s</u>	gardens
une voiture	a car
des voiture<u>s</u>	cars
un hôtel	a hotel
des hôtel<u>s</u>	hotels

➤ If the singular noun ends in -s, -x or -z, no further -s is added in the plural.

un fils	a son
des fils	sons
une voix	a voice
des voix	voices
un nez	a nose
des nez	noses

2 Plurals ending in -x

➤ The following nouns add an -x instead of an -s in the plural:

- nouns ending in -eau

un chapeau	a hat
des chapeau<u>x</u>	hats

- most nouns ending in -eu

un jeu	a game
des jeu<u>x</u>	games

- a FEW nouns ending in -ou (MOST nouns ending in -ou add -s as usual)

un bijou	a jewel
des bijou<u>x</u>	jewels
un caillou	a pebble
des caillou<u>x</u>	pebbles
un chou	a cabbage
des chou<u>x</u>	cabbages
un genou	a knee
des genou<u>x</u>	knees
un hibou	an owl
des hibou<u>x</u>	owls
un joujou	a toy
des joujou<u>x</u>	toys
un pou	a louse
des pou<u>x</u>	lice

Tip

Adding an -s or -x to the end of a noun does not usually change the way the word is pronounced. For example, professeur and professeurs and chapeau and chapeaux sound just the same when you say them out loud.

➤ If the singular noun ends in -al or -ail, the plural usually ends in -aux.

un journal	a newspaper
des journ<u>aux</u>	newspapers
un animal	an animal
des anim<u>aux</u>	animals
un travail	a job
des trav<u>aux</u>	jobs

For further explanation of grammatical terms, please see pages viii-xii.

> *Tip*
>
> The plural of un œil (*an eye*) is des yeux (*eyes*).

3 Plural versus singular

➤ A few words relating to clothing are plural in English but <u>NOT</u> in French.

<u>un</u> slip	pants
<u>un</u> short	shorts
<u>un</u> pantalon	trousers

➤ A few common words are plural in French but <u>NOT</u> in English.

<u>les</u> affaires	business
<u>les</u> cheveux	hair
<u>des</u> renseignements	information

Grammar Extra!

When nouns are made up of two separate words, they are called <u>compound nouns</u>, for example, les grands-parents (meaning *grandparents*), des ouvre-boîtes (meaning *tin-openers*). The rules for forming the plural of compound nouns are complicated and it is best to check in a dictionary to see what the plural is.

Key points

✔ Most French nouns form their plural by adding an -s to their singular form. If the singular noun ends in -s, -x or -z, no further -s is added in the plural.

✔ Most nouns ending in -eau or -eu add an -x in the plural.

✔ Most nouns ending in -ou take an -s in the plural, with a few exceptions.

✔ If the singular noun ends in -al or -ail, the plural usually ends in -aux.

✔ Adding an -s or -x to the end of a noun does not generally affect the way the word is pronounced.

✔ A few common words are plural in English but not in French, and vice versa.

ARTICLES

What is an article?
In English, an **article** is one of the words *the*, *a*, and *an* which is placed in front of a noun.

Different types of article

➤ There are three types of article:

- the <u>definite</u> article: *the* in English. This is used to identify a particular thing or person.

    I'm going to <u>the</u> supermarket.
    That's <u>the</u> woman I was talking to.

- the <u>indefinite</u> article: *a* or *an* in English, *some* or *any* (or no word at all) in the plural. This is used to refer to something unspecific, or that you do not really know about.

    Is there <u>a</u> supermarket near here?
    I need <u>a</u> day off.

- the <u>partitive</u> article: *some* or *any* (or no word at all) in English. This is used to talk about quantities or amounts.

    Can you lend me <u>some</u> sugar?
    They've got (<u>some</u>) problems.
    Did you buy <u>any</u> wine?

For further explanation of grammatical terms, please see pages viii-xii.

The definite article: le, la, l' and les

1 The basic rules

➤ In English we only have <u>one</u> definite article: *the*. In French, there is more than one definite article to choose from. All French nouns are either masculine or feminine and, just as in English, they can be either singular or plural. The word you choose for *the* depends on whether the noun it is used with is masculine or feminine, singular or plural. This may sound complicated, but it is not too difficult.

⇨ *For more information on **Nouns**, see page 1.*

	with masculine noun	with feminine noun
Singular	le (l')	la (l')
Plural	les	les

> ### Tip
> le and la change to l' when they are used in front of a word starting with a vowel and most words starting with h.

➤ le is used in front of <u>masculine singular nouns</u>.

le roi	the king
le chien	the dog
le jardin	the garden

➤ la is used in front of <u>feminine singular nouns</u>.

la reine	the queen
la souris	the mouse
la porte	the door

➤ l' is used in front of <u>singular nouns that start with a vowel</u> (*a, e, i, o,* or *u*), whether they are masculine or feminine.

l'ami (*masculine*)	the friend
l'eau (*feminine*)	the water
l'étage (*masculine*)	the floor

[*i*] Note that l' is also used in front of most words starting with h but some others take le or la instead.

l'hôpital	the hospital
le hamster	the hamster
la hi-fi	the stereo

> *Tip*
>
> It is a good idea to learn the <u>article</u> or the <u>gender</u> with the noun when you come across a word for the first time, so that you know whether it is masculine or feminine. A good dictionary will also give you this information.

➤ les is used in front of <u>plural nouns</u>, whether they are masculine or feminine and whatever letter they start with.

<u>les</u> chiens	the dogs
<u>les</u> portes	the doors
<u>les</u> amis	the friends
<u>les</u> hôtels	the hotels

i Note that you have to make the noun plural too, just as you would in English. In French, as in English, you usually add an -s.

➪ *For more information on **Forming plurals**, see page 9.*

> *Tip*
>
> When les is used in front of a word that starts with a consonant, you DO NOT say the s on the end of les: **les chiens** *the dogs*.
> When les is used in front of a word that starts with a vowel, most words starting with h, and the French word y, you DO pronounce the s on the end of **les**. It sounds like the z in the English word *zip*: **les amis** *the friends*, **les hôtels** *the hotels*.

2 Using à with le, la, l' and les

➤ The French word à is translated into English in several different ways, including *at* or *to*. There are special rules when you use it together with le and les.

➪ *For more information on the preposition à, see page 163.*

➤ When à is followed by le, the two words become au.

<u>au</u> cinéma	to/at the cinema
<u>au</u> professeur	to the teacher

➤ When à is followed by les, the two words become aux.

    aux maisons   to the houses

    aux étudiants   to the students

➤ When à is followed by la or l', the words do not change.

    à la bibliothèque   to/at the library

    à l'hôtel   to/at the hotel

Tip

le and la change to l' when they are used in front of a word starting with a vowel and most words starting with h.

---

3 Using de with le, la, l' and les

➤ The French word de is translated into English in several different ways, including *of* and *from*. There are special rules when you use it together with le and les.

➪ *For more information on the preposition de, see page 166.*

➤ When de is followed by le, the two words become du.

    du cinéma   from/of the cinema

    du professeur   from/of the teacher

➤ When de is followed by les, the two words become des.

    des maisons   from/of the houses

    des étudiants   from/of the students

➤ When de is followed by la or l', the words do not change.

    de la bibliothèque   from/of the library

    de l'hôtel   from/of the hotel

Tip

le and la change to l' when they are used in front of a word starting with a vowel and most words starting with h.

> **Key points**
> ✔ With masculine singular nouns → use le.
> ✔ With feminine singular nouns → use la.
> ✔ With nouns starting with a vowel, most nouns beginning with h and the French word y → use l'.
> ✔ With plural nouns → use les.
> ✔ à + le = au
>   à + les = aux
>   de + le = du
>   de + les = des

4 | Using the definite article

➤ The definite article in French (le, la, l' and les) is used in more or less the same way as we use *the* in English, but it is also used in French in a few places where you might not expect it.

➤ The definite article is used with words like *prices*, *flu* and *time* that describe qualities, ideas or experiences (called <u>abstract nouns</u>) rather than something that you can touch with your hand. Usually, *the* is missed out in English with this type of word.

<u>Les</u> prix montent.	Prices are rising.
J'ai <u>la</u> grippe.	I've got flu.
Je n'ai pas <u>le</u> temps.	I don't have time.

[i] Note that there are some set phrases using avoir, avec or sans followed by a noun, where the definite article is <u>NOT</u> used.

avoir faim	to be hungry (*literally: to have hunger*)
avec plaisir	with pleasure
sans doute	probably (*literally: without doubt*)

➤ You also use the definite article when you are talking about things like *coffee* or *computers* that you can touch with your hand (called <u>concrete nouns</u>) if you are talking generally about that thing. Usually, *the* is missed out in English with this type of word.

Je n'aime pas <u>le</u> café.	I don't like coffee.
<u>Les</u> ordinateurs coûtent très cher.	Computers are very expensive.
<u>Les</u> professeurs ne gagnent pas beaucoup.	Teachers don't earn very much.

➤ If you are talking about a part of your body, you usually use a word like *my* or *his* in English, but in French you usually use the definite article.

Tourne <u>la</u> tête à gauche.	Turn your head to the left.
Il s'est cassé <u>le</u> bras.	He's broken his arm.
J'ai mal à <u>la</u> gorge.	My throat hurts.

➤ In French you have to use the definite article in front of the names of countries, continents and regions.

<u>la</u> Bretagne	Brittany
<u>l'</u>Europe	Europe
<u>La</u> France est très belle.	France is very beautiful.
J'ai acheté ce poster <u>au</u> Japon.	I bought this poster in Japan.
Je viens <u>des</u> États-Unis.	I come from the United States.

ℹ Note that if the name of the country comes after the French word en, meaning *to* or *in*, you do not use the definite article. en is used with the names of countries, continents and regions that are feminine in French.

Je vais <u>en Écosse</u> le mois prochain.	I'm going to Scotland next month.
Il travaille <u>en Allemagne</u>.	He works in Germany.

➪ *For more information on the preposition en, see page 168.*

➤ You often use the definite article with the name of school subjects, languages and sports.

Tu aimes <u>les</u> maths?	Do you like maths?
J'apprends <u>le</u> français depuis trois ans.	I've been learning French for three years.
Mon sport préféré, c'est <u>le</u> foot.	My favourite sport is football.

ℹ Note that the definite article is not used after en.

Comment est-ce qu'on dit 'fils' <u>en anglais</u>?	How do you say 'fils' in English?
Sophie est nulle <u>en chimie</u>.	Sophie's no good at chemistry.

➤ When you use the verb parler (meaning *to speak*) in front of the name of the language, you do not always need to use the definite article in French.

Tu parles espagnol?	Do you speak Spanish?
Il parle bien <u>l'</u>anglais.	He speaks English well.

➤ You use le with dates, and also with the names of the days of the week and the seasons when you are talking about something that you do regularly or that is a habit.

Elle part le 7 mai.	She's leaving on the seventh of May.
Je vais chez ma grand-mère le dimanche.	I go to my grandmother's on Sundays.

[*i*] Note that you do not use the definite article after en.

En hiver nous faisons du ski.   In winter we go skiing.

➤ You often find the definite article in phrases that tell you about prices and rates.

6 euros le kilo	6 euros a kilo
3 euros la pièce	3 euros each
On roulait à 100 kilomètres à l'heure.	We were doing 100 kilometres an hour.

Key points

✔ The definite article is used in French with:
- abstract nouns
- concrete nouns (*when you are saying something that is true about a thing in general*)
- parts of the body
- countries, continents and regions
- school subjects, languages and sports
- dates
- days of the week and the seasons (*when you are talking about something that you do regularly or that is a habit*)
- prices and rates

For further explanation of grammatical terms, please see pages viii-xii.

The indefinite article: un, une and des

1 | The basic rules

➤ In English we have the indefinite article *a*, which changes to *an* in front of a word that starts with a vowel. In the plural we say either *some*, *any* or nothing at all.

➤ In French, you choose from **un**, **une** and **des**, depending on whether the noun is masculine or feminine, and singular or plural.

	with masculine noun	with feminine noun
Singular	un	une
Plural	des	des

➤ **un** is used in front of <u>masculine singular nouns</u>.

un roi	a king
un chien	a dog
un jardin	a garden

➤ **une** is used in front of <u>feminine singular nouns</u>.

une reine	a queen
une souris	a mouse
une porte	a door

➤ **des** is used in front of <u>plural nouns</u>, whether they are masculine or feminine, and whatever letter they start with.

des chiens	(some/any) dogs
des souris	(some/any) mice
des amis	(some/any) friends

[*i*] Note that **des** is also a combination of **de** + **les** and has other meanings, such as saying who something belongs to or where something is from.

➪ *For more information on des, see page 166.*

> ### Tip
> When **des** is used in front of a word that starts with a consonant (any letter except *a, e, i, o* or *u*), you DO NOT say the s on the end of des: **des chiens** *(some/any) dogs.*
> When **des** is used in front of a word that starts with a vowel, and most words starting with **h**, you DO pronounce the s on the end. It sounds like the *z* in the English word *zip*: **des amis** *(some/any) friends,* **des hôtels** *(some/any) hotels.*

2 **The indefinite article in negative sentences**

➤ In English we use words like *not* and *never* to indicate that something is not happening or is not true. The sentences that these words are used in are called <u>negative</u> sentences.

> I <u>don't</u> know him.
>
> I <u>never</u> do my homework on time.

➤ In French, you use word pairs like **ne … pas** (meaning *not*) and **ne … jamais** (meaning *never*) to say that something is not happening or not true. When **un**, **une** or **des** is used after this type of expression, it has to be changed to **de**.

> **Je <u>n'</u>ai <u>pas de</u> vélo.**   I don't have a bike.
>
> **Nous <u>n'</u>avons <u>pas de</u> cousins.**   We don't have any cousins.

⮕ *For more information on **Negatives**, see page 138.*

> ## Tip
>
> **de** changes to **d'** in front of a word starting with a vowel and most words starting with **h**.
>
> **Je n'ai pas <u>d'</u>ordinateur.**   I don't have a computer.
>
> **Il n'y a pas <u>d'</u>horloge dans la salle.** There isn't a clock in the room.

Grammar Extra!

There are some very common adjectives, like **beau**, **bon** and **petit**, that can come <u>BEFORE</u> the noun instead of after it. When an adjective comes before a plural noun, **des** changes to **de**.

> **J'ai reçu <u>de</u> beaux cadeaux.**   I got some lovely presents.
>
> **Cette région a <u>de</u> très jolis**   This area has some very pretty
> **villages.**   villages.

⮕ *For more information on **Word order with adjectives**, see page 32.*

---

3 **The meaning of des**

➤ **des** can mean different things in English, depending on the sentence. *Some* is often the best word to use.

> **J'ai un chien, deux chats et**   I've got a dog, two cats and
> **<u>des</u> souris.**   <u>some</u> mice.
>
> **Tu veux <u>des</u> chips?**   Would you like <u>some</u> crisps?

For further explanation of grammatical terms, please see pages viii-xii.

➤ In questions and negative sentences **des** means *any*, or is not translated at all.

Tu as des frères?	Have you got <u>any</u> brothers?
Il n'y a pas d'œufs.	There aren't <u>any</u> eggs.
Avez-vous des timbres?	Do you have stamps?

> *Tip*
>
> As an English speaker, you will know what sounds right in your own language. The important thing to remember is that **des** can <u>NEVER</u> be missed out in French, even if there is no word in English.

4 Using the indefinite article

➤ The indefinite article is used in French in much the same way as we use *a*, *some* and *any* in English, but there are two places where the indefinite article is <u>NOT</u> used:

- with the adjective **quel** (meaning *what a*), in sentences like

Quel dommage!	What <u>a</u> shame!
Quelle surprise!	What <u>a</u> surprise!
Quelle bonne idée!	What <u>a</u> good idea!

⇨ *For more information on quel, see page 148.*

- when you say what jobs people do

Il est professeur.	He's <u>a</u> teacher.
Ma mère est infirmière.	My mother's <u>a</u> nurse.

> *Tip*
>
> When you use **c'est** (to mean *he/she is*), you <u>DO</u> use **un** or **une**. When you use **ce sont** (to mean *they are*), you <u>DO</u> use **des**.
>
> | | |
> |---|---|
> | **C'est un médecin.** | He's/She's a doctor. |
> | **Ce sont des acteurs.** | They're actors. |
>
> ⇨ *For more information on c'est and ce sont, see page 65.*

Key points
- ✔ With masculine singular nouns → use **un**.
- ✔ With feminine singular nouns → use **une**.
- ✔ With plural nouns → use **des**.
- ✔ **un**, **une** and **des** → change to **de** or **d'** in negative sentences.
- ✔ The indefinite article is not usually used when you say what jobs people do, or in exclamations with **quel**.

The partitive article: du, de la, de l' and des

☐1 The basic rules

➤ du, de la, de l' and des can all be used to give information about the amount or quantity of a particular thing. They are often translated into English as *some* or *any*.

➤ In French, you choose between du, de la, de l' and des, depending on whether the noun is masculine or feminine, singular or plural.

	with masculine noun	with feminine noun
Singular	du (de l')	de la (de l')
Plural	des	des

> *Tip*
>
> de + le and de la change to de l' when they are used in front of a word starting with a vowel, most words starting with h, and the French word y.

➤ du is used in front of <u>masculine singular nouns</u>.

| <u>du</u> beurre | (some/any) butter |
| <u>du</u> jus d'orange | (some/any) orange juice |

🛈 Note that du is also a combination of de + le and has other meanings, such as saying who something belongs to or where something is from.

⇨ *For more information on du, see page 166.*

➤ de la is used in front of <u>feminine singular nouns</u>.

| <u>de la</u> viande | (some/any) meat |
| <u>de la</u> margarine | (some/any) margarine |

➤ de l' is used in front of <u>singular nouns that start with a vowel</u> and most nouns starting with h, whether they are masculine or feminine.

<u>de l'</u>argent (*masculine*)	(some/any) money
<u>de l'</u>eau (*feminine*)	(some/any) water
<u>de l'</u>herbe (*feminine*)	(some/any) grass

➤ **des** is used in front of <u>plural nouns,</u> whether they are masculine or feminine and whatever letter they start with.

des gâteaux	(some/any) cakes
des lettres	(some/any) letters
des hôtels	(some/any) hotels

$\boxed{i}$ Note that **des** is also a combination of **de + les** and has other meanings, such as saying who something belongs to or where something is from.

⇨ *For more information on des, see page 166.*

2 The partitive article in negative sentences

➤ In French, you use word pairs like **ne ... pas** (meaning *not*) and **ne ... jamais** (meaning *never*) to say that something is not happening or not true. In this type of expression, **du, de la, de l'** and **des** all change to **de**.

Nous <u>n'</u>avons <u>pas</u> <u>de</u> beurre.	We don't have any butter.
Je <u>ne</u> mange <u>jamais</u> <u>de</u> viande.	I never eat meat.
Il <u>n'</u>y a <u>pas</u> <u>de</u> timbres.	There aren't any stamps.

⇨ *For more information on Negatives, see page 138.*

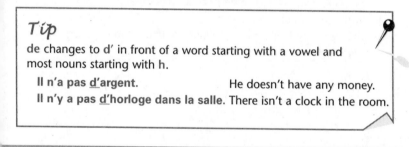

Tip

de changes to **d'** in front of a word starting with a vowel and most nouns starting with h.

Il n'a pas <u>d'</u>argent.   He doesn't have any money.
Il n'y a pas <u>d'</u>horloge dans la salle. There isn't a clock in the room.

Grammar Extra!

There are some very common adjectives, like **beau, bon** and **petit**, that can come BEFORE the noun instead of after it. When an adjective comes before a plural noun, **des** changes to **de**.

J'ai reçu de beaux cadeaux.   I got some lovely presents.
Cette région a de très jolis villages.   This area has some very pretty villages.

⇨ *For more information on Word order with adjectives, see page 32.*

3 **The meaning of du, de la, de l' and des**

➤ du, de la, de l' and des are often translated into English as *some* or *any*, but there are times when no word is used in English to translate the French.

Il me doit <u>de l'</u>argent.	He owes me (some) money.
Je vais acheter <u>de la</u> farine et <u>du</u> beurre pour faire un gâteau.	I'm going to buy (some) flour and butter to make a cake.
Est-ce qu'il y a <u>des</u> lettres pour moi?	Are there any letters for me?
Elle ne veut pas <u>de</u> beurre.	She doesn't want any butter.
Je ne prends pas <u>de</u> lait.	I don't take milk.

Tip

Remember that du, de la, de l' and des can <u>NEVER</u> be missed out in French, even if there is no word in English.

Key points

✔ With masculine singular nouns → use du.
✔ With feminine singular nouns → use de la.
✔ With singular nouns starting with a vowel and some nouns beginning with h → use de l'.
✔ With plural nouns → use des.
✔ du, de la, de l' and des → change to de or d' in negative sentences.

For further explanation of grammatical terms, please see pages viii-xii.

ADJECTIVES

> **What is an adjective?**
> An **adjective** is a 'describing' word that tells you more about a person or thing, such as their appearance, colour, size or other qualities, for example, *pretty*, *blue*, *big*.

Using adjectives

➤ Adjectives are words like *clever*, *expensive* and *silly* that tell you more about a noun (a living being, thing or idea). They can also tell you more about a pronoun, such as *he* or *they*. Adjectives are sometimes called 'describing words'. They can be used right next to a noun they are describing, or can be separated from the noun by a verb like *be*, *look*, *feel* and so on.

    a <u>clever</u> girl
    an <u>expensive</u> coat
    a <u>silly</u> idea
    He's just being <u>silly</u>.

⇨ *For more information on **Nouns** and **Pronouns**, see pages 1 and 42.*

➤ In English, the only time an adjective changes its form is when you are making a comparison.

    She's <u>cleverer</u> than her brother.
    That's the <u>silliest</u> idea I ever heard!

➤ In French, however, most adjectives <u>agree</u> with what they are describing. This means that their endings change depending on whether the person or thing you are referring to is masculine or feminine, and singular or plural.

un mot français	a French word
une chanson française	a French song
des traditions françaises	French traditions

➤ In English we put adjectives <u>BEFORE</u> the noun they describe, but in French you usually put them <u>AFTER</u> it.

    un chat <u>noir</u>   a <u>black</u> cat

⇨ *For further information, see* **Word order with adjectives** *on page 32.*

Key points

✔ Most French adjectives change their form, according to whether the person or thing they are describing is masculine or feminine, singular or plural.

✔ In French adjectives usually go after the noun they describe.

Making adjectives agree

1 The basic rules

➤ In dictionaries, regular French adjectives are usually shown in the masculine singular form. You need to know how to change them to make them agree with the noun or pronoun that they are describing.

➤ To make an adjective agree with the noun or pronoun it describes, you simply add the following endings in most cases:

	with masculine noun	with feminine noun
Singular	-	-e
Plural	-s	-es

un chat <u>noir</u>	a black cat
une chemise <u>noire</u>	a black shirt
des chats <u>noirs</u>	black cats
des chemises <u>noires</u>	black shirts

2 Making adjectives feminine

➤ With most adjectives you add an -e to the masculine singular form to make it feminine.

un chat noir a black cat → une chemise noir<u>e</u> a black shirt
un sac lourd a heavy bag → une valise lourd<u>e</u> a heavy suitcase

➤ If the adjective already ends in an -e in the masculine, you do not add another -e.

un sac jaune a yellow bag → une chemise jaune a yellow shirt
un garçon sage a good boy → une fille sage a good girl

➤ Some changes to endings are a little more complicated but still follow a regular pattern. Sometimes you have to double the consonant as well as adding an -e. On the next page there is a table showing these changes.

Masculine ending	Feminine ending	Example	Meaning
-f	-ve	neuf/neuve	new
-x	-se	heureux/heureuse	happy
-er	-ère	cher/chère	dear, expensive
-an	-anne	paysan/paysanne	farming, country
-en	-enne	européen/européenne	European
-on	-onne	bon/bonne	good, right
-el	-elle	cruel/cruelle	cruel
-eil	-eille	pareil/pareille	similar
-et	-ette	net/nette	clear
	-ète	complet/complète	complete, full

un **bon** repas a good meal → de **bonne** humeur in a good mood

un homme **cruel** a cruel man → une remarque **cruelle** a cruel remark

Tip

If a masculine adjective ends in a vowel (*a, e, i, o* or *u*), its pronunciation does not change when an -e is added to form the feminine. For example, joli and jolie are both pronounced the same.

If a masculine adjective ends with a consonant that is not pronounced, such as -d, -s or -t, you <u>DO</u> pronounce that consonant when an -e is added in the feminine. For example, in chaud (meaning *hot, warm*), you cannot hear the d when it is said out loud; in the feminine form chaude, you can hear the d sound.

This is also true when you have to double the consonant before the -e is added, for example, gros (meaning *big, fat*), where you cannot hear the s, and the feminine form grosse, where you can hear the s sound.

Some masculine adjectives, such as bon (meaning *good*) or italien (meaning *Italian*), end in what is called a <u>nasal vowel</u> and an -n. With these words, you pronounce the vowel 'through your nose' but do not say the n. When the consonant is doubled and an -e is added in the feminine – bonne, italienne – the vowel becomes a normal one instead of a nasal vowel and you do pronounce the n.

For further explanation of grammatical terms, please see pages viii-xii.

➤ Some very common adjectives have irregular feminine forms.

Masculine form	Feminine form	Meaning
blanc	blanche	white, blank
doux	douce	soft, sweet, mild, gentle
faux	fausse	untrue
favori	favorite	favourite
frais	fraîche	fresh, chilly, cool
gentil	gentille	nice, kind
grec	grecque	Greek
gros	grosse	big, fat
long	longue	long
nul	nulle	useless
roux	rousse	red, red-haired
sec	sèche	dry, dried
turc	turque	Turkish

mon sport <u>favori</u> my favourite sport → ma chanson <u>favorite</u> my favourite song

un ami <u>grec</u> a Greek (male) friend → une amie <u>grecque</u> a Greek (female) friend

➤ A very small group of French adjectives have an <u>extra</u> masculine singular form that is used in front of words that begin with a vowel (*a, e, i, o* or *u*) and most words beginning with h. These adjectives also have an irregular feminine form.

Masculine form in front of a word beginning with a consonant	Masculine form in front of a word beginning with a vowel or most words beginning with h	Feminine form	Meaning
beau	bel	belle	lovely, beautiful, good-looking, handsome
fou	fol	folle	mad
nouveau	nouvel	nouvelle	new
vieux	vieil	vieille	old

un <u>bel</u> appartement — a beautiful flat
le <u>Nouvel</u> An — New Year
un <u>vieil</u> arbre — an old tree

3 Making adjectives plural

➤ With most adjectives you add an -s to the masculine singular or feminine singular form to make it plural.

un chat noir a black cat → **des chats noirs** black cats
une valise lourde a heavy suitcase → **des valises lourdes** heavy suitcases

> *Tip*
>
> When an adjective describes a masculine <u>and</u> a feminine noun or pronoun, use the masculine plural form of the adjective.
>
> **La maison et le jardin sont <u>beaux</u>.** — The house and garden are beautiful.
>
> **Sophie et son petit ami sont très <u>gentils</u>.** — Sophie and her boyfriend are very nice.

➤ If the masculine singular form already ends in an -s or an -x, you do not add an -s.

un fromage français a French cheese → **des fromages français** French cheeses
un homme dangereux a dangerous man → **des hommes dangereux** dangerous men

➤ If the masculine singular form ends in -eau or -al, the masculine plural is usually -eaux or -aux.

le nouveau professeur the new teacher → **les nouv<u>eaux</u> professeurs** the new teachers
le rôle principal the main role → **les rôles princip<u>aux</u>** the main roles

> *Tip*
>
> Adding an -s or an -x does not change the pronunciation of a word. For example, noir and noirs sound just the same, as do nouveau and nouveaux.
>
> When the -s or -x ending comes before a word starting with a vowel or most words starting with h, you have to pronounce the s or x on the end of the adjective. It sounds like the z in the English word *zip*.
>
> **les anciens <u>é</u>lèves** — the former pupils
> **de grands <u>h</u>ôtels** — big hotels

4 **Invariable adjectives**

➤ A small number of adjectives (mostly relating to colours) do not change in the feminine or plural. They are called <u>invariable</u> because their form NEVER changes, no matter what they are describing. These adjectives are often made up of more than one word – for example, bleu marine (meaning *navy blue*), or else come from the names of fruit or nuts – for example, orange (meaning *orange*), marron (meaning *brown*).

des chaussures <u>marron</u>	brown shoes
une veste <u>bleu marine</u>	a navy blue jacket

Key points

✔ To make an adjective agree with a feminine singular noun or pronoun, you usually add -e to the masculine singular. If the adjective already ends in an -e, no further -e is added.

✔ Several adjectives ending in a consonant double their consonant as well as adding -e in the feminine.

✔ beau, fou, nouveau and vieux have an irregular feminine form and an extra masculine singular form that is used in front of words that begin with a vowel and most words beginning with h: bel, fol, nouvel, vieil.

✔ To make an adjective agree with a masculine plural noun or pronoun, you usually add -s to the masculine singular. If the adjective already ends in an -s or an -x, no further -s is added.

✔ If the adjective ends in -eau or -al, the masculine plural is usually -eaux or -aux.

✔ To make an adjective agree with a feminine plural noun or pronoun, you usually add -es to the masculine singular.

✔ Some adjectives relating to colours never change their form.

Word order with adjectives

1 **The basic rules**

➤ When adjectives are used right beside the noun they are describing, they go <u>BEFORE</u> it in English. French adjectives usually go <u>AFTER</u> the noun.

| l'heure <u>exacte</u> | the <u>right</u> time |
| la page <u>suivante</u> | the <u>following</u> page |

➤ Adjectives describing colours, shapes or nationalities always go <u>AFTER</u> the noun.

des cravates <u>rouges</u>	red ties
une table <u>ronde</u>	a round table
un mot <u>français</u>	a French word

➤ Some very common adjectives usually come <u>BEFORE</u> the noun.

beau	lovely, beautiful, good-looking, handsome
bon	good, right
court	short
grand	tall, big, long, great
gros	big, fat
haut	high
jeune	young
joli	pretty
long	long
mauvais	bad, poor
meilleur	better
nouveau	new
petit	small, little
premier	first
vieux	old
une belle journée	a lovely day
Bonne chance!	Good luck!

➤ There is a small group of common adjectives whose meaning changes depending on whether they come before the noun or go after it.

Adjective	Example before noun	Meaning	Example after noun	Meaning
ancien	un ancien collègue	a <u>former</u> colleague	un fauteuil ancien	an <u>antique</u> chair
cher	Chère Julie	<u>Dear</u> Julie	une robe chère	an <u>expensive</u> dress
propre	ma propre chambre	my <u>own</u> bedroom	un mouchoir propre	a <u>clean</u> handkerchief

For further explanation of grammatical terms, please see pages viii-xii.

Tip

dernier (meaning *last*) and prochain (meaning *next*) go <u>AFTER</u>
nouns relating to time, for example, semaine (meaning *week*) and
mois (meaning *month*). Otherwise they go <u>BEFORE</u> the noun.

la semaine <u>dernière</u>	last week
la <u>dernière</u> fois que je t'ai vu	the last time I saw you
la semaine <u>prochaine</u>	next week
la <u>prochaine</u> fois que j'y vais	the next time I go there

Grammar Extra!

When certain adjectives are used with certain nouns, they may take on a meaning you
wouldn't have guessed. You may need to check these in your dictionary and learn them.
Here are a few:

mon petit ami	my boyfriend
les petits pois	peas
les grandes vacances	the summer holidays
une grande personne	an adult, a grown-up

2 Using more than one adjective

➤ In French you can use more than one adjective at a time to describe
someone or something. If one of the adjectives usually comes <u>BEFORE</u> the
noun and the other usually goes <u>AFTER</u> the noun, the word order follows
the usual pattern.

une <u>jeune</u> femme <u>blonde</u>	a young blonde woman
un <u>nouveau</u> film <u>intéressant</u>	an interesting new film

➤ If both adjectives usually come <u>AFTER</u> the noun, they are joined together
with et (meaning *and*).

un homme mince <u>et</u> laid	a thin, ugly man
une personne intelligente <u>et</u> drôle	an intelligent, funny person

Key points

✔ Most French adjectives go after the noun they describe.
✔ Some very common adjectives usually come before the noun:
bon/mauvais, court/long, grand/petit, jeune/nouveau/vieux,
gros, haut, beau, joli, premier, meilleur.
✔ The meaning of some adjectives such as ancien, cher and propre
varies according to the position in the sentence.

Comparatives and superlatives of adjectives

1 Making comparisons using comparative adjectives

> **What is a comparative adjective?**
> A **comparative adjective** in English is one with *-er* on the end of it or
> *more* or *less* in front of it, that is used to compare people or things, for
> example, *slower, less important, more beautiful.*

➤ In French, to say that something is *easier, more expensive* and so on, you use
plus (meaning *more*) before the adjective.

Cette question est <u>plus</u> facile.	This question is easier.
Cette veste est <u>plus</u> chère.	This jacket is more expensive.

➤ To say something is *less expensive, less complicated* and so on, you use
moins (meaning *less*) before the adjective.

Cette veste est <u>moins</u> chère.	This jacket is less expensive.
un projet <u>moins</u> compliqué	a less complicated plan

➤ To introduce the person or thing you are making the comparison with, use
que (meaning *than*).

Elle est plus petite <u>que</u> moi.	She's smaller than me.
Cette question est plus facile <u>que</u> la première.	This question is easier than the first one.

➤ To say that something or someone is *as … as* something or someone else,
use aussi … que.

Il est <u>aussi</u> inquiet <u>que</u> moi.	He's as worried as me.
Cette ville n'est pas <u>aussi</u> grande <u>que</u> Bordeaux.	This town isn't as big as Bordeaux.

2 Making comparisons using superlative adjectives

> **What is a superlative adjective?**
> A **superlative adjective** in English is one with *-est* on the end of it or
> *most* or *least* in front of it, that is used to compare people or things, for
> example, *thinnest, most beautiful, least interesting.*

➤ In French, to say that something or someone is *easiest, prettiest, most
expensive* and so on, you use:

- le plus with <u>masculine singular</u> adjectives

- la plus with <u>feminine singular</u> adjectives
- les plus with <u>plural</u> adjectives (for both masculine and feminine)

le guide <u>le plus</u> utile	the <u>most</u> useful guidebook
la question <u>la plus</u> facile	the easi<u>est</u> question
<u>les plus</u> grands hôtels	the bigg<u>est</u> hotels
<u>les plus</u> petites voitures	the small<u>est</u> cars

➤ To say that something or someone is *the least easy*, *the least pretty*, *the least expensive* and so on, you use:

- le moins with <u>masculine singular</u> adjectives
- la moins with <u>feminine singular</u> adjectives
- les moins with <u>plural</u> adjectives (for both masculine and feminine).

le guide <u>le moins</u> utile	the <u>least</u> useful guidebook
Cette question est <u>la moins</u> facile.	This question is the <u>least</u> easy (*or* the hard<u>est</u>).
les mois <u>les moins</u> agréables	the <u>least</u> pleasant months
<u>les moins</u> belles photos	the <u>least</u> attractive photos

---

Tip

When the adjective comes <u>AFTER</u> the noun, you repeat the definite article (le, la or les).

    les mois <u>les</u> moins agréables   the least pleasant months

When the adjective comes <u>BEFORE</u> the noun, you do not repeat the definite article.

    les moins belles photos   the least attractive photos

⮑ *For more information on **Word order with adjectives**, see page 32.*

➤ In phrases like *the biggest hotel in London* and *the oldest person in the village*, you use de to translate *in*.

le plus grand hôtel <u>de</u> Londres	the biggest hotel in London
la personne la plus âgée <u>du</u> village	the oldest person in the village

⮑ *For more information on de and du, see page 166.*

---

3 | **Irregular comparative and superlative adjectives**

➤ Just as English has some irregular comparative and superlative forms – *better* instead of '*more good*', and *worst* instead of '*most bad*' – French also has a few irregular forms.

Adjective	Meaning	Comparative	Meaning	Superlative	Meaning
bon	good	meilleur	better	le meilleur	the best
mauvais	bad	pire plus mauvais	worse	le pire le plus mauvais	the worst
petit	small	moindre plus petit	smaller, lesser	le moindre le plus petit	the smallest, the least, the slightest

J'ai une <u>meilleure</u> idée.   I've got a <u>better</u> idea.

Il ne fait pas <u>le moindre</u> effort.   He doesn't make the <u>slightest</u> effort.

Tip

Choose the right form of the adjective to match the noun or pronoun, depending on whether it is masculine or feminine, singular or plural. Don't forget to change le to la or les in superlatives.

Grammar Extra!

bien and its comparative and superlative forms mieux and le mieux can be both adjectives and adverbs.

Il est <u>bien</u>, ce restaurant. (=*adjective*) This restaurant is good.

Elle va <u>mieux</u> aujourd'hui. (=*adverb*) She's better today.

⇨ *For more information on Adverbs, see page 152.*

Key points

✔ To compare people or things in French you use plus + adjective, moins + adjective or aussi ... que.

✔ *than* in comparatives is translated by que.

✔ French superlatives are formed with le/la/les plus + adjective and le/la/les moins + adjective.

✔ *in* after superlatives is translated by de.

✔ bon, mauvais and petit have irregular comparatives and superlatives: bon/meilleur/le meilleur, mauvais/pire/le pire, petit/moindre/le moindre.

Demonstrative adjectives ce, cette, cet and ces

> **What is a demonstrative adjective?**
> A **demonstrative adjective** is one of the words *this, that, these* and *those* used with a noun in English to point out a particular thing or person, for example, *this woman, that dog.*

➤ In French you use ce to point out a particular thing or person. Like all adjectives in French, ce changes its form depending on whether you are referring to a noun that is masculine or feminine, singular or plural.

	Masculine	**Feminine**	**Meaning**
Singular	ce (cet)	cette	this that
Plural	ces	ces	these those

Tip

cet is used in front of masculine singular nouns which begin with a vowel and most words beginning with h.

cet oiseau	this/that bird
cet hôpital	this/that hospital

➤ ce comes <u>BEFORE</u> the noun it refers to.

Combien coûte <u>ce</u> manteau?	How much is this/that coat?
Comment s'appelle <u>cette</u> entreprise?	What's this/that company called?
<u>Ces</u> livres sont très intéressants.	These/Those books are very interesting.
<u>Ces</u> couleurs sont jolies.	These/Those colours are pretty.

➤ If you want to emphasize the difference between something that is close to you and something that is further away, you can add:

● -ci on the end of the noun for things that are closer

Prends cette valise-<u>ci</u>.	Take this case.

- -là on the end of the noun for things that are further away

Est-ce que tu reconnais cette personne-là?	Do you recognize that person?

Key points

✔ The adjective ce corresponds to *this* and *that* in the singular, and *these* and *those* in the plural.

✔ The forms are ce and cette in the singular, and ces in the plural. cet is used with masculine singular nouns beginning with a vowel and most words beginning with h.

✔ You can add -ci on the end of the noun for things that are closer, or -là for things that are further away, to emphasize their nearness or distance.

For further explanation of grammatical terms, please see pages viii-xii.

Possessive adjectives

> **What is a possessive adjective?**
> In English a **possessive adjective** is one of the words *my, your, his, her, its, our* or *their* used with a noun to show that one person or thing belongs to another.

➤ Here are the French possessive adjectives. Like all French adjectives, these agree with the noun they refer to.

with masculine singular noun	with feminine singular noun	with plural noun (masculine or feminine)	Meaning
mon	ma (mon)	mes	my
ton	ta (ton)	tes	your
son	sa (son)	ses	his her its one's
notre	notre	nos	our
votre	votre	vos	your
leur	leur	leurs	their

> ## *Tip*
> You use mon, ton and son with feminine singular nouns in front of words that begin with a vowel and most words beginning with h. This makes them easier to say.
>
> | | |
> |---|---|
> | **mon** assiette | my plate |
> | **ton** histoire | your story |
> | **son** erreur | his/her mistake |
> | **mon** autre sœur | my other sister |

➤ Possessive adjectives come <u>BEFORE</u> the noun they describe.

Voilà **mon** mari.	There's my husband.
Mon frère et **ma** sœur habitent à Glasgow.	My brother and sister live in Glasgow.
Est-ce que **tes** voisins vendent **leur** maison?	Are your neighbours selling their house?
Rangez **vos** affaires.	Put your things away.

> *Tip*
>
> Possessive adjectives agree with what they describe, <u>NOT</u> with the
> person who owns that thing. For example, sa can mean *his, her, its*
> and *one's*, but can only ever be used with a feminine singular noun.
>
> | | |
> |---|---|
> | Paul cherche <u>sa</u> montre. | Paul's looking for <u>his</u> watch. |
> | Paul cherche <u>ses</u> lunettes. | Paul's looking for <u>his</u> glasses. |
> | Catherine a appelé <u>son</u> frère. | Catherine called <u>her</u> brother. |
> | Catherine a appelé <u>sa</u> sœur. | Catherine called <u>her</u> sister. |

➤ The equivalent of *your* in French is ton/ta/tes for someone you call tu, or
  votre/vos for someone you call vous.

⇨ *For more information on the difference between tu and vous, see page 43.*

[*i*] Note that possessive adjectives are <u>not</u> normally used with parts of
  the body. Use le, la, l' or les instead.

  J'ai mal <u>à la main</u>.   My hand hurts.

⇨ *For more information on **Articles**, see page 12.*

Key points

✔ The French possessive adjectives are:
  - mon/ton/son/notre/votre/leur in the masculine singular
  - ma/ta/sa/notre/votre/leur in the feminine singular
  - mes/tes/ses/nos/vos/leurs in the plural

✔ Possessive adjectives come before the noun they refer to. They
  agree with what they describe, rather than with the person who
  owns that thing.

✔ You use mon, ton and son with feminine singular nouns when
  the following word begins with a vowel. You also use them with
  most words beginning with h.

✔ Possessive adjectives are not normally used with parts of the body.
  Use le, la, l' or les instead.

Indefinite adjectives

> **What is an indefinite adjective?**
> An **indefinite adjective** is one of a small group of adjectives that are used to talk about people or things in a general way without saying exactly who or what they are, for example, *several, all, every*.

➤ In French, this type of adjective comes <u>BEFORE</u> the noun it refers to. Here are the most common French indefinite adjectives:

Masculine singular	Feminine singular	Masculine plural	Feminine plural	Meaning
autre	autre	autres	autres	other
chaque	chaque	-	-	every, each
même	même	mêmes	mêmes	same
-	-	quelques	quelques	some, a few
tout	toute	tous	toutes	all, every

J'ai d'<u>autres</u> projets.	I've got other plans.
J'y vais <u>chaque</u> année.	I go every year.
J'ai le <u>même</u> manteau.	I have the same coat.
Il a <u>quelques</u> amis à Paris.	He has some friends in Paris.
Il reste <u>quelques</u> bouteilles.	There are a few bottles left.
Il travaille <u>tout</u> le temps.	He works all the time.

> *Tip*
> You can also use **tout** to talk about how often something happens.
> tous les jours — every day
> tous les deux jours — every other day

ℹ️ Note that these words can also be used as <u>pronouns</u>, standing in place of a noun instead of being used with one. chaque and quelques have a slightly different form when they are used in this way.

➪ *For more information on **Pronouns**, see page 42.*

> **Key points**
> ✔ The most common French indefinite adjectives are autre, chaque, même, quelques and tout.
> ✔ They come before the noun when they are used in this way.

PRONOUNS

What is a pronoun?
A **pronoun** is a word you use instead of a noun, when you do not need or want to name someone or something directly, for example, *it, you, none.*

➤ There are several different types of pronoun:

- <u>Personal pronouns</u> such as *I, you, he, her* and *they*, which are used to refer to yourself, the person you are talking to, or other people and things. They can be either <u>subject pronouns</u> (*I, you, he* and so on) or <u>object pronouns</u> (*him, her, them* and so on).

- <u>Possessive pronouns</u> like *mine* and *yours*, which show who someone or something belongs to.

- <u>Indefinite pronouns</u> like *someone* or *nothing,* which refer to people or things in a general way without saying exactly who or what they are.

- <u>Relative pronouns</u> like *who, which* or *that,* which link two parts of a sentence together.

- <u>Demonstrative pronouns</u> like *this* or *those,* which point things or people out.

- <u>Reflexive pronouns</u>, a type of object pronoun that forms part of French reflexive verbs like **se laver** (meaning *to wash*) or **s'appeler** (meaning *to be called*).

⇨ *For more information on **Reflexive verbs**, see page 88.*

- The two French pronouns, **en** and **y**, which are used in certain constructions.

- The pronouns **qui?** (meaning *who?, whom?*), **que?** (meaning *what?*), **quoi?** (meaning *what?*) and **lequel?** (meaning *which one?*), which are used in asking questions.

⇨ *For more information on **Questions**, see page 142.*

➤ Pronouns often stand in for a noun to save repeating it.
> I finished my homework and gave <u>it</u> to my teacher.
> Do you remember Jack? I saw <u>him</u> at the weekend.

➤ Word order with personal pronouns is usually different in French and English.

For further explanation of grammatical terms, please see pages viii-xii.

Personal pronouns: subject

What is a subject pronoun?
A **subject pronoun** is a word such as *I, he, she* and *they*, which performs the action expressed by the verb. Pronouns stand in for nouns when it is clear who is being talked about, for example, *My brother isn't here at the moment. He'll be back in an hour.*

1 Using subject pronouns

➤ Here are the French subject pronouns:

Singular	Meaning	Plural	Meaning
je (j')	I	nous	we
tu	you	vous	you
il	he it	ils	they (*masculine*)
elle	she it	elles	they (*feminine*)
on	one (we/you/they)		

<u>Je</u> pars en vacances demain.	I'm going on holiday tomorrow.
<u>Nous</u> habitons à Nice.	We live in Nice.

> ### Tip
> je changes to j' in front of words beginning with a vowel, most words beginning with h, and the French word y.
>
> **J'arrive!**   I'm just coming!
> **Bon, j'y vais.**   Right, I'm off.

2 tu or vous?

➤ In English we have only <u>one</u> way of saying *you*. In French, there are <u>two</u> words: tu and vous. The word you use depends on:
  - whether you are talking to one person or more than one person
  - whether you are talking to a friend or family member, or someone else

➤ If you are talking to one person <u>you know well</u>, such as a friend, a young person or a relative, use tu.

  <u>Tu</u> me prêtes ce CD?   Will you lend me this CD?

➤ If you are talking to one person <u>you do not know so well</u>, such as your teacher, your boss or a stranger, use **vous**.

> <u>Vous</u> pouvez entrer. You may come in.

> *Tip*
>
> If you are in doubt as to which form of *you* to use, it is safest to use **vous** so you will not offend anybody.

➤ If you are talking to <u>more than one person</u>, you have to use **vous**, no matter how well you know them.

> <u>Vous</u> comprenez, les enfants? Do you understand, children?

[i] Note that the adjectives you use with **tu** and **vous** have to agree in the feminine and plural forms.

> Vous êtes <u>certain</u>, Monsieur Leclerc? (*masculine singular*) Are you sure, Mr Leclerc?
>
> Vous êtes <u>certains</u>, les enfants? (*masculine plural*) Are you sure, children?

Grammar Extra!

Any past participles (the form of the verb ending in -é, -i or -u in French) used with **être** in tenses such as the perfect also have to agree in the feminine and plural forms.

> Vous êtes <u>partie</u> quand, Estelle? (*feminine singular*) When did you leave, Estelle?
>
> Estelle et Sophie – vous êtes <u>parties</u> quand? (*feminine plural*) Estelle and Sophie – when did you leave?

⇨ For more information on the **Past participle**, see page 111.

---

3 il/elle and ils/elles

➤ In English we generally refer to things (such as *table, book, car*) only as *it*. In French, **il** (meaning *he, it*) and **elle** (meaning *she, it*) are used to talk about a thing, as well as about a person or an animal. You use **il** for <u>masculine nouns</u> and **elle** for <u>feminine nouns.</u>

> <u>Il</u> est déjà parti. He's already left.
>
> <u>Elle</u> est actrice. She's an actress.
>
> <u>Il</u> mord, ton chien? Does your dog bite?
>
> Prends cette chaise. <u>Elle</u> est plus confortable. Take this chair. It's more comfortable.

➤ **il** is also used to talk about the weather, the time and in certain other set phrases.

Il pleut.	It's raining.
Il est deux heures.	It's two o'clock.
Il faut partir.	We/You have to go.

➤ **ils** (meaning *they*) and **elles** (meaning *they*) are used in the plural to talk about things, as well as about people or animals. Use **ils** for <u>masculine nouns</u> and **elles** for <u>feminine nouns</u>.

Ils vont appeler ce soir.	They're going to phone tonight.
'Où sont Anne et Rachel?' – '**Elles** sont à la piscine.'	'Where are Anne and Rachel?' – 'They're at the swimming pool.'
'Est-ce qu'il reste des billets?' – 'Non, <u>ils</u> sont tous vendus.'	'Are there are any tickets left?' – 'No, they're all sold.'
'Tu aimes ces chaussures?' – 'Non, <u>elles</u> sont affreuses!'	'Do you like those shoes?' – 'No, they're horrible!'

➤ If you are talking about a masculine and a feminine noun, use **ils**.

Que font <u>ton père et ta mère</u> quand <u>ils</u> partent en vacances?	What do your father and mother do when they go on holiday?
'Où sont <u>le poivre et la moutarde</u>?' – '**Ils** sont déjà sur la table.'	'Where are the pepper and the mustard?' – 'They're already on the table.'

4	**on**

➤ **on** is frequently used in informal, everyday French to mean *we*.

On va à la plage demain.	We're going to the beach tomorrow.
On y va?	Shall we go?

➤ **on** can also have the sense of *someone* or *they*.

On m'a volé mon porte-monnaie.	Someone has stolen my purse.
On m'a dit que tu étais malade.	They told me you were ill.

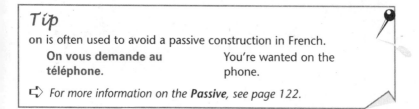

Tip

on is often used to avoid a passive construction in French.

On vous demande au téléphone.	You're wanted on the phone.

➪ *For more information on the **Passive**, see page 122.*

➤ You can also use **on** as we use *you* in English when we mean people in general.

On peut visiter le château en été.	You can visit the castle in the summer.
D'ici on peut voir les côtes françaises.	From here you can see the French coast.

Tip

The form of the verb you use with **on** is the same as the **il/elle** form.

⇨ *For more information on **Verbs**, see pages 69–137.*

Key points

✔ The French subject pronouns are: **je** (**j'**), **tu**, **il**, **elle**, **on** in the singular, and **nous**, **vous**, **ils**, **elles** in the plural.

✔ To say *you* in French, use **tu** if you are talking to one person you know well or to a young person. Use **vous** if you are talking to one person you do not know so well or to more than one person.

✔ **il/ils** (masculine singular/plural) and **elle/elles** (feminine singular/plural) are used to refer to things, as well as to people or animals. **il** is also used in certain set phrases.

✔ If there is a mixture of masculine and feminine nouns, use **ils**.

✔ **on** can mean *we*, *someone*, *you*, *they*, or people in general. It is often used instead of a passive construction.

Personal pronouns: direct object

> **What is a direct object pronoun?**
> A **direct object pronoun** is a word such as *me, him, us* and *them,* which is used instead of the noun to stand in for the person or thing most directly affected by the action expressed by the verb.

1 Using direct object pronouns

➤ Direct object pronouns stand in for nouns when it is clear who or what is being talked about, and save having to repeat the noun.

> I've lost my glasses. Have you seen <u>them</u>?
> 'Have you met Jo?' – 'Yes, I really like <u>her</u>!'

➤ Here are the French direct object pronouns:

Singular	Meaning	Plural	Meaning
me (m')	me	nous	us
te (t')	you	vous	you
le (l')	him it	les	them (*masculine and feminine*)
la (l')	her it		

Ils vont <u>nous</u> aider.	They're going to help us.
Je <u>la</u> vois.	I can see her/it.
'Tu aimes les carottes?' – 'Non, je <u>les</u> déteste!'	'Do you like carrots?' – 'No, I hate them!'

[i] Note that you cannot use direct object pronouns after a preposition like à or de, or when you want to emphasize something.

⇨ *For more information on **Emphatic pronouns**, see page 51.*

Tip

me changes to m', te to t', and le/la to l' in front of words beginning with a vowel, most words beginning with h, and the French word y.

Je <u>t'</u>aime.	I love you.
Tu <u>m'</u>entends?	Can you hear me?

➤ In orders and instructions **moi** is used instead of **me**, and **toi** is used instead of **te**.

Aidez-<u>moi</u>!	Help me!
Assieds-<u>toi</u>.	Sit down.

➤ **le** is sometimes used to refer back to an idea or information that has already been given. The word *it* is often missed out in English.

'Ta chemise est très sale.' –	'Your shirt's very dirty.' –
'Je <u>le</u> sais.'	'I know.'

2 Word order with direct object pronouns

➤ The direct object pronoun usually comes <u>BEFORE</u> the verb.

Je <u>t'</u>aime.	I love you.
<u>Les</u> voyez-vous?	Can you see them?
Elle ne <u>nous</u> connaît pas.	She doesn't know us.

i Note that in orders and instructions the direct object pronoun comes <u>AFTER</u> the verb.

Asseyez-<u>vous</u>.	Sit down.

➤ In tenses like the perfect that are formed with **avoir** or **être** and the past participle (the part of the verb that ends in -é, -i or -u in French), the direct object pronoun comes <u>BEFORE</u> the part of the verb that comes from **avoir** or **être**.

Il <u>m'</u>a vu.	He saw me.

➤ When a verb like **vouloir** (meaning *to want*) or **pouvoir** (meaning *to be able to, can*) is followed by another verb in the infinitive (the '*to*' form of the verb), the direct object pronoun comes <u>BEFORE</u> the infinitive.

Il voudrait <u>la</u> revoir.	He'd like to see her again.
Puis-je <u>vous</u> aider?	Can I help you?

> **Key points**
> ✔ The French direct object pronouns are: me (m'), te (t'), le/la (l') in the singular, and nous, vous, les in the plural.
> ✔ Except in orders and instructions the direct object pronoun comes before the verb.

Personal pronouns: indirect object

> **What is an indirect object pronoun?**
> When a verb has two objects (a <u>direct</u> one and an <u>indirect</u> one), the
> **indirect object pronoun** is used instead of a noun to show the person or
> thing the action is intended to benefit or harm, for example, *me* in *He
> gave me a book; Can you get me a towel?*

1 Using indirect object pronouns

➤ It is important to understand the difference between direct and indirect
object pronouns in English, as they can have different forms in French:

- an <u>indirect object</u> answers the question *who to/for?* or *to/for
  what?*

  He gave me a book. → *Who did he give the book to?* → me (=*indirect
  object pronoun*)

  Can you get me a towel? → *Who can you get a towel for?* → me
  (=*indirect object pronoun*)

- if something answers the question *what* or *who*, then it is the <u>direct
  object</u> and **NOT** the indirect object

  He gave me a book. → *What did he give me?* → a book (=*direct
  object*)

  Can you get me a towel? → *What can you get me?* → a towel (=*direct
  object*)

➤ Here are the French indirect object pronouns:

Singular	Meaning	Plural	Meaning
me (m')	me, to me, for me	nous	us, to us, for us
te (t')	you, to you, for you	vous	you, to you, for you
lui	him, to him, for him it, to it, for it	leur	them, to them, for them (*masculine and feminine*)
lui	her, to her, for her it, to it, for it		

Il <u>nous</u> écrit tous les jours.   He writes to us every day.
Qu'est-ce que tu <u>lui</u> as acheté?   What did you buy him?

> *Tip*
> me changes to m' and te to t' in front of words beginning with a vowel, most words beginning with h, and the French word y.
>
> Il m'a donné un livre.   He gave me a book.
> Tu m'apportes une serviette?   Can you get me a towel?

➤ The pronouns shown in the table are used instead of the preposition à with a noun.

J'écris à Suzanne. I'm writing to Suzanne. → Je lui écris. I'm writing to her.
Donne du lait au chat. Give the cat some milk. → Donne-lui du lait. Give it some milk.

➤ Some French verbs like demander à (meaning *to ask*) and téléphoner à (meaning *to phone*) take an indirect object while English uses a direct object.

Il leur téléphone tous les soirs.   He phones them every evening.

➤ On the other hand, some French verbs like attendre (meaning *to wait for*), chercher (meaning *to look for*) and regarder (meaning *to look at*) take a direct object to translate an English preposition + pronoun.

Je les attends devant la gare.   I'll wait for them outside the station.

2 Word order with indirect object pronouns

➤ The indirect object pronoun usually comes BEFORE the verb.

Dominique vous écrit une lettre. Dominique's writing you a letter.
Il ne nous parle pas.   He doesn't speak to us.
Il ne veut pas me répondre.   He won't answer me.

i Note that in orders and instructions telling someone to do something, the indirect object pronoun comes AFTER the verb.

Donne-lui ça!   Give her that!

Key points
✔ The French indirect object pronouns are: me (m'), te (t'), lui in the singular, and nous, vous, leur in the plural.
✔ Except in orders and instructions telling someone to do something, the direct object pronoun comes before the verb.

Emphatic pronouns

What is an emphatic pronoun?
An **emphatic pronoun** is used instead of a noun when you want to emphasize something, for example *Is this for _me_?*

1 Using emphatic pronouns

➤ In French, there is another set of pronouns which you use after prepositions, when you want to emphasize something and in certain other cases. These are called <u>emphatic pronouns</u> or <u>stressed pronouns</u>.

Singular	Meaning	Plural	Meaning
moi	I me	nous	we us
toi	you	vous	you
lui	he him	eux	they (*masculine*) them
elle	she her	elles	they (*feminine*) them
soi	oneself (yourself, ourselves)		

Je pense souvent à <u>toi</u>.	I often think about you.
C'est pour <u>moi</u>?	Is this for me?
Venez avec <u>moi</u>.	Come with me.
Il a besoin de <u>nous</u>.	He needs us.

➤ soi (meaning *oneself*) is used with the subject pronoun on and with words like tout le monde (meaning *everyone*) or chacun (meaning *each one*).

Il faut avoir confiance en <u>soi</u>.	You have to have confidence in yourself.
Tout le monde est rentré chez <u>soi</u>.	Everyone went home.

2 When to use emphatic pronouns

➤ Emphatic pronouns are used in the following circumstances:

- after a preposition

C'est <u>pour moi</u>?	Is this for me?

- for emphasis, especially where a contrast is involved

<u>Toi</u>, tu ressembles à ton père, mais <u>elle</u> non.

You look like your father, she doesn't.

Il m'énerve, <u>lui</u>!

He's getting on my nerves!

- on their own without a verb

'Qui a cassé la fenêtre?' – '<u>Lui</u>.'

'Who broke the window?' – 'He did.'

'Je suis fatiguée.' – '<u>Moi</u> aussi.'

'I'm tired.' – 'Me too.'

- after c'est and ce sont (meaning *it is*)

C'est <u>toi</u>, Simon?

Is that you, Simon?

Ce sont <u>eux</u>.

It's them.

⇨ *For more information on c'est and ce sont, see page 65.*

- in comparisons

Tu es plus jeune que <u>moi</u>.

You're younger than me.

Il est moins grand que <u>toi</u>.

He's smaller than you (are).

- when the subject of the sentence is made up of two pronouns, or of a pronoun and a noun

<u>Mon père et elle</u> ne s'entendent pas.

My father and she don't get on.

Grammar Extra!

You can add -même or -mêmes to the emphatic pronouns when you particularly want to emphasize something. These forms correspond to English *myself*, *ourselves* and so on.

Form with -même	Meaning
moi-même	myself
toi-même	yourself
lui-même	himself, itself
elle-même	herself, itself
soi-même	oneself (yourself, ourselves)
nous-mêmes	ourselves
vous-même vous-mêmes	yourself yourselves
eux-mêmes	themselves (*masculine*)
elles-mêmes	themselves (*feminine*)

Je l'ai fait <u>moi-même</u>.

I did it myself.

Elle l'a choisi <u>elle-même</u>.

She chose it herself.

Key points

✔ The French emphatic pronouns are: moi, toi, lui, elle, soi in the singular, and nous, vous, eux, elles in the plural.

✔ They are used:
- after a preposition
- for emphasis
- on their own without a verb
- after c'est and ce sont
- in comparisons
- when the subject of the sentence is made up of two pronouns, or of a pronoun and a noun

✔ You can add -même or -mêmes to the emphatic pronouns when you particularly want to emphasize something.

Possessive pronouns

> **What is a possessive pronoun?**
> A **possessive pronoun** is one of the words *mine, yours, hers, his, ours* or
> *theirs*, which are used instead of a noun to show that one person or thing
> belongs to another, for example, *Ask Carole if this pen is <u>hers</u>*.

➤ Here are the French possessive pronouns:

Masculine singular	Feminine singular	Masculine plural	Feminine plural	Meaning
le mien	la mienne	les miens	les miennes	mine
le tien	la tienne	les tiens	les tiennes	yours
le sien	la sienne	les siens	les siennes	his hers
le nôtre	la nôtre	les nôtres	les nôtres	ours
le vôtre	la vôtre	les vôtres	les vôtres	yours
le leur	la leur	les leurs	les leurs	theirs

Ces CD-là, ce sont <u>les miens</u>.	Those CDs are mine.
Heureusement que tu as tes clés. J'ai oublié <u>les miennes</u>.	It's lucky you've got your keys. I forgot mine.

Tip

In French, possessive pronouns agree with what they describe,
<u>NOT</u> with the person who owns that thing. For example, le sien
can mean *his* or *hers*, but can only be used to replace a masculine
singular noun.

'C'est <u>le vélo</u> de Paul?' – 'Oui, c'est <u>le sien</u>.'	'Is that Paul's bike?' – 'Yes, it's <u>his</u>.'
'C'est <u>le vélo</u> d'Isabelle?' – 'Oui, c'est <u>le sien</u>.'	'Is that Isabelle's bike?' – 'Yes, it's <u>hers</u>.'

Grammar Extra!

Remember that à with the definite article le becomes au, and à with les becomes aux, so:

> à + le mien → au mien
> à + les miens → aux miens
> à + les miennes → aux miennes

Tu préfères ce manteau <u>au mien</u>?   Do you prefer this coat to mine?

Remember that de with the definite article le becomes du, and de with les becomes des, so:

> de + le mien → du mien
> de + les miens → des miens
> de + les miennes → des miennes

J'ai oublié mes clés. J'ai besoin <u>des tiennes</u>.   I've forgotten my keys. I need yours.

⇨ For more information on **Articles**, see page 12.

Key points

✔ The French possessive pronouns are le mien, le tien, le sien for singular subject pronouns, and le nôtre, le vôtre and le leur for plural subject pronouns. Their forms change in the feminine and the plural.

✔ In French, the pronoun you choose has to agree with the noun it replaces, and <u>not</u> with the person who owns that thing.

en and y

➤ en and y do not usually refer to people. How we translate them into English depends on where en and y are found in French.

1 en

➤ en is used with verbs and phrases normally followed by de to avoid repeating the same word.

Si tu as un problème, tu peux m'**en** parler.	If you've got a problem, you can talk to me about it. (*en replaces de in parler de quelque chose*)
Est-ce que tu peux me prêter ce livre? J'**en** ai besoin.	Can you lend me that book? I need it. (*en replaces de in avoir besoin de quelque chose*)
Il a un beau jardin et il **en** est très fier.	He's got a beautiful garden and is very proud of it. (*en replaces de in être fier de quelque chose*)

➤ en can also replace the <u>partitive article</u> (du, de la, de l', des).

Je n'ai pas d'argent. Tu **en** as?	I haven't got any money. Have you got any?
'Tu peux me prêter des timbres?' – 'Non, je dois **en** acheter.'	'Can you lend me some stamps?' – 'No, I need to buy some.'

⇨ *For more information on the **Partitive article**, see page 22.*

➤ en is also used:
- as a preposition
- with the present participle of verbs

⇨ *For more information on **Prepositions** and the **Present participle**, see pages 162 and 125.*

➤ When en is used with avoir, with il y a or with numbers, it is often not translated in English but can <u>NEVER</u> be missed out in French.

'Est-ce que tu as un dictionnaire?' – 'Oui, j'**en** ai un.'	'Have you got a dictionary?' – 'Yes, I've got one.'
'Combien d'élèves y a-t-il dans ta classe?' – 'Il y **en** a trente.'	'How many pupils are there in your class?' – 'There are thirty.'
J'**en** veux deux.	I want two (of them).

2 y

➤ y is used with verbs and phrases normally followed by à to avoid repeating the same word.

'Je pensais à l'examen.' – 'Mais arrête d'y penser!'	'I was thinking about the exam.' – 'Well, stop thinking about it!' (*y replaces à in penser à quelque chose*)
'Je ne m'attendais pas à ça.' – 'Moi, je m'y attendais.'	'I wasn't expecting that.' – 'Well, I was expecting it.' (*y replaces à in s'attendre à quelque chose*)

➤ y can also mean *there*. It can be used to replace phrases that would use prepositions such as dans (meaning *in*) and sur (meaning *on*).

Elle y passe tout l'été.	She spends the whole summer there.
Regarde dans le tiroir. Je pense que les clés y sont.	Look in the drawer. I think the keys are in there.

3 Word order with en and y

➤ en and y usually come <u>BEFORE</u> the verb.

J'en veux.	I want some.
Elle en a parlé avec moi.	She talked to me about it.
En êtes-vous content?	Are you pleased with it/them?
Comment fait-on pour y aller?	How do you get there?
N'y pense plus.	Don't think about it any more.

➤ In orders and instructions telling someone to do something, en or y come <u>AFTER</u> the verb and are attached to it with a hyphen (-).

Prenez-en.	Take some.
Restez-y.	Stay there.

Tip

The final -s of -er verbs is usually dropped in the tu form used for orders and instructions. When an -er verb in the tu form is used before en or y, however, the -s is not dropped, to make it easier to say.

Donne des bonbons à ton frère.	Give some sweets to your brother.
<u>Donnes-en</u> à ton frère.	Give some to your brother.
Va dans ta chambre!	Go to your room!
<u>Vas-y!</u>	Go on!

➩ *For more information on the Imperative, see page 85.*

➤ en and y come <u>AFTER</u> other direct or indirect object pronouns.

Donnez-<u>leur-en</u>.	Give them some.
Il <u>m'en</u> a parlé.	He spoke to me about it.

⇨ *For more information on **Direct object pronouns** and **Indirect object pronouns**, see pages 47 and 49.*

Key points

✔ en is used with verbs and expressions normally followed by de to avoid repeating the same word.

✔ en can also replace the partitive article.

✔ When en is used with avoir and il y a or with numbers, it is often not translated in English but can never be missed out in French.

✔ y is used with verbs and expressions normally followed by à to avoid repeating the same word.

✔ y can also mean *there* and may replace expressions that would be used with dans and sur or some other preposition indicating a place.

✔ en and y usually come before the verb, except in orders and instructions telling someone to do something, when en or y follows the verb and is attached to it with a hyphen.

✔ en and y come after other direct or indirect object pronouns.

Using different types of pronoun together

➤ Sometimes you find a direct object pronoun and an indirect object pronoun in the same sentence.

He gave me *(indirect object)* <u>them</u> *(direct object)*.

He gave <u>them</u> *(direct object)* to <u>me</u> *(indirect object)*.

➤ When this happens in French, you have to put the indirect and direct object pronouns in a certain order.

Indirect	Direct	Indirect	
me	le		
te	la	lui	en
nous	les	leur	y
vous			

Dominique <u>vous l'</u>envoie demain.	Dominique's sending it to you tomorrow.
Il <u>te les</u> a montrés?	Has he shown them to you?
Je <u>les lui</u> ai lus.	I read them to him/her.
Ne <u>la leur</u> donne pas.	Don't give it to them.
Elle ne <u>m'en</u> a pas parlé.	She didn't speak to me about it.

Key points
✔ If a direct and an indirect object pronoun are used in the same sentence, you usually put the indirect object pronoun before the direct object pronoun.
✔ With lui and leur, this order is reversed and you put the direct object pronoun before the indirect object pronoun.

Indefinite pronouns

> **What is an indefinite pronoun?**
> An **indefinite pronoun** is one of a small group of pronouns such as
> *everything, nobody* and *something* which are used to refer to people or
> things in a general way without saying exactly who or what they are.

➤ Here are the most common French indefinite pronouns:

- chacun (*masculine singular*)/chacune (*feminine singular*) each, everyone

Nous avons <u>chacun</u> donné dix euros.	We each gave ten euros.
<u>Chacun</u> fait ce qu'il veut.	Everyone does what they like.
Toutes les villas ont <u>chacune</u> leur piscine.	Each villa has its own swimming pool.

- personne nobody/no one, anybody/anyone

Il <u>n</u>'y a <u>personne</u> à la maison.	There's no one at home.
Elle <u>ne</u> veut voir <u>personne</u>.	She doesn't want to see anybody.

⇨ *For more information on **Negatives**, see page 138.*

Tip
You can use personne on its own to answer a question.

Qui sait la réponse? <u>Personne</u>.	Who knows the answer? No one.

If the sentence contains a verb you have to use ne with it.

Personne <u>n</u>'est venu.	Nobody came.

- quelque chose something, anything

J'ai <u>quelque chose</u> pour toi.	I've got something for you.
Avez-vous <u>quelque chose</u> à déclarer?	Do you have anything to declare?

- quelqu'un somebody/someone, anybody/anyone

Il y a <u>quelqu'un</u> à la porte.	There's someone at the door.
<u>Quelqu'un</u> a vu mon parapluie?	Has anybody seen my umbrella?

- rien nothing, anything

Elle n'a <u>rien</u> dit.	She didn't say anything.
<u>Rien</u> n'a changé.	Nothing's changed.

⇨ *For more information on **Negatives**, see page 138.*

For further explanation of grammatical terms, please see pages viii-xii.

> ## Tip
>
> You can use rien on its own to answer a question.
>
> 'Qu'est-ce tu as acheté?' –   'What did you buy?' –
> 'Rien.'   'Nothing.'
>
> If the sentence contains a verb you have to use ne with it.
>
> Il n'a rien mangé.   He's eaten nothing.

- tout everything

    Il organise tout.   He's organizing everything.
    Tout va bien?   Is everything OK?

- tous (*masculine plural*)/toutes (*feminine plural*) all

    Je les connais tous.   I know them all.
    Elles sont toutes arrivées?   Are they all here?

➤ You can use quelque chose de/rien de and quelqu'un de/personne de
with adjectives if you want to say *nothing interesting*, *something new* and
so on.

    rien d'intéressant   nothing interesting

> ### Key points
>
> ✔ rien and personne can be used on their own to answer
>   questions, but need to be used with ne when there is a verb in
>   the sentence.
> ✔ quelque chose/rien and quelqu'un/personne can be followed
>   by de + adjective.

Relative pronouns: qui, que, lequel, auquel, duquel

> **What is a relative pronoun?**
> In English a **relative pronoun** is one of the words *who*, *which* and *that* (and the more formal *whom*) which can be used to introduce information that makes it clear which person or thing is being talked about, for example, *The man who has just come in is Ann's boyfriend; The vase that you broke was quite valuable.*
> Relative pronouns can also introduce further information about someone or something, for example, *Peter, who is a brilliant painter, wants to study art; Jane's house, which was built in 1890, needs a lot of repairs.*

➤ In French, the relative pronouns are qui, que, lequel, auquel, and duquel.

1 qui and que

➤ qui and que can both refer to people or things.

	Relative pronoun	Meaning
Subject	qui	who which that
Direct object	que	who, whom which that

Mon frère, <u>qui</u> a vingt ans, est à l'université.	My brother, who's twenty, is at university.
Est-ce qu'il y a un bus <u>qui</u> va au centre-ville?	Is there a bus that goes to the town centre?
Les amis <u>que</u> je vois le plus sont Léa et Mehdi.	The friends (that) I see most are Léa and Mehdi.
Voilà la maison <u>que</u> nous voulons acheter.	That's the house (which) we want to buy.

> *Tip*
> que changes to qu' in front of a word beginning with a vowel and most words beginning with h.

➤ **qui** is also used after a preposition such as **à**, **de** or **pour** to talk about people.

> la personne <u>à qui</u> il parle   the person he is speaking to
>
> les enfants <u>pour qui</u> j'ai acheté   the children I bought sweets for
> des bonbons

> ## Tip
>
> In English we often miss out the object pronouns *who*, *which* and *that*. For example, we can say both *the friends <u>that</u> I see most*, or *the friends I see most*, and *the house <u>which</u> we want to buy*, or *the house we want to buy*. In French you can <u>NEVER</u> miss out **que** or **qui** in this way.

2 lequel, laquelle, lesquels, lesquelles

➤ **lequel** (meaning *which*) is used after a preposition such as **à**, **de** or **pour** to talk about <u>things</u>. It has to agree with the noun it replaces.

	Masculine	Feminine	Meaning
Singular	lequel	laquelle	which
Plural	lesquels	lesquelles	which

> le livre <u>pour lequel</u> elle est   the book she is famous for
> connue
>
> la table <u>sur laquelle</u> j'ai mis   the table I put my bag on
> mon sac

➤ Remember that **à** and **de** combine with the definite article **le** to become **au** and **du**, and with **les** to become **aux** and **des**. **lequel/lesquels/lesquelles** combine with **à** and **de** as shown in the table. **laquelle** doesn't change.

	+ lequel	+ laquelle	+ lesquels	+ lesquelles	Meaning
à	auquel	à laquelle	auxquels	auxquelles	to which
de	duquel	de laquelle	desquels	desquelles	of which

⇨ *For more information on* à *and* de, *see pages 14 and 15.*

Grammar Extra!

dont means *whose, of whom, of which, about which* and so on. It can refer to people or things, but its form <u>NEVER</u> changes.

la femme <u>dont</u> la voiture est en panne	the woman whose car has broken down
les films <u>dont</u> tu parles	the films you're talking about

Key points

✔ qui and que can both refer to people or things: qui is the subject of the part of the sentence it is found in; que is the object.

✔ In English we often miss out the object pronouns *who, which* and *that,* but in French you can <u>never</u> miss out que or qui.

✔ After a preposition you use qui if you are referring to people, and lequel if you are referring to things – lequel agrees with the noun it replaces.

✔ à + lequel → auquel
   à + lesquels → auxquels
   à + lesquelles → auxquelles

✔ de + lequel → duquel
   de + lesquels → desquels
   de + lesquelles → desquelles

For further explanation of grammatical terms, please see pages viii-xii.

Demonstrative pronouns: ce, cela/ça, ceci, celui

> **What is a demonstrative pronoun?**
> In English a **demonstrative pronoun** is one of the words *this, that, these,* and *those* used instead of a noun to point people or things out, for example, <u>*That*</u> *looks fun.*

1 <u>ce</u>

➤ ce is usually used with the verb être (meaning *to be*) in the expressions c'est (meaning *it's, that's*), c'était (meaning *it was, that was*), ce sont (meaning *it's, that's*) and so on.

<u>C'</u>est moi.	It's me.
<u>C'</u>était mon frère.	That was my brother.
<u>Ce</u> sont eux.	It's them.

> ### Tip
>
> ce becomes c' when it is followed by a part of the verb that starts with e or é.
> ce becomes ç' when it is followed by a part of the verb that starts with a.
>
> | | |
> |---|---|
> | <u>Ç'</u>a été difficile. | It was difficult. |
>
> Note that after c'est and ce sont and so on you have to use the emphatic form of the pronoun, for example, moi instead of je, eux instead of ils and so on.
>
> | | |
> |---|---|
> | C'est <u>moi</u>. | It's me. |
>
> ⇨ *For more information on **Emphatic pronouns**, see page 51.*

➤ ce is used:

- with a noun or a question word to identify a person or thing

Qui est-<u>ce</u>?	Who is it?, Who's this/that?
<u>Ce</u> sont des professeurs.	They're teachers.
Qu'est-ce que <u>c'</u>est?	What's this/that?
<u>C'</u>est un ouvre-boîte.	It's a tin-opener.

- with an adjective to refer to a statement, idea and so on that cannot be classed as either masculine or feminine

<u>C</u>'est très intéressant.	That's/It's very interesting.
<u>C</u>'est dangereux.	That's/It's dangerous.
<u>Ce</u> n'est pas grave.	It doesn't matter.

- for emphasis

<u>C</u>'est moi qui ai téléphoné.	It was me who phoned.
<u>Ce</u> sont les enfants qui ont fait le gâteau.	It was the children who made the cake.

2 cela, ça and ceci

➤ cela and ça mean *it, this* or *that*. Both refer to a statement, an idea or an object. ça is used instead of cela in everyday, informal French.

<u>Ça</u> ne fait rien.	It doesn't matter.
Écoute-moi <u>ça</u>!	Listen to this!
<u>Cela</u> dépend.	That/It depends.
Je n'aime pas <u>cela</u>.	I don't like that.
Donne-moi <u>ça</u>!	Give me that!

Tip

ça and cela are used in a more general way than il and elle, which are usually linked to a noun that has already been mentioned.

<u>Ça</u> te plaît d'aller à l'étranger?	Do you like going abroad?
<u>Elle</u> te plaît, <u>ma nouvelle voiture</u>?	Do you like my new car?

➤ ceci means *this* and is not as common as cela and ça. It is used to talk about something that has not yet been mentioned.

Lisez <u>ceci</u>.	Read this.

➤ ceci is also used to hand or show someone something.

Prends <u>ceci</u>. Tu en auras besoin.	Take this. You'll need it.

3 celui, celle, ceux, celles

➤ celui and celle mean *the one*; ceux and celles mean *the ones*. The form you choose depends on whether the noun it is replacing is masculine or feminine, and singular or plural.

For further explanation of grammatical terms, please see pages viii-xii.

	Masculine	Feminine	Meaning
Singular	celui	celle	the one
Plural	ceux	celles	the ones

➤ celui and its other forms are used before:

- qui, que or dont

'Quelle robe préférez-vous?'	'Which dress do you like best?'
– 'Celle qui est en vitrine.'	– 'The one in the window.'
Prends ceux que tu préfères.	Take the ones you like best.
celui dont je t'ai parlé	the one I told you about

- prepositions like à, dans and so on.

celui proche de la fontaine	the one near the fountain

➤ celui and its other forms can be used with de to show who something belongs to. In English, we would use 's.

Je n'ai pas d'appareil photo mais je peux emprunter celui de ma sœur.	I haven't got a camera but I can borrow my sister's.
Comparez vos réponses à celles de votre voisin.	Compare your answers with your neighbour's.

➤ You can add the endings -ci and -là to celui and its other forms to emphasize the difference between something that is close to you and something that is further away.

- use -ci for something that is closer to you
- use -là for something that is further away

	Masculine	Feminine	Meaning
Singular	celui-ci	celle-ci	this, this one
	celui-là	celle-là	that, that one
Plural	ceux-ci	celles-ci	these, these ones
	ceux-là	celles-là	those, those ones

On prend quel fromage? Celui-ci ou celui-là?	Which cheese shall we get? This one or that one?
Ces chemises ont deux poches mais celles-là n'en ont pas.	These shirts have two pockets but those have none.

> **Key points**
>
> ✔ ce is often found in the expressions c'est, ce sont and so on.
> ✔ ce is also used:
>   - to identify a person or thing
>   - to refer to a statement, idea and so on that cannot be classed as either masculine or feminine
>   - for emphasis
> ✔ cela and ça mean *it, this* or *that*; ceci means *this*, but is not as common.
> ✔ celui and celle mean *the one*; ceux and celles mean *the ones*. They are often found with the endings -ci and -là and are used to distinguish between things which are close and things which are further away.

VERBS

What is a verb?
A **verb** is a 'doing' word which describes what someone or something does, what someone or something is, or what happens to them, for example, *be*, *sing*, *live*.

The three conjugations

➤ Verbs are usually used with a noun, with a pronoun such as *I*, *you* or *she*, or with somebody's name. They can relate to the present, the past and the future; this is called their <u>tense</u>.

⇨ *For more information on **Nouns** and **Pronouns**, see pages 1 and 42.*

➤ Verbs are either:
  - <u>regular</u>; their forms follow the normal rules
  - <u>irregular</u>; their forms do not follow the normal rules

➤ Regular English verbs have a <u>base form</u> (the form of the verb without any endings added to it, for example, *walk*). The base form can have *to* in front of it, for example, *to walk*. This is called the <u>infinitive</u>. You will find one of these forms when you look a verb up in your dictionary.

➤ French verbs also have an infinitive, which ends in -er, -ir or -re, for example, donner (meaning *to give*), finir (meaning *to finish*), attendre (meaning *to wait*). <u>Regular</u> French verbs belong to one of these three verb groups, which are called <u>conjugations</u>. We will look at each of these three conjugations in turn on the next few pages.

➤ English verbs have other forms apart from the base form and infinitive: a form ending in -s (*walks*), a form ending in -ing (*walking*), and a form ending in -ed (*walked*).

➤ French verbs have many more forms than this, which are made up of endings added to a <u>stem</u>. The stem of a verb can usually be worked out from the infinitive.

➤ French verb endings change, depending on who you are talking about: je (*I*), tu (*you*), il/elle/on (*he/she/one*) in the singular, or nous (*we*), vous (*you*) and ils/elles (*they*) in the plural. French verbs also have different forms depending on whether you are referring to the present, future or past.

➤ Some verbs in French do not follow the normal rules, and are called <u>irregular verbs</u>. These include some very common and important verbs like **avoir** (meaning *to have*), **être** (meaning *to be*), **faire** (meaning *to do, to make*) and **aller** (meaning *to go*). There is information on many of these irregular verbs in the following sections.

⇨ For **Verb tables**, see supplement.

> ### Key points
> ✔ French verbs have different forms depending on what noun or pronoun they are used with, and on their tense.
> ✔ They are made up of a stem and an ending. The stem is usually based on the infinitive.
> ✔ Regular verbs fit into one of three patterns or conjugations: -er, -ir, or -re verbs.
> ✔ Irregular verbs do not follow the normal rules.

For further explanation of grammatical terms, please see pages viii-xii.

The present tense

> **What is the present tense?**
> The **present tense** is used to talk about what is true at the moment, what happens regularly and what is happening now, for example, I'm a student, I _travel_ to college by train, I'm _studying_ languages.

▶ You use a verb in the present tense to talk about:

- things that are happening now
  It's raining.
  The phone's ringing.

- things that happen all the time or at certain intervals, or things that you do as a habit
  It always snows in January.
  I play football on Saturdays.

- things that are true at the present time:
  She's not very well.
  It's a beautiful house.

▶ There is more than one way to express the present tense in English. For example, you can say either I give, I am giving, or occasionally I do give. In French you use the same form (je donne) for all of these!

▶ In English you can also use the present tense to talk about something that is going to happen in the near future. You can do the same in French.

Je vais en France le mois prochain.	I'm going to France next month.
Nous prenons le train de dix heures.	We're getting the ten o'clock train.

> *Tip*
> Although English sometimes uses parts of the verb to be to form the present tense of other verbs (for example, I am listening, she's talking), French NEVER uses the verb être in this way.

The present tense: regular -er (first conjugation) verbs

➤ If an infinitive in French ends in -er, it means the verb belongs to the <u>first conjugation</u>, for example, donner, aimer, parler.

➤ To know which form of the verb to use in French, you need to work out what the stem of the verb is and then add the correct ending. The stem of -er verbs in the present tense is formed by taking the <u>infinitive</u> and chopping off -er.

Infinitive	Stem (without -er)
donner (*to give*)	donn-
aimer (*to like, to love*)	aim-
parler (*to speak, to talk*)	parl-

➤ Now you know how to find the stem of a verb, you can add the correct ending. Which one you choose will depend on whether you are referring to je, tu, il, elle, on, nous, vous, ils or elles.

⇨ *For more information on **Pronouns**, see page 42.*

➤ Here are the present tense endings for -er verbs:

Pronoun	Ending	Add to stem, e.g. donn-	Meanings
je (j')	-e	je donn<u>e</u>	I give I am giving
tu	-es	tu donn<u>es</u>	you give you are giving
il elle on	-e	il donn<u>e</u> elle donn<u>e</u> on donn<u>e</u>	he/she/it/one gives he/she/it/one is giving
nous	-ons	nous donn<u>ons</u>	we give we are giving
vous	-ez	vous donn<u>ez</u>	you give you are giving
ils elles	-ent	ils donn<u>ent</u> elles donn<u>ent</u>	they give they are giving

Marie <u>regarde</u> la télé.	Marie is watching TV.
Le train <u>arrive</u> à deux heures.	The train arrives at 2 o'clock.

Tip

je changes to j' in front of a word starting with a vowel (*a, e, i, o* or *u*), most words starting with h, and the French word y.

📋 Note that there are a few regular -er verbs that are spelled slightly differently from the way you might expect.

⇨ *For more information on **Spelling changes in** -er **verbs**, see page 78.*

Key points

✔ Verbs ending in -er belong to the first conjugation and form their present tense stem by losing the -er from the infinitive.
✔ The present tense endings for -er verbs are:
-e, -es, -e, -ons, -ez, -ent.

The present tense: regular -ir (second conjugation) verbs

➤ If an infinitive ends in -ir, it means the verb belongs to the <u>second conjugation</u>, for example, finir, choisir, remplir.

➤ The stem of -ir verbs in the present tense is formed by taking the <u>infinitive</u> and chopping off -ir.

Infinitive	Stem (without -ir)
finir *(to finish)*	fin-
choisir *(to choose)*	chois-
remplir *(to fill, to fill in)*	rempl-

➤ Now add the correct ending, depending on whether you are referring to je, tu, il, elle, on, nous, vous, ils or elles.

⇨ *For more information on **Pronouns**, see page 42.*

➤ Here are the present tense endings for -ir verbs:

Pronoun	Ending	Add to stem, e.g. fin-	Meanings
je (j')	-is	je fin<u>is</u>	I finish I am finishing
tu	-is	tu fin<u>is</u>	you finish you are finishing
il elle on	-it	il fin<u>it</u> elle fin<u>it</u> on fin<u>it</u>	he/she/it/one finishes he/she/it/one is finishing
nous	-issons	nous fin<u>issons</u>	we finish we are finishing
vous	-issez	vous fin<u>issez</u>	you finish you are finishing
ils elles	-issent	ils fin<u>issent</u> elles fin<u>issent</u>	they finish they are finishing

Le cours <u>finit</u> à onze heures.
Je <u>finis</u> mes devoirs.

The lesson finishes at eleven o'clock.
I'm finishing my homework.

Tip

je changes to j' in front of a word starting with a vowel, most
words starting with h, and the French word y.

➤ The nous and vous forms of -ir verbs have an extra syllable.

tu fi|nis   (*two syllables*)
vous fi|ni|ssez   (*three syllables*)

Key points

✔ Verbs ending in -ir belong to the second conjugation and form
their present tense stem by losing the -ir from the infinitive.

✔ The present tense endings for -ir verbs are:
-is, -is, -it, -issons, -issez, -issent.

✔ Remember the extra syllable in the nous and vous forms.

The present tense: regular -re (third conjugation) verbs

➤ If an infinitive ends in -re, it means the verb belongs to the <u>third conjugation</u>, for example, attendre, vendre, entendre.

➤ The stem of -re verbs in the present tense is formed by taking the <u>infinitive</u> and chopping off -re.

Infinitive	Stem (without -re)
attendre (*to wait*)	attend-
vendre (*to sell*)	vend-
entendre (*to hear*)	entend-

➤ Now add the correct ending, depending on whether you are referring to je, tu, il, elle, on, nous, vous, ils or elles.

⮕ *For more information on **Pronouns**, see page 42.*

➤ Here are the present tense endings for -re verbs:

Pronoun	Ending	Add to stem, e.g. attend-	Meanings
je (j')	-s	j'attend<u>s</u>	I wait I am waiting
tu	-s	tu attend<u>s</u>	you wait you are waiting
il elle on	-	il attend elle attend on attend	he/she/it/one waits he/she/it/one is waiting
nous	-ons	nous attend<u>ons</u>	we wait we are waiting
vous	-ez	vous attend<u>ez</u>	you wait you are waiting
ils elles	-ent	ils attend<u>ent</u> elles attend<u>ent</u>	they wait they are waiting

J'<u>attends</u> ma sœur. I'm waiting for my sister.

Chaque matin nous <u>attendons</u> le train ensemble. Every morning we wait for the train together.

Tip

je changes to j' in front of a word starting with a vowel, most words starting with h, and the French word y.

Key points

✔ Verbs ending in -re belong to the third conjugation and form their present tense stem by losing the -re from the infinitive.

✔ The present tense endings for -re verbs are:
-s, -s, -, -ons, -ez, -ent.

The present tense: spelling changes in -er verbs

➤ Learning the patterns shown on pages 72–73 means you can now work out the forms of most -er verbs. A few verbs, though, involve a small spelling change. This is usually to do with how a word is pronounced. In the tables below the form(s) with the irregular spelling is/are <u>underlined</u>.

1 Verbs ending in -cer

➤ With verbs such as lancer (meaning *to throw*), which end in -cer, c becomes ç before an a or an o. This is so the letter c is still pronounced as in the English word *ice*.

Pronoun	Example verb: lancer
je	lance
tu	lances
il elle on	lance
nous	<u>lançons</u>
vous	lancez
ils elles	lancent

2 Verbs ending in -ger

➤ With verbs such as manger (meaning *to eat*), which end in -ger, g becomes ge before an a or an o. This is so the letter g is still pronounced like the s in the English word *leisure*.

Pronoun	Example verb: manger
je	mange
tu	manges
il elle on	mange
nous	<u>mangeons</u>
vous	mangez
ils elles	mangent

3 | Verbs ending in -eler

► With verbs such as **appeler** (meaning *to call*), which end in -eler, the l doubles before -e, -es and -ent. The double consonant (ll) affects the pronunciation of the word. In **appeler**, the first e sounds like the vowel sound at the end of the English word *teacher*, but in **appelle** the first e sounds like the one in the English word *pet*.

Pronoun	Example verb: appeler
j'	<u>appelle</u>
tu	<u>appelles</u>
il elle on	<u>appelle</u>
nous	appelons
vous	appelez
ils elles	<u>appellent</u>

► The exceptions to this rule are **geler** (meaning *to freeze*) and **peler** (meaning *to peel*), which change in the same way as **lever** (*see page 81*).

► Verbs like this are sometimes called '<u>1, 2, 3, 6 verbs</u>' because they change in the first person singular (**je**), second person singular (**tu**), and third person singular and plural (**il/elle/on** and **ils/elles**).

4 | Verbs ending in -eter

► With verbs such as **jeter** (meaning *to throw*), which end in -eter, the t doubles before -e, -es and -ent. The double consonant (tt) affects the pronunciation of the word. In **jeter**, the first e sounds like the vowel sound at the end of the English word *teacher*, but in **jette** the first e sounds like the one in the English word *pet*.

Pronoun	Example verb: jeter
je	<u>jette</u>
tu	<u>jettes</u>
il elle on	<u>jette</u>
nous	jetons
vous	jetez
ils elles	<u>jettent</u>

➤ The exceptions to this rule include acheter (meaning *to buy*), which changes in the same way as lever (*see page 81*).

➤ Verbs like this are sometimes called '1, 2, 3, 6 verbs'.

5 **Verbs ending in -yer**

➤ With verbs such as nettoyer (meaning *to clean*), which end in -yer, the y changes to i before -e, -es and -ent.

Pronoun	Example verb: nettoyer
je	nettoie
tu	nettoies
il elle on	nettoie
nous	nettoyons
vous	nettoyez
ils elles	nettoient

➤ Verbs ending in -ayer, such as payer (meaning *to pay*) and essayer (meaning *to try*), can be spelled with either a y or an i. So je paie and je paye, for example, are both correct.

➤ Verbs like this are sometimes called '1, 2, 3, 6 verbs'.

6 **Changes involving accents**

➤ With verbs such as lever (meaning *to raise*), peser (meaning *to weigh*) and acheter (meaning *to buy*), e changes to è before the consonant + -e, -es and -ent. The accent changes the pronunciation too. In lever the first e sounds like the vowel sound at the end of the English word *teacher*, but in lève and so on the first e sounds like the one in the English word *pet*.

Pronoun	Example verb: lever
je	lève
tu	lèves
il elle on	lève
nous	levons
vous	levez
ils elles	lèvent

For further explanation of grammatical terms, please see pages viii-xii.

➤ With verbs such as **espérer** (meaning *to hope*), **régler** (meaning *to adjust*) and **préférer** (meaning *to prefer*), é changes to è before the consonant + -e, -es and -ent.

Pronoun	Example verb: espérer
j'	espère
tu	espères
il elle on	espère
nous	espérons
vous	espérez
ils elles	espèrent

➤ Verbs like this are sometimes called '1, 2, 3, 6 verbs'.

> **Key points**
> ✔ In verbs ending in -cer and -ger:
> c → ç and g → ge in the **nous** form.
> ✔ In verbs ending in -eler and -eter:
> l → ll and t → tt in all but the **nous** and **vous** forms.
> ✔ In verbs ending in -yer:
> y → i in all but the **nous** and **vous** forms (optional in -ayer verbs).

The present tense: irregular verbs

➤ Some verbs in French do not follow the normal rules. These verbs include some very common and important verbs like **avoir** (meaning *to have*), **être** (meaning *to be*), **faire** (meaning *to do, to make*) and **aller** (meaning *to go*). The present tense of these four verbs is given in full below.

⇨ For **Verb tables**, see supplement.

1 The present tense of avoir

Pronoun	avoir	Meaning: *to have*
j'	ai	I have
tu	as	you have
il elle on	a	he/she/it/one has
nous	avons	we have
vous	avez	you have
ils elles	ont	they have

J'**ai** deux sœurs.   I have two sisters.
Il **a** les yeux bleus.   He has blue eyes.
Elle **a** trois ans.   She's three.
Qu'est-ce qu'il y **a**?   What's the matter?

2 The present tense of être

Pronoun	être	Meaning: *to be*
je	suis	I am
tu	es	you are
il elle on	est	he/she/it/one is
nous	sommes	we are
vous	êtes	you are
ils elles	sont	they are

Je **suis** heureux.   I'm happy.
Mon père **est** instituteur.   My father's a primary school
                                    teacher.
Il **est** deux heures.   It's two o'clock.

3 The present tense of faire

Pronoun	faire	Meaning: *to do, to make*
je	fais	I do/make I am doing/making
tu	fais	you do/make you are doing/making
il elle on	fait	he/she/it/one does/makes he/she/it/one is doing/making
nous	faisons	we do/make we are doing/making
vous	faites	you do/make you are doing/making
ils elles	font	they do/make they are doing/making

Je <u>fais</u> un gâteau.	I'm making a cake.
Qu'est-ce que tu <u>fais</u>?	What are you doing?
Il <u>fait</u> **chaud.**	It's hot.
Ça ne <u>fait</u> **rien.**	It doesn't matter.

4 The present tense of aller

Pronoun	aller	Meaning: *to go*
je	vais	I go I am going
tu	vas	you go you are going
il elle on	va	he/she/it/one goes he/she/it/one is going
nous	allons	we go we are going
vous	allez	you go you are going
ils elles	vont	they go they are going

Je <u>vais</u> **à Londres.**	I'm going to London.
'Comment <u>allez</u>**-vous?' – 'Je** <u>vais</u> **bien.'**	'How are you?' – 'I'm fine.'
'Comment ça <u>va</u>?' – 'Ça <u>va</u> **bien.'**	'How are you?' – 'I'm fine.'

5 Irregular -ir verbs

➤ Many irregular verbs that end in -ir, such as partir (meaning *to go*) and tenir (meaning *to hold*), have a common pattern in the singular. The je and tu forms often end in -s, and the il/elle/on form often ends in -t.

Pronoun	partir	tenir
je	par<u>s</u>	tien<u>s</u>
tu	par<u>s</u>	tien<u>s</u>
il/elle/on	par<u>t</u>	tien<u>t</u>

    Je <u>pars</u> demain.   I'm leaving tomorrow.
    Elle <u>tient</u> le bébé.   She is holding the baby.

➪ *For **Verb tables**, see supplement.*

> **Key points**
> ✔ Some very important French verbs are irregular, including avoir, être, faire and aller. They are worth learning in full.
> ✔ The -s, -s, -t pattern occurs frequently in irregular -ir verbs.

The imperative

> **What is the imperative?**
> An **imperative** is a form of the verb used when giving orders and instructions, for example, *Shut the door!; Sit down!; Don't go!*

1 Using the imperative

➤ In French, there are two forms of the imperative that are used to give instructions or orders to someone. These correspond to **tu** and **vous**.

⟹ *For more information on the difference between tu and vous, see page 43.*

➤ There is also a form of the imperative that corresponds to **nous**. This means the same as *let's* in English. It is not used as often as the **tu** and **vous** forms.

2 Forming the present tense imperative

➤ For regular verbs, the imperative is the same as the **tu**, **nous** and **vous** forms of the present tense, except that you do not say the pronouns **tu**, **nous** and **vous**. Also, in the **tu** form of -er verbs like **donner**, the final -s is dropped.

Pronoun	-er verbs: donner	Meaning	-ir verbs: finir	Meaning	-re verbs: attendre	Meaning
tu	donne	give	finis	finish	attends	wait
nous	donnons	let's give	finissons	let's finish	attendons	let's wait
vous	donnez	give	finissez	finish	attendez	wait

Donne-moi ça! — Give me that!

Finissez vos devoirs et **allez** vous coucher. — Finish your homework and go to bed.

Attendons le bus. — Let's wait for the bus.

> *Tip*
>
> When a **tu** imperative comes before **en** or **y**, the final -s is kept to make the words easier to pronounce. The s is pronounced like the *z* in the English word *zip*:
>
> **Vas-y!** — Go on!
>
> **Donnes-en** à ton frère. — Give some to your brother.

3 | Where to put the object pronoun

➤ An object pronoun is a word like la (meaning *her/it*), me/moi (meaning *me*) or leur (meaning *to them*) that is used instead of a noun as the object of a sentence. In orders and instructions, the position of these object pronouns in the sentence changes depending on whether you are telling someone <u>TO DO</u> something or <u>NOT TO DO</u> something.

⤷ For more information on **Object pronouns**, see page 47.

➤ If you are telling someone <u>NOT TO DO</u> something, you put the object pronouns <u>BEFORE</u> the verb.

Ne me dérange pas.	Don't disturb me.
Ne leur parlons pas.	Let's not speak to them.
Ne le regardez pas.	Don't look at him/it.

➤ If you are telling someone <u>TO DO</u> something, you put the object pronouns <u>AFTER</u> the verb and join the two words with a hyphen. The word order is the same as in English.

Excusez-moi.	Excuse me.
Aide-nous.	Help us.
Attendons-la.	Let's wait for her/it.

➤ Orders and instructions telling someone to do something may contain <u>direct object</u> and <u>indirect object pronouns</u>. When this happens, the pronouns go in this order:

DIRECT		INDIRECT
le		moi
la	BEFORE	toi
les		lui
		nous
		vous
		leur

Prête-les moi!	Lend them to me! *or* Lend me them!
Donnez-la-nous!	Give it to us! *or* Give us it!

⤷ For imperatives using **Reflexive verbs**, see page 90.

4 **Imperative forms of irregular verbs**

➤ avoir (meaning *to have*), être (meaning *to be*), savoir (meaning *to know*) and vouloir (meaning *to want*) have irregular imperative forms.

Pronoun	avoir	être	savoir	vouloir
tu	aie	sois	sache	veuille
nous	ayons	soyons	sachons	veuillons
vous	ayez	soyez	sachez	veuillez

<u>Sois</u> sage.　　　　　　　　　Be good.

<u>Veuillez</u> fermer la porte.　　Please shut the door.

> **Key points**
> ✔ The imperative has three forms: tu, nous and vous.
> ✔ The forms are the same as the tu, nous and vous forms of the present tense, except that the final -s is dropped in the tu form of -er verbs.
> ✔ Object pronouns go before the verb when you are telling someone not to do something, but after the verb with a hyphen when you are telling someone to do something.
> ✔ avoir, être, savoir and vouloir have irregular imperative forms.

Reflexive verbs

What is a reflexive verb?
A **reflexive verb** is one where the subject and object are the same, and where the action 'reflects back' on the subject. It is used with a reflexive pronoun such as *myself*, *yourself* and *herself* in English, for example, *I washed myself; He shaved himself.*

1 Using reflexive verbs

➤ In French, reflexive verbs are much more common than in English, and many are used in everyday French. They are shown in dictionaries as se plus the infinitive (se means *himself, herself, itself, themselves* or *oneself*). se is called a <u>reflexive pronoun</u>.

> *Tip*
>
> se changes to s' in front of a word starting with a vowel, most words starting with h, and the French word y.

➤ Reflexive verbs are often used to describe things you do (to yourself) every day or that involve a change of some sort (going to bed, sitting down, getting angry, going to sleep). Some of the most common French reflexive verbs are listed here:

s'amuser	to play, to enjoy oneself
s'appeler	to be called
s'arrêter	to stop
s'asseoir	to sit down
se baigner	to go swimming
se coucher	to go to bed
se dépêcher	to hurry
s'habiller	to get dressed
s'intéresser à (quelque chose)	to be interested in (something)
se laver	to wash, to have a wash
se lever	to get up, to rise, to stand up
se passer	to take place, to happen, to go
se promener	to go for a walk
se rappeler	to remember
se réveiller	to wake up
se trouver	to be (situated)

Qu'est-ce qui <u>se passe</u>?	What's happening?
Le soleil <u>se lève</u> à cinq heures.	The sun rises at five o'clock.
<u>Asseyez-vous</u>!	Sit down!

i Note that se and s' are very rarely translated as *himself* and so on in English.

➤ Some French verbs can be used with a reflexive pronoun or without a reflexive pronoun, for example, the verbs appeler and s'appeler, and arrêter and s'arrêter. Sometimes, however, their meaning may change.

<u>Appelle</u> le chien.	<u>Call</u> the dog.
Je <u>m'appelle</u> Jacques.	I'<u>m called</u> Jacques.
Il <u>arrête</u> le moteur.	He <u>switches off</u> the engine.
Elle <u>s'arrête</u> devant une vitrine.	She <u>stops</u> in front of a shop window.

2 Forming the present tense of reflexive verbs

➤ To use a reflexive verb in French, you need to decide which reflexive pronoun to use. The forms shown in brackets in the table are used before a word starting with a vowel, most words starting with h, or the French word y.

Subject pronoun	Reflexive pronoun	Meaning
je	me (m')	myself
tu	te (t')	yourself
il elle on	se (s')	himself herself itself oneself
nous	nous	ourselves
vous	vous	yourself (*singular*) yourselves (*plural*)
ils elles	se (s')	themselves

Je <u>me lève</u> tôt.	I get up early.
Elle <u>s'habille</u>.	She's getting dressed.
Ils <u>s'intéressent</u> beaucoup aux animaux.	They're very interested in animals.

➤ The present tense forms of a reflexive verb work in just the same way as an ordinary verb, except that the reflexive pronoun is used as well.

Reflexive forms	Meaning
je me lave	I wash (myself)
tu te laves	you wash (yourself)
il se lave elle se lave on se lave	he washes (himself) she washes (herself) it washes (itself) one washes (oneself)
nous nous lavons	we wash (ourselves)
vous vous lavez	you wash (yourself) (*singular*) you wash (yourselves) (*plural*)
ils se lavent elles se lavent	they wash (themselves)

➤ Some reflexive verbs, such as s'asseoir (meaning *to sit down*), are irregular. Some of these irregular verbs are shown in the **Verb tables**.

⇨ *For **Verb tables**, see supplement.*

3 Where to put the reflexive pronoun

➤ In the present tense, the reflexive pronoun almost always comes <u>BEFORE</u> the verb.

> **Je me couche tôt.**   I go to bed early.
> **Comment t'appelles-tu?**   What's your name?

➤ When telling someone <u>NOT TO DO</u> something, you put the reflexive pronoun <u>BEFORE</u> the verb as usual.

> **Ne te lève pas.**   Don't get up.
> **Ne vous habillez pas.**   Don't get dressed.

➤ When telling someone <u>TO DO</u> something, you put the reflexive pronoun <u>AFTER</u> the verb and join the two words with a hyphen.

> **Lève-toi!**   Get up!
> **Dépêchez-vous!**   Hurry up!
> **Habillons-nous.**   Let's get dressed.

> **Tip**
>
> When you are telling someone <u>TO DO</u> something, te or t'
> changes to toi.
>
>   Assieds-<u>toi</u>.   Sit down.
>
> When you are telling someone <u>NOT TO DO</u> something, te or t' is
> used, not toi.
>
>   Ne te lève pas.   Don't get up.

⇨ *For more information on the **Imperative**, see page 85.*

4 *Each other* and *one another*

➤ The French reflexive pronouns nous, vous and se can be used to translate
the English phrase *each other* and *one another*.

Nous <u>nous</u> parlons tous les jours.	We speak to <u>each other</u> every day.
On <u>se</u> voit demain?	Shall we see <u>each other</u> tomorrow?
Les trois pays <u>se</u> ressemblent beaucoup.	The three countries are really like <u>one another</u>.

> **Key points**
> - ✔ A reflexive verb is made up of a reflexive pronoun and a verb.
> - ✔ The reflexive pronouns are: me, te, se, nous, vous, se (m', t', s', nous, vous, s' before a vowel, most words beginning with h and the French word y).
> - ✔ The reflexive pronoun comes before the verb, except when you are telling someone to do something.

The imperfect tense

> **What is the imperfect tense?**
> The **imperfect tense** is one of the verb tenses used to talk about the past, especially in descriptions, and to say what used to happen, for example, I _used to walk_ to school; It _was_ sunny at the weekend.

1 Using the imperfect tense

➤ The imperfect tense is used:

- to describe what things were like and how people felt in the past
  I _was_ very sad when she left.
  It _was pouring_ with rain.

- to say what used to happen or what you used to do regularly in the past
  We _used to get up_ very early in those days.
  I never _used to like_ milk.

- to indicate things that were happening or something that was true when something else took place
  I _was watching_ TV when the phone rang.
  As we _were looking_ out of the window, we saw someone walk across the lawn.

[_i_] Note that if you want to talk about an event or action that took place and was completed in the past, you use the perfect tense.

⇨ _For more information on the **Perfect tense**, see page 111._

➤ You can often recognize an imperfect tense in English because it uses a form like _were looking_ or _was raining_. The words _used to_ also indicate an imperfect tense.

> _Tip_
> Remember that you NEVER use the verb être to translate _was_ or _were_ in forms like _was raining_ or _were looking_ and so on. You change the French verb ending instead.

2 Forming the imperfect tense of -er verbs

➤ To form the imperfect tense of -er verbs, you use the same stem of the verb as for the present tense. Then you add the correct ending, depending on whether you are referring to je, tu, il, elle, on, nous, vous, ils or elles.

Pronoun	Ending	Add to stem, e.g. donn-	Meanings
je (j')	-ais	je donnais	I gave I was giving I used to give
tu	-ais	tu donnais	you gave you were giving you used to give
il elle on	-ait	il donnait elle donnait on donnait	he/she/it/one gave he/she/it/one was giving he/she/it/one used to give
nous	-ions	nous donnions	we gave we were giving we used to give
vous	-iez	vous donniez	you gave you were giving you used to give
ils elles	-aient	ils donnaient elles donnaient	they gave they were giving they used to give

Il portait toujours un grand chapeau noir.
He always wore a big black hat.

Nous habitions à Paris à cette époque.
We were living in Paris at that time.

Pour gagner un peu d'argent, je donnais des cours de français.
To earn a little money I used to give French lessons.

Tip
je changes to j' in front of a word starting with a vowel, most words starting with h, and the French word y.

3 **Forming the imperfect tense of -ir verbs**

➤ To form the imperfect tense of -ir verbs, you use the same stem of the verb as for the present tense. Then you add the correct ending, depending on whether you are referring to je, tu, il, elle, on, nous, vous, ils or elles.

Pronoun	Ending	Add to stem, e.g. fin-	Meanings
je (j')	-issais	je finissais	I finished I was finishing I used to finish
tu	-issais	tu finissais	you finished you were finishing you used to finish
il elle on	-issait	il finissait elle finissait on finissait	he/she/it/one finished he/she/it/one was finishing he/she/it/one used to finish
nous	-issions	nous finissions	we finished we were finishing we used to finish
vous	-issiez	vous finissiez	you finished you were finishing you used to finish
ils elles	-issaient	ils finissaient elles finissaient	they finished they were finishing they used to finish

Il **finissait** souvent ses devoirs avant le dîner.
He often finished his homework before dinner.

Cet après-midi-là ils **choisissaient** une bague de fiançailles.
That afternoon they were choosing an engagement ring.

4 **Forming the imperfect tense of -re verbs**

➤ To form the imperfect tense of -re verbs, you use the same stem of the verb as for the present tense. Then you add the correct ending, depending on whether you are referring to je, tu, il, elle, on, nous, vous, ils or elles. These endings are the same as for -er verbs.

Pronoun	Ending	Add to stem, e.g. attend-	Meanings
j' (j')	-ais	j'attend<u>ais</u>	I waited I was waiting I used to wait
tu	-ais	tu attend<u>ais</u>	you waited you were waiting you used to wait
il elle on	-ait	il attend<u>ait</u> elle attend<u>ait</u> on attend<u>ait</u>	he/she/it/one waited he/she/it/one was waiting he/she/it/one used to wait
nous	-ions	nous attend<u>ions</u>	we waited we were waiting we used to wait
vous	-iez	vous attend<u>iez</u>	you waited you were waiting you used to wait
ils elles	-aient	ils attend<u>aient</u> elles attend<u>aient</u>	they waited they were waiting they used to wait

Christine m'<u>attendait</u> tous les soirs à la sortie.	Christine used to wait for me every evening at the exit.
Je <u>vivais</u> seule après mon divorce.	I was living alone after my divorce.

5 Spelling changes in -er verbs

➤ As with the present tense, a few -er verbs change their spellings slightly when they are used in the imperfect tense. The forms with spelling changes have been <u>underlined</u> in the tables.

➤ With verbs such as lancer (meaning *to throw*), which end in -cer, c becomes ç before an a or an o. This is so that the letter c is still pronounced as in the English word *ice*.

Pronoun	Example verb: lancer
je	<u>lançais</u>
tu	<u>lançais</u>
il elle on	<u>lançait</u>
nous	lancions
vous	lanciez
ils elles	<u>lançaient</u>

➤ With verbs such as manger (meaning *to eat*), which end in -ger, g becomes ge before an a or an o. This is so the letter g is still pronounced like the s in the English word *leisure*.

Pronoun	Example verb: manger
je	<u>mangeais</u>
tu	<u>mangeais</u>
il elle on	<u>mangeait</u>
nous	mangions
vous	mangiez
ils elles	<u>mangeaient</u>

➤ These verbs follow the <u>1,2,3,6 pattern</u>. That is, they change in the first, second and third person singular, and in the third person plural.

6 Reflexive verbs in the imperfect tense

➤ The imperfect tense of reflexive verbs is formed just as for ordinary verbs, except that you add the reflexive pronoun (me, te, se, nous, vous, se).

Subject pronoun	Reflexive pronoun	Example with laver	Meaning
je	me (m')	lavais	I washed I was washing I used to wash
tu	te (t')	lavais	you washed you were washing you used to wash
il elle on	se (s')	lavait	he/she/it/one washed he/she/it/one was washing he/she/it/one used to wash
nous	nous	lavions	we washed we were washing we used to wash
vous	vous	laviez	you washed you were washing you used to wash
ils elles	se (s')	lavaient	they washed they were washing they used to wash

For further explanation of grammatical terms, please see pages viii-xii.

7 Irregular verbs in the imperfect tense

➤ One of the most common verbs that is irregular in the imperfect tense is
être.

Pronoun	être	Meaning
j'	étais	I was
tu	étais	you were
il elle on	était	he/she/it/one was
nous	étions	we were
vous	étiez	you were
ils elles	étaient	they were

J'**étais** heureux.	I was happy.
Mon père **était** instituteur.	My father was a primary school teacher.

➤ All other irregular verbs are formed by adding the imperfect endings to
the stem of the nous form of the present tense.

For example:

Verb	Present *nous* form	Imperfect
vouloir	voul-ons	je voulais, tu voulais, il voulait etc
pouvoir	pouv-ons	je pouvais, tu pouvais, il pouvait etc
lire	lis-ons	je lisais, tu lisais, il lisait

Key points

✔ The imperfect tense endings for -er and -re verbs are:
-ais, -ais, -ait, -ions, -iez, -aient.
✔ The imperfect tense endings for -ir verbs are:
-issais, -issais, -issait, -issions, -issiez, -issaient.
✔ In verbs ending in -cer and -ger:
c → ç and g → ge in all but the nous and vous forms.
✔ être is irregular in the imperfect tense.

The future tense

> **What is the future tense?**
> The **future tense** is a verb tense used to talk about something that will happen or will be true.

1 Using the future tense

➤ In English the future tense is often shown by *will* or its shortened form *'ll*.

What <u>will</u> you do?

The weather <u>will</u> be warm and dry tomorrow.

He'<u>ll</u> be here soon.

I'<u>ll</u> give you a call.

➤ Just as in English, you can use the present tense in French to refer to something that is going to happen in the future.

Je <u>prends</u> le train de dix heures.	I'm taking the ten o'clock train.
Nous <u>allons</u> à Paris la semaine prochaine.	We're going to Paris next week.

➤ In English we often use *going to* followed by an infinitive to talk about something that will happen in the immediate future. You can use the French verb aller (meaning *to go*) followed by an infinitive in the same way.

Tu <u>vas tomber</u> si tu continues.	You're going to fall if you carry on.
Il <u>va manquer</u> le train.	He's going to miss the train.

> *Tip*
>
> Remember that French has no direct equivalent of the word *will* in verb forms like *will rain* or *will look* and so on. You change the French verb ending instead to form the future tense.

2 Forming the future tense

➤ To form the future tense in French, you use:

- the <u>infinitive</u> of -er and -ir verbs, for example, donner, finir
- the <u>infinitive without the final e</u> of -re verbs: for example, attendr-

➤ Then add the correct ending to the stem, depending on whether you are talking about je, tu, il, elle, on, nous, vous, ils or elles. The endings are the same for -er, -ir and -re verbs.

[i] Note that apart from the nous and vous forms, the endings are the same as the present tense of avoir.

⇨ *For the present tense of avoir, see page 82.*

Pronoun	Ending	Add to stem, e.g. donner-, finir-, attendr-	Meanings
je (j')	-ai	je donnerai je finirai j'attendrai	I will give I will finish I will wait
tu	-as	tu donneras tu finiras tu attendras	you will give you will finish you will wait
il elle on	-a	il/elle/on donnera il/elle/on finira il/elle/on attendra	he/she/it/one will give he/she/it/one will finish he/she/it/one will wait
nous	-ons	nous donnerons nous finirons nous attendrons	we will give we will finish we will wait
vous	-ez	vous donnerez vous finirez vous attendrez	you will give you will finish you will wait
ils elles	-ont	ils/elles donneront ils/elles finiront ils/elles attendront	they will give they will finish they will wait

Elle te <u>donnera</u> mon adresse. — She'll give you my address.
Le cours <u>finira</u> à onze heures. — The lesson will finish at eleven o'clock.
Nous t'<u>attendrons</u> devant le cinéma. — We'll wait for you in front of the cinema.

Tip
je changes to j' in front of a word starting with a vowel, most words starting with h, and the French word y.

3 Spelling changes in -er verbs

➤ As with the present and imperfect tenses, a few -er verbs change their spellings slightly in the future tense. The forms with spelling changes have been <u>underlined</u> in the tables.

➤ With verbs such as **appeler** (meaning *to call*), which end in -eler, the
l doubles throughout the future tense. The double consonant (ll) affects
the pronunciation of the word. In **appeler**, the first e sounds like the vowel
sound at the end of the English word *teacher*, but in **appellerai** the first
e sounds like the one in the English word *pet*.

Pronoun	Example verb: appeler
j'	appellerai
tu	appelleras
il elle on	appellera
nous	appellerons
vous	appellerez
ils elles	appelleront

➤ The exceptions to this rule are **geler** (meaning *to freeze*) and **peler**
(meaning *to peel*), which change in the same way as **lever** (*see page 101*).

➤ With verbs such as **jeter** (meaning *to throw*), that end in -eter, the t
doubles throughout the future tense. The double consonant (tt) affects the
pronunciation of the word. In **jeter**, the first e sounds like the vowel sound
at the end of the English word *teacher*, but in **jetterai** the first e sounds like
the one in the English word *pet*.

Pronoun	Example verb: jeter
je	jetterai
tu	jetteras
il elle on	jettera
nous	jetterons
vous	jetterez
ils elles	jetteront

➤ The exceptions to this rule include **acheter** (meaning *to buy*), which
changes in the same way as **lever** (*see page 101*).

➤ With verbs such as **nettoyer** (meaning *to clean*), that end in -yer, the y changes to i throughout the future tense.

Pronoun	Example verb: nettoyer
je	nettoierai
tu	nettoieras
il elle on	nettoiera
nous	nettoierons
vous	nettoierez
ils elles	nettoieront

➤ Verbs ending in -ayer, such as **payer** (meaning *to pay)* and **essayer** (meaning *to try*), can be spelled with either a y or an i. So **je paierai** and **je payerai**, for example, are both correct.

➤ With verbs such as **lever** (meaning *to raise*), **peser** (meaning *to weigh*) and **acheter** (meaning *to buy*), e changes to è throughout the future tense. In **lever** the first e sounds like the vowel sound at the end of the English word *teacher*, but in **lèverai** and so on the first e sounds like the one in the English word *pet*.

Pronoun	Example verb: lever
je	lèverai
tu	lèveras
il elle on	lèvera
nous	lèverons
vous	lèverez
ils elles	lèveront

4 Reflexive verbs in the future tense

➤ The future tense of reflexive verbs is formed in just the same way as for ordinary verbs, except that you have to remember to give the reflexive pronoun (me, se, nous, vous, se).

Subject pronoun	Reflexive pronoun	Example with laver	Meaning
je	me (m')	laverai	I will wash
tu	te (t')	laveras	you will wash
il elle on	se (s')	lavera	he/she/it/one will wash
nous	nous	laverons	we will wash
vous	vous	laverez	you will wash
ils elles	se (s')	laveront	they will wash

Tip

me changes to m', te to t' and se to s' before a vowel, most words starting with h and the French word y.

5 Irregular verbs in the future tense

➤ There are some verbs that <u>do not</u> use their infinitives as the stem for the future tense, including avoir, être, faire and aller, which are shown in full on pages 103–104.

➤ Other irregular verbs include:

Verb	Meaning	je	tu	il/elle/on	nous	vous	ils/elles
devoir	to have to, must	devrai	devras	devra	devrons	devrez	devront
pouvoir	to be able to, can	pourrai	pourras	pourra	pourrons	pourrez	pourront
savoir	to know	saurai	sauras	saura	saurons	saurez	sauront
tenir	to hold	tiendrai	tiendras	tiendra	tiendrons	tiendrez	tiendront
venir	to come	viendrai	viendras	viendra	viendrons	viendrez	viendront
voir	to see	verrai	verras	verra	verrons	verrez	verront
vouloir	to want	voudrai	voudras	voudra	voudrons	voudrez	voudront

For further explanation of grammatical terms, please see pages viii-xii.

➤ il faut becomes il faudra (meaning *it will be necessary to*).

➤ il pleut becomes il pleuvra (meaning *it will rain*).

➤ This is the future tense of avoir:

Pronoun	avoir	Meaning: *to have*
j'	aurai	I will have
tu	auras	you will have
il elle on	aura	he/she/it/one will have
nous	aurons	we will have
vous	aurez	you will have
ils elles	auront	they will have

➤ This is the future tense of être:

Pronoun	être	Meaning: *to be*
je	serai	I will be
tu	seras	you will be
il elle on	sera	he/she/it/one will be
nous	serons	we will be
vous	serez	you will be
ils elles	seront	they will be

➤ This is the future tense of faire:

Pronoun	faire	Meaning: *to do, to make*
je	ferai	I will do/make
tu	feras	you will do/make
il elle on	fera	he/she/it/one will do/make
nous	ferons	we will do/make
vous	ferez	you will do/make
ils elles	feront	they will do/make

➤ This is the future tense of aller:

Pronoun	aller	Meaning: *to go*
j'	irai	I will go
tu	iras	you will go
il elle on	ira	he/she/it/one will go
nous	irons	we will go
vous	irez	you will go
ils elles	iront	they will go

⇨ *For **Verb tables**, see supplement.*

> ### Key points
> ✔ You can use a present tense in French to talk about something that will happen or be true in the future, just as in English.
> ✔ You can use aller with an infinitive to refer to things that will happen in the immediate future.
> ✔ The stem is the same as the infinitive for -er, -ir and -re verbs, except that the final -e of -re verbs is lost.
> ✔ The future tense endings are the same for -er, -ir and -re verbs: -ai, -as, -a, -ons, -ez, -ont.
> ✔ In verbs ending in -eler and -eter:
> l → ll and t → tt throughout the future tense.
> ✔ In verbs ending in -yer:
> y → i throughout the future tense (optional in -ayer verbs).
> ✔ Some verbs are irregular in the future tense. It is worth learning these in full.

The conditional

> **What is the conditional?**
> The **conditional** is a verb form used to talk about things that would
> happen or that would be true under certain conditions, for example,
> I _would help_ you if I could.
> It is also used to say what you would like or need, for example, _Could you
> give_ me the bill?

1 Using the conditional

➤ You can often recognize a conditional in English by the word _would_ or its
shortened form _'d_.

    I <u>would</u> be sad if you left.

    If you asked him, he'<u>d</u> help you.

➤ You use the conditional for:
  - asking for something formally and politely, especially in shops
    I'<u>d</u> <u>like</u> a kilo of pears, please.
  - saying what you would like
    I'<u>d</u> <u>like</u> to go to the United States.
  - making a suggestion
    I <u>could</u> <u>come</u> and pick you up.
  - giving advice
    You <u>should</u> <u>say</u> you're sorry.

> _Tip_
>
> There is no direct French translation of _would_ in verb forms like
> _would be, would like, would help_ and so on. You change the French
> verb ending instead.

2 Forming the conditional

➤ To form the conditional in French, you have to use:
  - the infinitive of -er and -ir verbs, for example, donner-, finir-
  - the infinitive without the final e of -re verbs, for example, attendr-

➤ Then add the correct ending to the stem, depending on whether you are
talking about je, tu, il, elle, on, nous, vous, ils or elles. The endings are
the same for all verbs. They are the same as the -er and -re endings for the
<u>IMPERFECT TENSE</u>, but the stem is the same as that of the <u>FUTURE TENSE</u>.

⇨ _For more information on the **Imperfect tense** and the **Future tense**, see pages
92 and 98._

Pronoun	Ending	Add to stem, e.g. donner-, finir-, attendr-	Meanings
je (j')	-ais	je donner<u>ais</u> je finir<u>ais</u> j'attendr<u>ais</u>	I would give I would finish I would wait
tu	-ais	tu donner<u>ais</u> tu finir<u>ais</u> tu attendr<u>ais</u>	you would give you would finish you would wait
il elle on	-ait	il/elle/on donner<u>ait</u> il/elle/on finir<u>ait</u> il/elle/on attendr<u>ait</u>	he/she/it/one would give he/she/it/one would finish he/she/it/one would wait
nous	-ions	nous donner<u>ions</u> nous finir<u>ions</u> nous attendr<u>ions</u>	we would give we would finish we would wait
vous	-iez	vous donner<u>iez</u> vous finir<u>iez</u> vous attendr<u>iez</u>	you would give you would finish you would wait
ils elles	-aient	ils/elles donner<u>aient</u> ils/elles finir<u>aient</u> ils/elles attendr<u>aient</u>	they would give they would finish they would wait

J'<u>aimerais</u> aller aux États Unis.   I'd like to go to the United States.

Tip

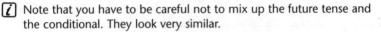

je changes to j' in front of a word starting with a vowel, most words starting with h, and the French word y.

i Note that you have to be careful not to mix up the future tense and the conditional. They look very similar.

FUTURE	CONDITIONAL
je donnerai	je donnerais
je finirai	je finirais
j'attendrai	j'attendrais
j'aimerai	j'aimerais
je voudrai	je voudrais
je viendrai	je viendrais
je serai	je serais

3 **Spelling changes in -er verbs**

➤ As with the future tense, a few -er verbs change their spellings slightly in the conditional. The forms with spelling changes have been <u>underlined</u> in the tables below.

➤ With verbs such as appeler (meaning *to call*), which end in -eler, the l doubles throughout the conditional. The double consonant (ll) affects the pronunciation of the word. In appeler, the first e sounds like the vowel sound at the end of the English word *teacher*, but in appellerais the first e sounds like the one in the English word *pet*.

Pronoun	Example verb: appeler
j'	<u>appellerais</u>
tu	<u>appellerais</u>
il elle on	<u>appellerait</u>
nous	<u>appellerions</u>
vous	<u>appelleriez</u>
ils elles	<u>appelleraient</u>

➤ The exceptions to this rule are geler (meaning *to freeze*) and peler (meaning *to peel*), which change in the same way as lever (*see page 108*).

➤ With verbs such as jeter (meaning *to throw*), which end in -eter, the t doubles throughout the conditional. The double consonant (tt) affects the pronunciation of the word. In jeter, the first e sounds like the vowel sound at the end of the English word *teacher*, but in jetterais the first e sounds like the one in the English word *pet*.

Pronoun	Example verb: jeter
je	<u>jetterais</u>
tu	<u>jetterais</u>
il elle on	<u>jetterait</u>
nous	<u>jetterions</u>
vous	<u>jetteriez</u>
ils elles	<u>jetteraient</u>

➤ The exceptions to this rule include acheter (meaning *to buy*), which changes in the same way as lever (*see page 108*).

➤ With verbs such as **nettoyer** (meaning *to clean*), that end in -yer, the y changes to i throughout the conditional.

Pronoun	Example verb: nettoyer
je	nettoierais
tu	nettoierais
il elle on	nettoierait
nous	nettoierions
vous	nettoieriez
ils elles	nettoieraient

➤ Verbs ending in -ayer, such as **payer** (meaning *to pay*) and **essayer** (meaning *to try*), can be spelled with either a y or an i. So **je paierais** and **je payerais**, for example, are both correct.

➤ With verbs such as **lever** (meaning *to raise*), **peser** (meaning *to weigh*) and **acheter** (meaning *to buy*), e changes to è throughout the conditional. In lever the first e sounds like the vowel sound at the end of the English word *teacher*, but in lèverais and so on the first e sounds like the one in the English word *pet*.

Pronoun	Example verb: lever
je	lèverais
tu	lèverais
il elle on	lèverait
nous	lèverions
vous	lèveriez
ils elles	lèveraient

4 Reflexive verbs in the conditional

➤ The conditional of reflexive verbs is formed in just the same way as for ordinary verbs, except that you have to remember to give the reflexive pronoun (me, te, se, nous, vous, se).

Subject pronoun	Reflexive pronoun	Example with laver	Meaning
je	me (m')	laverais	I would wash
tu	te (t')	laverais	you would wash
il elle on	se (s')	laverait	he/she/it would wash
nous	nous	laverions	we would wash
vous	vous	laveriez	you would wash
ils elles	se (s')	laveraient	they would wash

Tip

me changes to m', te to t' and se to s' before a vowel, most words starting with h and the French word y.

5 Irregular verbs in the conditional

➤ The same verbs that are irregular in the future tense are irregular in the conditional, including: avoir, être, faire, aller, devoir, pouvoir, savoir, tenir, venir, voir, vouloir.

⇨ *For more information on **Irregular verbs in the future tense**, see page 102.*

➤ To form the conditional of an irregular verb, use the same stem as for the future tense, for example:

  avoir → aur-
  être → ser-

➤ Then add the usual endings for the conditional.

Infinitive	Future stem	Conditional endings	Conditional form
avoir	aur-	-ais, -ais, -ait, -ions, -iez, -aient	j'aurais, tu aurais, il/elle/on aurait, nous aurions, vous auriez, ils/elles auraient
être	ser-	-ais, -ais, -ait, -ions, -iez, -aient	je serais, tu serais, il/elle/on serait, nous serions, vous seriez, ils/elles seraient
faire	fer-	-ais, -ais, -ait, -ions, -iez, -aient	je ferais, tu ferais, il/elle/on ferait nous ferions, vous feriez, ils/elles feraient
aller	ir-	-ais, -ais, -ait, -ions, -iez, -aient	j'irais, tu irais, il/elle/on irait, nous irions, vous iriez, ils/elles iraient

J'<u>irais</u> si j'avais le temps.　　　　I would go if I had time.

Je <u>voudrais</u> un kilo de poires, 　　I'd like a kilo of pears, please.
s'il vous plaît.

Tu <u>devrais</u> t'excuser.　　　　　　You should say you're sorry.

> **Key points**
> ✔ The conditional endings are the same for -er, -ir and -re verbs:
>   -ais, -ais, -ait, -ions, -iez, -aient.
> ✔ The conditional endings are the same as the endings for the
>   imperfect tense of -er and -re verbs, but the stem is the same as
>   the stem of the future tense.
> ✔ In verbs ending in -eler and -eter:
>   l → ll and t → tt throughout the conditional.
> ✔ In verbs ending in -yer:
>   y → i throughout the conditional (optional in -ayer verbs).
> ✔ The same verbs that are irregular in the future are irregular in the
>   conditional. It is worth learning these in full.

For further explanation of grammatical terms, please see pages viii-xii.

The perfect tense

> **What is the perfect tense?**
> The **perfect** is one of the verb tenses used in French to talk about the past, especially about actions that took place and were completed in the past.

1 Using the perfect tense

➤ In English there are two types of past tense: _I gave_, _I finished_, and _I have given_, _I have finished_. Both types are translated by the French perfect.

> _Tip_
>
> The perfect tense is the tense you will need most to talk about things that have happened or were true in the past. It is used to talk about actions that took place and WERE COMPLETED in the past.
> Use the imperfect tense for regular events and in most descriptions.
>
> ⇨ _For more information on the **Imperfect tense**, see page 92._

2 Forming the perfect tense

➤ The imperfect, future and conditional tenses in French are made up of just one word, for example, je donne, tu finissais or il attendra. The perfect tense has TWO parts to it:

- the present tense of the verb avoir (meaning _to have_) or être (meaning _to be_)
- a part of the main verb called the past participle, such as _given_, _finished_ and _done_ in English

➤ In other words, the perfect tense in French is like the form _I have done_ in English.

⇨ _For more information on forming the present tense of avoir and être, see page 82._

3 Forming the past participle

➤ To form the past participle of regular verbs, you use the infinitive of the verb:

- For -er verbs, you replace the -er at the end of the infinitive with é.

Infinitive	Take off -er	Add -é
donner (to give)	donn-	donné
tomber (to fall)	tomb-	tombé

- For -ir verbs, you replace the -ir at the end of the infinitive with -i.

Infinitive	Take off -ir	Add -i
finir (to finish)	fin-	fini
partir (to leave, to go)	part-	parti

- For -re verbs, you replace the -re at the end of the infinitive with -u.

Infinitive	Take off -re	Add -u
attendre (to wait)	attend-	attendu
descendre (to go down, to come down, to get off)	descend-	descendu

4 Verbs that form their perfect tense with avoir

➤ Most verbs form their perfect tense with avoir, for example donner:

Pronoun	avoir	Past participle	Meaning
j'	ai	donné	I gave I have given
tu	as	donné	you gave you have given
il elle on	a	donné	he/she/it/one gave he/she/it/one has given
nous	avons	donné	we gave we have given
vous	avez	donné	you gave you have given
ils elles	ont	donné	they gave they have given

Elle **a donné** son numéro de téléphone à Claude.	She gave Claude her phone number.
Il **a acheté** un ordinateur.	He's bought a computer.
Je n'**ai** pas **regardé** la télé hier.	I didn't watch TV yesterday.

Tip

je changes to j' in front of a word starting with a vowel, most words starting with h, and the French word y.

➤ The perfect tense of -ir verbs like finir is formed in the same way, except for the different ending of the past participle: j'ai fini, tu as fini and so on.

➤ The perfect tense of -re verbs like attendre is formed in the same way, except for the past participle: j'ai attendu, tu as attendu and so on.

5 **avoir or être?**

➤ MOST verbs form their perfect tense with avoir; these include donner as shown on page 112.

➤ There are two main groups of verbs which form their perfect tense with être instead of avoir:

● all reflexive verbs

➪ *For more information on **Reflexive verbs**, see page 88.*

● a group of verbs that are mainly used to talk about movement or a change of some kind, including these ones:

aller	to go
venir	to come
arriver	to arrive, to happen
partir	to leave, to go
descendre	to go down, to come down, to get off
monter	to go up, to come up
entrer	to go in, to come in
sortir	to go out, to come out
mourir	to die
naître	to be born
devenir	to become
rester	to stay
tomber	to fall

Je <u>suis allé</u> au match de football hier.	I went to the football match yesterday.
Il <u>est sorti</u> acheter un journal.	He's gone out to buy a newspaper.
Vous <u>êtes descendu</u> à quelle station?	Which station did you get off at?

Grammar Extra!

Some of the verbs on the previous page take avoir when they are used with a direct object, for example:

descendre quelque chose	to get something down, to bring something down, to take something down
monter quelque chose	to go up something, to come up something
sortir quelque chose	to take something out
Est-ce que tu <u>as descendu</u> les bagages?	Did you bring the bags down?
Elle <u>a monté</u> les escaliers.	She went up the stairs.
Elle <u>a sorti</u> son porte-monnaie de son sac.	She took her purse out of her handbag.

⇨ *For more information on **Direct objects**, see page 47.*

6 | **Verbs that form their perfect tense with** être

➤ When a verb takes être, the past participle <u>ALWAYS</u> agrees with the subject of the verb; that is, the endings change in the feminine and plural forms.

	Masculine endings	Examples	Feminine endings	Examples
Singular	-	tombé parti descendu	-e	tomb<u>ée</u> part<u>ie</u> descend<u>ue</u>
Plural	-s	tombé<u>s</u> parti<u>s</u> descendu<u>s</u>	-es	tomb<u>ées</u> part<u>ies</u> descend<u>ues</u>

Est-ce ton frère est <u>allé</u> à l'étranger?	Did your brother go abroad?
Elle est <u>venue</u> avec nous.	She came with us.
Ils sont <u>partis</u> à six heures.	They left at six o'clock.
Mes cousines sont <u>arrivées</u> hier.	My cousins arrived yesterday. *(The cousins are female.)*

➤ Here are the perfect tense forms of tomber in full:

Pronoun	avoir	Past participle	Meaning
je	suis	tombé (*masculine*) tombée (*feminine*)	I fell/I have fallen
tu	es	tombé (*masculine*) tombée (*feminine*)	you fell/you have fallen
il	est	tombé	he/it fell, he/it has fallen
elle	est	tombée	she/it fell, she/it has fallen
on	est	tombé (*singular*) tombés (*masculine plural*) tombées (*feminine plural*)	one fell/one has fallen, we fell/we have fallen
nous	sommes	tombés (*masculine*) tombées (*feminine*)	we fell/we have fallen
vous	êtes	tombé (*masculine singular*) tombée (*feminine singular*) tombés (*masculine plural*) tombées (*feminine plural*)	you fell/you have fallen
ils	sont	tombés	they fell/they have fallen
elles	sont	tombées	they fell/they have fallen

Grammar Extra!

When the subject of the sentence is masculine and feminine, such as Marcel et Marie, the past participle has a masculine plural ending.

Marcel et Marie sont <u>tombés</u> amoureux.   Marcel and Marie fell in love.

➤ The perfect tense of -ir verbs like partir is formed in the same way, except for the past participle: je suis parti(e), tu es parti(e) and so on.

➤ The perfect tense of -re verbs like descendre is formed in the same way, except for the past participle: je suis descendu(e), tu es descendu(e) and so on.

Grammar Extra!

When a verb takes avoir, the past participle usually stays in the masculine singular form, as shown in the table for donner, and does not change for the feminine or plural forms.

Il a <u>fini</u> sa dissertation.	He's finished his essay.
Elles ont <u>fini</u> leur dissertation.	They've finished their essay.

In one particular case, however, the past participle of verbs with avoir does change in the feminine and plural forms. In the sentences above, dissertation is the direct object of the verb finir. When the direct object comes <u>AFTER</u> the verb, as it does in the examples above, then the past participle doesn't change. If the direct object comes <u>BEFORE</u> the verb, however, the past participle has to change to agree with that direct object.

<u>la</u> dissertation qu'il a fini<u>e</u> hier	the essay that he finished yesterday
<u>la</u> dissertation qu'elles ont fini<u>e</u> hier	the essay that they finished yesterday

Since object pronouns usually come BEFORE the verb, the past participle changes to agree with the pronoun.

Il a bu son thé? – Oui, il <u>l'</u>a <u>bu</u>.	Did he drink his tea? – Yes, he's drunk it.
Il a bu sa limonade? – Oui, il <u>l'</u>a <u>bue</u>.	Did he drink his lemonade? – Yes, he's drunk it.

> *Tip*
>
> Remember that with verbs taking être, it is the <u>subject</u> of the verb that tells you what ending to add to the past participle. Compare this with the rule for verbs taking avoir that have a direct object; in their case, it is the <u>direct object</u> coming before the verb that tells you what ending to add to the past participle.

For further explanation of grammatical terms, please see pages viii-xii.

7 The perfect tense of reflexive verbs

▶ Here is the perfect tense of the reflexive verb **se laver** (meaning *to wash (oneself), to have a wash, to get washed*) in full. Remember that all reflexive verbs take **être**, and so the past participle of reflexive verbs usually agrees with the subject of the sentence.

Subject pronoun	Reflexive pronoun	Present tense of être	Past participle	Meaning
je	me	suis	lavé (*masculine*) lavée (*feminine*)	I washed myself
tu	t'	es	lavé (*masculine*) lavée (*feminine*)	you washed yourself
il	s'	est	lavé	he washed himself
elle	s'	est	lavée	she washed herself
on	s'	est	lavé (*singular*) lavés (*masculine plural*) lavées (*feminine plural*)	one washed oneself we washed ourselves
nous	nous	sommes	lavés (*masculine*) lavées (*feminine*)	we washed ourselves
vous	vous	êtes	lavé (*masculine singular*) lavée (*feminine singular*) lavés (*masculine plural*) lavées (*feminine plural*)	you washed yourself (*singular*) you washed yourselves (*plural*)
ils	se	sont	lavés	they washed themselves
elles	se	sont	lavées	they washed themselves

Tip

When **on** means *we*, and masculine and feminine are involved, the past participle has a masculine ending. You can use either the masculine singular or the masculine plural.

On s'est déjà lavé.
On s'est déjà lavés. We've already washed.

Grammar Extra!

The past participle of reflexive verbs <u>DOES NOT</u> change if the direct object (la jambe in the example below) <u>FOLLOWS</u> the verb.

> **Elle s'<u>est cassé</u> la jambe.**　　　　She's broken her leg.

8 Irregular verbs in the perfect tense

➤ Some past participles are irregular. There aren't too many, so try to learn them.

avoir (meaning *to have*)	→ **eu**
devoir (meaning *to have to, must*)	→ **dû**
dire (meaning *to say, to tell*)	→ **dit**
être (meaning *to be*)	→ **été**
faire (meaning *to do, to make*)	→ **fait**
mettre (meaning *to put*)	→ **mis**
pouvoir (meaning *to be able to, can*)	→ **pu**
prendre (meaning *to take*)	→ **pris**
savoir (meaning *to know*)	→ **su**
tenir (meaning *to hold*)	→ **tenu**
venir (meaning *to come*)	→ **venu**
voir (meaning *to see*)	→ **vu**
vouloir (meaning *to want*)	→ **voulu**

➤ **il pleut** becomes **il a plu** (*it rained*).

➤ **il faut** becomes **il a fallu** (*it was necessary*).

> **Key points**
> ✔ The perfect tense describes things that happened and were completed in the past. It is not used for things that happened regularly or in descriptions.
> ✔ The perfect tense is formed with the present tense of **avoir** or **être** and a past participle.
> ✔ Most verbs take **avoir** in the perfect tense. All reflexive verbs and a small group of verbs referring to movement or change take **être**.
> ✔ The past participle ends in **-é** for **-er** verbs, in **-i** for **-ir** verbs, and in **-u** for **-re** verbs.
> ✔ With verbs that take **avoir**, the past participle does not usually change. With verbs that take **être**, including reflexive verbs, the past participle changes in the feminine and plural.

For further explanation of grammatical terms, please see pages viii-xii.

Grammar Extra!

The pluperfect tense

What is the pluperfect tense?
The **pluperfect** is a verb tense which describes something that <u>had</u> happened or <u>had</u> been true at a point in the past, for example, *I'd forgotten to finish my homework.*

1 Using the pluperfect tense

➤ Examples of the pluperfect tense in English are *I had arrived, you'd fallen.*

Elle <u>avait essayé</u> des douzaines de pulls.	She <u>had tried on</u> dozens of jumpers.
Nous <u>avions</u> déjà <u>commencé</u> à manger quand il est arrivé.	We'd already <u>started</u> eating when he arrived.
J'<u>étais arrivée</u> la première.	I <u>had arrived</u> first.
Mes parents s'<u>étaient couchés</u> tôt.	My parents <u>had gone</u> to bed early.

2 Forming the pluperfect tense

➤ Like the perfect tense, the pluperfect tense in French has <u>two</u> parts to it:

- the <u>imperfect</u> tense of the verb avoir (meaning *to have*) or être (meaning *to be*)
- the past participle

➤ If a verb takes avoir in the perfect tense, then it will take avoir in the pluperfect too. If a verb takes être in the perfect, then it will take être in the pluperfect too.

➡ *For more information on the **Imperfect tense** and the **Perfect tense**, see pages 92 and 111.*

3 Verbs taking avoir

➤ Here are the pluperfect tense forms of donner (meaning *to give*) in full.

Pronoun	avoir	Past participle	Meaning
j'	avais	donné	I had given
tu	avais	donné	you had given
il elle on	avait	donné	he/she/it/one had given
nous	avions	donné	we had given
vous	aviez	donné	you had given
ils elles	avaient	donné	they had given

➤ The pluperfect tense of -ir verbs like finir (meaning *to finish*) is formed in the same way, except for the ending of the past participle: j'avais fini, tu avais fini and so on.

➤ The pluperfect tense of -re verbs like attendre (meaning *to wait*) is formed in the same way, except for the past participle: j'avais attendu, tu avais attendu and so on.

4 **Verbs taking être**

➤ Here are the pluperfect tense forms of **tomber** (meaning *to fall*) in full. When a verb takes être in the pluperfect tense, the past participle <u>always</u> agrees with the subject of the verb; that is, the endings change in the feminine and plural forms.

Pronoun	être	Past participle	Meaning
j'	étais	tombé (*masculine*) tombée (*feminine*)	I had fallen
tu	étais	tombé (*masculine*) tombée (*feminine*)	you had fallen
il	était	tombé	he/it had fallen
elle	était	tombée	she/it had fallen
on	était	tombé (*singular*) tombés (*masculine plural*) tombées (*feminine plural*)	one had fallen we had fallen
nous	étions	tombés (*masculine*) tombées (*feminine*)	we had fallen
vous	étiez	tombé (*masculine singular*) tombée (*feminine singular*) tombés (*masculine plural*) tombées (*feminine plural*)	you had fallen
ils	étaient	tombés	they had fallen
elles	étaient	tombées	they had fallen

➤ The pluperfect tense of -ir verbs like **partir** (meaning *to leave, to go*) is formed in the same way, except for the past participle: j'étais parti(e), tu étais parti(e) and so on.

➤ The pluperfect tense of -re verbs like **descendre** (meaning *to come down, to go down, to get off*) is formed in the same way, except for the past participle: j'étais descendu(e), tu étais descendu(e) and so on.

Tip

When **on** means *we*, the past participle can agree with the subject of the sentence, but it is optional.

On était <u>tombées</u>.   We had fallen. (*feminine*)

5 **Reflexive verbs in the pluperfect tense**

➤ Reflexive verbs in the pluperfect tense are formed in the same way as in the perfect tense, but with the imperfect tense of the verb être (*see page 97*).

⇨ *For more information on the **Perfect tense of reflexive verbs**, see page 117.*

6 Irregular verbs in the pluperfect tense

➤ Irregular past participles are the same as for the perfect tense (*see page 118*).

> **Key points**
> ✔ The pluperfect tense describes things that had happened or were true at a point in the past before something else happened.
> ✔ It is formed with the imperfect tense of avoir or être and the past participle.
> ✔ The rules for agreement of the past participle are the same as for the perfect tense.

The passive

> **What is the passive?**
> The **passive** is a form of the verb that is used when the subject of the verb is the person or thing that is affected by the action, for example, *I was given, we were told, it had been made.*

1 Using the passive

➤ In a normal, or *active* sentence, the 'subject' of the verb is the person or thing that carries out the action described by the verb. The 'object' of the verb is the person or thing that the verb 'happens' to.

Ryan *(subject)* hit *(active verb)* me *(object)*.

➤ In English, as in French, you can turn an <u>active</u> sentence round to make a <u>passive</u> sentence.

I *(subject)* was hit *(passive verb)* by Ryan *(agent)*.

➤ Very often, however, you cannot identify who is carrying out the action indicated by the verb.

I was hit in the face.

The trees will be chopped down.

I've been chosen to represent the school.

> ## Tip
> There is a very important difference between French and English in sentences containing an <u>indirect object</u>. In English we can quite easily turn a normal (active) sentence with an indirect object into a passive sentence.
>
> **Active**
> Someone *(subject)* gave *(active verb)* me *(indirect object)* a book *(direct object)*.
>
> **Passive**
> I *(subject)* was given *(passive verb)* a book *(direct object)*.
>
> In French, an indirect object can <u>NEVER</u> become the subject of a passive verb.
>
> ➪ *For more information on* **Direct** *and* **Indirect objects,** *see pages 47 and 49.*

➤ In English we use the verb *to be* with the past participle (*was hit, was given*) to form the passive. In French the passive is formed in exactly the same way, using être and the past participle. The past participle agrees with the subject of the passive verb; that is, the endings change in the feminine and plural forms.

Elle <u>est encouragée</u> **par ses parents.**	She is encouraged by her parents.
Vous <u>êtes</u> **tous bien** <u>payés</u>.	You are all well paid. (*'you' here is plural and refers to men, or men and women*)
Les portes <u>ont été fermées</u>.	The doors have been closed.

⇨ *For more information on the **Past participle**, see page 111.*

➤ Here is the present tense of the -er verb aimer (meaning *to like, to love*) in its passive form.

Pronoun	Present tense of être	Past participle	Meaning
je	suis	aimé (*masculine*) aimée (*feminine*)	I am loved
tu	es	aimé (*masculine*) aimée (*feminine*)	you are loved
il	est	aimé	he/it is loved
elle	est	aimée	she/it is loved
on	est	aimé (*singular*) aimés (*masculine plural*) aimées (*feminine plural*)	one is loved we are loved
nous	sommes	aimés (*masculine*) aimées (*feminine*)	we are loved
vous	êtes	aimé (*masculine singular*) aimée (*feminine singular*) aimés (*masculine plural*) aimées (*feminine plural*)	you are loved
ils	sont	aimés	they are loved
elles	sont	aimées	they are loved

➤ The passive of -ir verbs is formed in the same way, except that the past participle is different. For example, elle est remplie (meaning *it is full*).

➤ The passive of -re verbs is formed in the same way, except that the past participle is different. For example, il est défendu (meaning *it is forbidden*).

Grammar Extra!

When on means *we*, the past participle can agree with the subject of the sentence, but it is optional.

> **On est <u>aimés</u> de tout le monde.** · We're loved by everyone. (*masculine*)

➤ You can form other tenses of the passive by changing the tense of the verb être.

> Imperfect: j'étais aimé(e) I was loved
> Future: tu seras aimé(e) you will be loved
> Perfect: il a été aimé he was loved

⇨ *For more information on the **Imperfect, future** and **perfect tenses**, see pages 92, 98 and 111.*

➤ Irregular past participles are the same as for the perfect tense (*see page 118*).

3 Avoiding the passive

➤ Passives are not as common in French as in English. There are <u>two</u> main ways that French speakers express the same idea.

- by using the pronoun **on** (meaning *someone* or *they*) with a normal, active verb

> **On leur a envoyé une lettre.**   They were sent a letter. (*literally: Someone sent them a letter.*)
>
> **On m'a dit que tu ne venais pas.**   I was told that you weren't coming. (*literally: They told me you weren't coming.*)

⇨ *For more information on **Pronouns**, see page 42.*

- by using a reflexive verb

> **Les melons <u>se vendent</u> 2 euros la pièce.**   Melons are sold for 2 euros each.

⇨ *For more information on **Reflexive verbs**, see page 88.*

Key points

✔ The present tense of the passive is formed by using the present tense of être with the past participle.

✔ The past participle always agrees with the <u>subject</u> of the passive verb.

✔ You can sometimes avoid a passive construction by using a reflexive verb or the pronoun on.

Grammar Extra!

The present participle

What is a present participle?
The **present participle** is a verb form ending in *-ing* which is used in English to form verb tenses, and which may be used as an adjective or a noun, for example, *What are you <u>doing</u>?; the <u>setting</u> sun; <u>Swimming</u> is easy!*

1 | Using the present participle

➤ Present participles are not as common in French as in English, because they are not used to form tenses. The main uses of the present participle in French are:

● as a verb, on its own, corresponding to the English *-ing* form. It <u>DOES NOT</u> agree with the subject of the verb when it is used in this way.

<u>Habitant</u> près de Paris, je vais assez souvent en ville.	Living close to Paris, I go into town quite often.
Ils m'ont suivi, <u>criant</u> mon nom.	They followed me, shouting my name.

● as a verb, after the preposition en. The present participle <u>DOES NOT</u> agree with the subject of the verb when it is used in this way. The subject of the two parts of the sentence is always the same. en can be translated in a number of different ways.

<u>En attendant</u> sa sœur, Richard s'est endormi.	While waiting for his sister Richard fell asleep.
Appelle-nous <u>en arrivant</u> chez toi.	Call us when you get home.
<u>En appuyant</u> sur ce bouton, on peut imprimer ses documents.	By pressing this button, you can print your documents.
Il s'est blessé <u>en essayant</u> de sauver un chat.	He hurt himself trying to rescue a cat.

⇨ *For more information on the preposition en, see page 168.*

● as an adjective, as in English. As with all adjectives in French, the ending <u>DOES</u> change in the feminine and plural forms.

le soleil <u>couchant</u>	the setting sun
l'année <u>suivante</u>	the following year
Ces enfants sont <u>énervants</u>.	Those children are annoying.
des chaises <u>pliantes</u>	folding chairs

> *Tip*
> The French present participle is <u>NEVER</u> used to translate English verb forms
> like *I was walking, we are leaving.*
>
> ⇨ *For more information on the **Imperfect tense** and the **Present tense**, see
> pages 92 and 111.*

➤ English verbs describing movement that are followed by an adverb such as *out* or
down, or a preposition such as *across* or *up* are often translated by a verb + en +
present participle.

Il **est sorti en courant**.   He ran out. (*literally*: He came out
running.)

J'**ai traversé** la rue **en boîtant**.   I limped across the street. (*literally*:
I crossed the street limping.)

2 Forming the present participle

➤ To form the present participle of regular -er, -ir and -re verbs, you use the nous form
of the present tense and replace the -ons ending with -ant.

nous form of present tense	Take off -ons	Add -ant
donnons	donn-	donnant
lançons	lanç-	lançant
mangeons	mange-	mangeant
finissons	finiss-	finissant
partons	part-	partant
attendons	attend-	attendant
descendons	descend-	descendant

3 Irregular verbs

➤ Three verbs have an irregular present participle:

    avoir (meaning *to have*) → ayant
    être (meaning *to be*)   → étant
    savoir (meaning *to know*) → sachant

> **Key points**
> ✔ Present participles are never used to form tenses in French, but they can
> be used as verbs, either on their own or after en.
> ✔ They can also be used as adjectives, in which case they agree with the
> noun they describe.
> ✔ They are formed by taking the nous form of the present tense and
> replacing the -ons ending with -ant. The exceptions are avoir, être and
> savoir.

Impersonal verbs

> **What is an impersonal verb?**
> An **impersonal verb** is one that does not refer to a real person or thing and where the subject is represented by *it*, for example, *It's going to rain; It's ten o'clock.*

➤ Impersonal verbs are only used with il (meaning *it*) and in the infinitive. They are called impersonal verbs because il does not really refer to a real person, animal or thing, just like *it* and *there* in English in the examples below.

Il pleut.	It's raining.
Il va pleuvoir.	It's going to rain.
Il y a un problème.	There's a problem.
Il pourrait y avoir un problème.	There could be a problem.

➤ There are also some very common verbs that can be used in this way in addition to their normal meanings, for example, avoir, être and faire.

Infinitive	Expression	Meaning
avoir + noun	il y a	there is (*singular*) there are (*plural*)
être + time	il est	it is
faire + noun	il fait jour il fait nuit	it's daylight it's dark
falloir + noun	il faut	we/you *etc.* need it takes
falloir + infinitive	il faut	we/you *etc.* have to
manquer	il manque	there is … missing (*singular*) there are … missing (*plural*)
paraître	il paraît que	it appears that it seems that
rester + noun	il reste	there is … left (*singular*) there are … left (*plural*)
sembler	il semble que	it appears that it seems that
valoir mieux + infinitive	il vaut mieux	it would be better to

Il y a quelqu'un à la porte.	There's somebody at the door.
Il est deux heures.	It's two o'clock.
Il faut partir.	I've/We've *etc.* got to go.
Il manque cent euros.	100 euros are missing.
Il reste du pain.	There's some bread left.
Il vaut mieux ne rien dire.	It would be better to say nothing.

➤ Several impersonal verbs relate to the weather.

Infinitive	Expression	Meaning
faire + adjective	il fait beau	the weather's lovely
	il fait mauvais	the weather's bad
faire + noun	il fait du vent	it's windy
	il fait du soleil	it's sunny
geler	il gèle	it's freezing
neiger	il neige	it's snowing
pleuvoir	il pleut	it's raining

Grammar Extra!

There is another group of useful expressions that start with an impersonal il. These are followed by a form of the verb called the <u>subjunctive</u>.

il faut que	
Il faut que je <u>parte</u>.	I've got to go.
il est nécessaire que	
Il est nécessaire qu'on le <u>fasse</u>.	We have to do it.
il est possible que	
Il est possible qu'il <u>vienne</u>.	He might come.
il est dommage que	
Il est dommage que tu ne l'<u>aies</u> pas vu.	It's a shame you didn't see him.

➪ For more information on the **Subjunctive**, see page 129.

Key points

✔ Impersonal verbs can only be used in the infinitive and the il form.

✔ il faut, il y a, il est and il fait with expressions relating to the weather are very common.

Grammar Extra!

The subjunctive

What is the subjunctive?
The **subjunctive** is a verb form that is used in certain circumstances to express some sort of feeling, or to show there is doubt about whether something will happen or whether something is true. It is only used occasionally in modern English, for example, *If I <u>were</u> you, I wouldn't bother.; So <u>be</u> it.*

1 Using the subjunctive

➤ In French the subjunctive is used after certain verbs and conjunctions when two parts of a sentence have different subjects.

I'm afraid <u>he</u> won't come back.
(The subject of the first part of the sentence is 'I'; the subject of the second part of the sentence is 'he'.)

➤ Sometimes, in a sentence like *We want her to be happy*, you use the infinitive of the verb in English (*to be*). This is <u>NOT</u> possible in French when there is a different subject in the two parts of the sentence (*we* and *her*). You have to use a subjunctive for the second verb.

Nous voulons être heureux. We want to be happy.
(No change of subject, so you can just use an infinitive – être – in French.)

Nous voulons qu'elle soit heureuse. We want her to be happy.
(Subject changes from nous to elle, so you have to use a subjunctive – soit – in French.)

➤ In the case of impersonal verbs, the infinitive can be used instead of the subjunctive.

Il faut que tu <u>viennes</u> à l'heure.   →   Il faut <u>venir</u> à l'heure.
  (*using subjunctive*)   (*using infinitive*)
You have to come on time.

Il vaut mieux que tu <u>restes</u> chez toi.   →   Il vaut mieux <u>rester</u> chez toi.
  (*using subjunctive*)   (*using infinitive*)
It's better that you stay at home.

2 Coming across the subjunctive

➤ The subjunctive has several tenses but you are only likely to come across the present subjunctive occasionally in your reading.

➤ You may see a subjunctive after certain verbs when you are:

- wishing something: vouloir que and désirer que (meaning *to wish that, to want*), aimer mieux que and préférer que (meaning *to prefer that*)
- fearing something: avoir peur que (meaning *to be afraid that*)
- giving your opinion: croire que (meaning *to think that*)

- saying how you feel: regretter que (meaning *to be sorry that*), être content que (meaning *to be pleased that*), être surpris que (meaning *to be surprised that*) and so on

> Je suis content que vous les <u>aimiez</u>.
>
> I'm pleased you like them.
>
> J'ai peur qu'il ne <u>revienne</u> pas.
>
> I'm afraid he won't come back.

➤ You may see a subjunctive after certain verbal expressions starting with il, such as il faut que (meaning *it is necessary that*) and il vaut mieux que (meaning *it is better that*).

> Il faut que je sois <u>prudent</u>.
>
> I need to be careful.

⇨ *For a list of some expressions requiring the subjunctive, see page 128.*

3 Forming the present subjunctive of -er verbs

➤ To form the stem of the present subjunctive you take the <u>infinitive</u> and chop off -er, just as for the present tense. Then you add the correct ending, depending on whether you are referring to je, tu, il, elle, on, nous, vous, ils or elles.

➤ For -er verbs the endings are the same as for the ordinary present tense, apart from the nous and vous forms, which have an extra i, as in the imperfect tense.

Pronoun	Ending	Add to stem, e.g. donn-	Meanings
je (j')	-e	je donne	I give
tu	-es	tu donnes	you give
il elle on	-e	il donne elle donne on donne	he/she/it/one gives
nous	-ions	nous donnions	we give
vous	-iez	vous donniez	you give
ils elles	-ent	ils donnent elles donnent	they give

> *Tip*
>
> je changes to j' in front of a word starting with a vowel, most words starting with h, and the French word y.

4 Forming the present subjunctive of -ir verbs

➤ To form the stem of the present subjunctive you take the <u>infinitive</u> and chop off -ir, just as for the present tense. Then you add the correct ending, depending on whether you are referring to to je, tu, il, elle, on, nous, vous, ils or elles.

Pronoun	Ending	Add to stem, e.g. fin-	Meanings
je (j')	-isse	je fin<u>isse</u>	I finish
tu	-isses	tu fin<u>isses</u>	you finish
il elle on	-isse	il fin<u>isse</u> elle fin<u>isse</u> on fin<u>isse</u>	he/she/it/one finishes
nous	-issions	nous fin<u>issions</u>	we finish
vous	-issiez	vous fin<u>issiez</u>	you finish
ils elles	-issent	ils fin<u>issent</u> elles fin<u>issent</u>	they finish

> *Tip*
>
> je changes to j' in front of a word starting with a vowel, most words starting with h, and the French word y.

5 Forming the present subjunctive of -re verbs

➤ To form the stem of the present subjunctive you take the <u>infinitive</u> and chop off -re, just as for the present tense. Then you add the correct ending, depending on whether you are referring to je, tu, il, elle, on, nous, vous, ils or elles.

Pronoun	Ending	Add to stem, e.g. attend-	Meanings
je (j')	-e	j'attend<u>e</u>	I wait
tu	-es	tu attend<u>es</u>	you wait
il elle on	-e	il attend<u>e</u> elle attend<u>e</u> on attend<u>e</u>	he/she/it/one waits
nous	-ions	nous attend<u>ions</u>	we wait
vous	-iez	vous attend<u>iez</u>	you wait
ils elles	-ent	ils attend<u>ent</u> elles attend<u>ent</u>	they wait

> *Tip*
>
> je changes to j' in front of a word starting with a vowel, most words starting with h, and the French word y.

6 Irregular verbs in the subjunctive

➤ Some important verbs have irregular subjunctive forms.

Verb	Meaning	je (j')	tu	il/elle/on	nous	vous	ils/elles
aller	to go	aille	ailles	aille	allions	alliez	aillent
avoir	to have	aie	aies	ait	ayons	ayez	aient
devoir	to have to, must	doive	doives	doive	devions	deviez	doivent
dire	to say, to tell	dise	dises	dise	disions	disiez	disent
être	to be	sois	sois	soit	soyons	soyez	soient
faire	to do, to make	fasse	fasses	fasse	fassions	fassiez	fassent
pouvoir	to be able to, can	puisse	puisses	puisse	puissions	puissiez	puissent
prendre	to take	prenne	prennes	prenne	prenions	preniez	prennent
savoir	to know	sache	saches	sache	sachions	sachiez	sachent
venir	to come	vienne	viennes	vienne	venions	veniez	viennent
vouloir	to want to	veuille	veuilles	veuille	voulions	vouliez	veuillent

(apprendre and comprendre also behave like this – j'apprenne, tu apprennes and so on)

Key points

✔ After certain verbs you have to use a subjunctive in French when there is a different subject in the two clauses. These verbs mostly relate to wishing, fearing, and saying what you think or what you feel or saying that you are uncertain. A subjunctive is also found after certain verbal expressions that start with il.

✔ The stem of the present tense subjunctive is the same as the stem used for the ordinary present tense.

✔ The present tense subjunctive endings for -er and -re verbs are: -e, -es, -e, -ions, -iez and -ent.

✔ The present tense subjunctive endings for -ir verbs are: -isse, -isses, -isse, -issions, -issiez and -issent.

Verbs followed by an infinitive

1 Linking two verbs together

➤ Many verbs in French can be followed by another verb in the infinitive. The infinitive is the form of the verb that is found in the dictionary, such as donner (meaning *to give*), finir (meaning *to finish*) and attendre (meaning *to wait*).

➤ There are three main ways that verbs can be linked together:

- with no linking word
  Vous voulez attendre?   Would you like to wait?
- with the preposition à
  J'apprends à nager.   I'm learning to swim.
- with the preposition de
  Essayez de venir.   Try to come.

⇨ *For more information on **Prepositions after adjectives**, and on **Prepositions after verbs**, see pages 183 and 178.*

2 Verbs followed by an infinitive with no preposition

➤ A number of verbs and groups of verbs can be followed by an infinitive with no preposition. The following important group of verbs are all very irregular, but they crop up so frequently that they are worth learning in full:

- devoir (*to have to, must, to be due to*)
  Tu <u>dois être</u> fatiguée.   You must be tired.
  Elle <u>doit partir</u>.   She has to leave.
  Le nouveau centre commercial <u>doit ouvrir</u> en mai.   The new shopping centre is due to open in May.

- pouvoir (*can, may*)
  Je <u>peux</u> t'<u>aider</u>, si tu veux.   I can help you, if you like.
  <u>Puis</u>-je <u>venir</u> vous voir samedi?   May I come and see you on Saturday?

- savoir (*to know how to, can*)
  Tu <u>sais conduire</u>?   Can you drive?
  Je <u>sais faire</u> les omelettes.   I know how to make omelettes.

- vouloir (*to want*)
  Élise <u>veut rester</u> un jour de plus.   Élise wants to stay one more day.
  Ma voiture ne <u>veut</u> pas démarrer.   My car won't start.
  <u>Voulez</u>-vous <u>boire</u> quelque chose?   Would you like something to drink?
  Je <u>voudrais acheter</u> un ordinateur.   I'd like to buy a computer.

➤ **falloir** (meaning *to be necessary*) and **valoir mieux** (meaning *to be better*) are only used in the infinitive and with **il**.

> <u>Il faut prendre</u> une décision.   We/you *etc*. have to make a decision.
> <u>Il vaut mieux téléphoner</u> avant.   It's better to ring first.

⇨ *For more information on **Impersonal verbs**, see page 127.*

➤ The following common verbs can also be followed by an infinitive <u>without</u> a preposition:

adorer	to love
aimer	to like, to love
aimer mieux	to prefer
désirer	to want
détester	to hate
envoyer	to send
espérer	to hope
faire	to make (faire faire quelque chose means to have something done)
laisser	to let
préférer	to prefer
sembler	to seem

J'<u>espère</u> te <u>voir</u> la semaine prochaine.	I hope to see you next week.
Ne me <u>fais</u> pas <u>rire</u>!	Don't make me laugh!
J'<u>ai fait réparer</u> mes chaussures.	I've had my shoes mended.
Je <u>préfère manger</u> à la cantine.	I prefer to eat in the canteen.

➤ Some of these verbs combine with infinitives to make set phrases with a special meaning.

aller chercher quelque chose	to go and get something
laisser tomber quelque chose	to drop something
vouloir dire quelque chose	to mean something

<u>Va chercher</u> ton papa!	Go and get your dad!
Paul <u>a laissé tomber</u> le vase.	Paul dropped the vase.
Qu'est-ce que ça <u>veut dire</u>?	What does that mean?

➤ Verbs that relate to seeing or hearing, such as **voir** (meaning *to see*), **regarder** (meaning *to watch, to look at*), **écouter** (meaning *to listen to*) and **entendre** (meaning *to hear*) can be followed by an infinitive.

Il nous <u>a vus arriver</u>.	He saw us arrive.
On <u>entend chanter</u> les oiseaux.	You can hear the birds singing.

For further explanation of grammatical terms, please see pages viii-xii.

▶ Verbs that relate to movement of some kind and do not have a direct object, such as aller (meaning *to go*) and venir (meaning *to come*), can be followed by an infinitive.

Je <u>vais voir</u> Nicolas ce soir.	I'm going to see Nicolas tonight.
<u>Viens voir</u>!	Come and see!

3 | **Verbs followed by à + infinitive**

▶ There are some common verbs that can be followed by à and an infinitive.

s'amuser <u>à</u> faire quelque chose	to have fun doing something
apprendre <u>à</u> faire quelque chose	to learn to do something
commencer <u>à</u> faire quelque chose	to begin to do something
continuer <u>à</u> faire quelque chose	to go on doing something
s'habituer <u>à</u> faire quelque chose	to get used to doing something
J'apprends <u>à</u> skier.	I'm learning to ski.
Il a commencé <u>à</u> pleuvoir.	It began to rain.

▶ Some verbs can be followed by a person's name or by a noun relating to a person, and then by à and an infinitive. Sometimes you need to put à in front of the person too.

aider quelqu'un <u>à</u> faire quelque chose	to help someone do something
apprendre <u>à</u> quelqu'un <u>à</u> faire quelque chose	to teach someone to do something
inviter quelqu'un <u>à</u> faire quelque chose	to invite someone to do something

4 | **Verbs followed by de + infinitive**

▶ There are some common verbs that can be followed by de and an infinitive.

arrêter <u>de</u> faire quelque chose, s'arrêter <u>de</u> faire quelque chose	to stop doing something
commencer <u>de</u> faire quelque chose	to start doing something
continuer <u>de</u> faire quelque chose	to go on doing something
décider <u>de</u> faire quelque chose	to decide to do something
se dépêcher <u>de</u> faire quelque chose	to hurry to do something
essayer <u>de</u> faire quelque chose	to try to do something
s'excuser <u>d'</u>avoir fait quelque chose	to apologize for doing something
finir <u>de</u> faire quelque chose	to finish doing something
oublier <u>de</u> faire quelque chose	to forget to do something
proposer <u>de</u> faire quelque chose	to suggest doing something
refuser <u>de</u> faire quelque chose	to refuse to do something
suggérer <u>de</u> faire quelque chose	to suggest doing something

| J'**ai décidé de** lui écrire. | I decided to write to her. |
| Je leur **ai suggéré de** partir de bonne heure. | I suggested that they set off early. |

➤ The following verbs meaning asking or telling are also followed by de and an infinitive. Sometimes you need to put à in front of the person you are asking or telling.

commander **à** quelqu'un **de** faire quelque chose	to order someone to do something
demander **à** quelqu'un **de** faire quelque chose	to ask someone to do something
dire **à** quelqu'un **de** faire quelque chose	to tell someone to do something
empêcher quelqu'un **de** faire quelque chose	to prevent someone from doing something
remercier quelqu'un **de** faire quelque chose	to thank someone for doing something

Grammar Extra!

If it is important to emphasize that something is going on at a particular time, you can use the phrase être en train de faire quelque chose.

| Il **est en train de travailler**. Est-ce que vous pouvez rappeler plus tard? | He's working. Can you call back later? |

If you want to say you have just done something, you can use the phrase venir de faire quelque chose. In English you use the <u>PAST</u> tense, but in French you use the <u>PRESENT</u> tense.

| Élisabeth **vient de partir**. | Élisabeth has just left. |

Key points

✔ Many French verbs can be followed by another verb in the infinitive.

✔ The two verbs may be linked by nothing at all, or by the prepositions à or de.

✔ The construction in French does not always match the English exactly. It's best to learn these constructions when you learn a new verb.

For further explanation of grammatical terms, please see pages viii-xii.

Other uses of the infinitive

→ The infinitive can be used in many other ways:

- after certain adjectives
  content de happy to
  prêt à ready to

Il est toujours <u>prêt à rendre</u> service.	He's always ready to help.

- after certain prepositions

<u>Pour aller</u> à la gare?	How do you get to the station?
Il est parti <u>sans dire</u> au revoir.	He left without saying goodbye.

- after certain set phrases involving a verb plus a noun
  avoir envie de <u>faire</u> quelque chose   to feel like doing something
  avoir besoin de <u>faire</u> quelque chose to need to do something
  avoir peur de faire quelque chose   to be frightened of doing
                                       something

J'ai besoin de <u>changer</u> de l'argent.	I need to change some money.

- in instructions that are aimed at the general public – for example, on signs or in cookery books

<u>Ajouter</u> le sel et le poivre, et bien <u>mélanger</u>.	Add the salt and pepper, and mix well.
<u>Conserver</u> au frais.	Keep refrigerated.

- as the subject or object of a sentence, when the infinitive corresponds to the -ing form in English used as a noun

<u>Fumer</u> n'est pas bon pour la santé.	Smoking isn't good for your health.
J'adore <u>lire</u>.	I love reading.

Tip

You can use the verb faire with an infinitive to refer to something you are having done by someone else.

Je dois <u>faire réparer</u> ma voiture.	I have to get my car repaired.

Key points

✔ Infinitives are found after certain adjectives, prepositions and set phrases, and in instructions to the general public.
✔ They can also function like nouns, as the subject or object of another verb.

NEGATIVES

What is a negative?
A **negative** question or statement is one which contains a word such as
not, *never* or *nothing* and is used to say that something is not happening,
is not true or is absent.

1 Using negatives

➤ In English we use words like *not, no, nothing* and *never* to show a negative.
> I'm <u>not</u> very pleased.
> Dan <u>never</u> rang me.
> <u>Nothing</u> ever happens here!
> There's <u>no</u> milk left.

➤ *Not* is often abbreviated and combined with certain English verbs – for
example, *can't, won't, didn't, hasn't.*
> He <u>isn't</u> joking.
> She <u>didn't</u> say.

➤ In French, if you want to make something negative, you generally use a pair
of words, for example, ne … pas (meaning *not*). The verb goes in the
middle.

ne … pas	not
ne … rien	nothing, not … anything
ne … personne	nobody, no one, not … anybody, not … anyone
ne … jamais	never, not … ever
ne … plus	no longer, no more, not … any longer, not … any more

Je <u>ne</u> fume <u>pas</u>.	I don't smoke.
<u>Ne</u> changez <u>rien</u>.	Don't change anything.
Je <u>ne</u> vois <u>personne</u>.	I can't see anybody.
Elle <u>n'</u>arrive <u>jamais</u> à l'heure.	She never arrives on time.
Il <u>ne</u> travaille <u>plus</u> ici.	He's no longer working here.

Tip
ne changes to n' in front of a word that starts with a vowel, most
words beginning with h and the French word y.

In English, *didn't* is often used to make a statement negative.

> I went to his party. → I did<u>n't</u> go to his party.
>
> We saw David at the weekend. → We did<u>n't</u> see David at the weekend.

Note that the French verb faire is <u>NEVER</u> used in this way.

- non plus is the equivalent of English *neither* in phrases like *me neither, neither do I* and so on.

'Je n'aime pas les hamburgers.' – 'Moi <u>non plus</u>.'	'I don't like hamburgers.' – 'Me neither.'
Il n'y va pas et moi <u>non plus</u>.	He isn't going and neither am I.

- The French word ne is missed out when negatives are used without a verb to answer a question.

'Qui a téléphoné?' – '<u>Personne</u>.'	'Who rang?' – 'Nobody.'
'Qu'est-ce que tu fais cet après-midi?' – '<u>Rien</u>.'	'What are you doing this afternoon?' – 'Nothing.'

> ## Tip
>
> In everyday conversation French native speakers often miss out the word ne. Be careful about doing this yourself in formal situations.
>
> | | |
> |---|---|
> | Je peux pas venir ce soir. | I can't come tonight. |
> | Il me l'a pas dit. | He didn't tell me. |

Grammar Extra!

Sometimes you will find two of these negative expressions combined.

Ils ne font jamais rien d'intéressant.	They never do anything interesting.
Je ne connais plus personne à Nice.	I don't know anyone in Nice any more.

2 | Word order with negatives

- Negative expressions in French 'sandwich' the verb in the present tense and in other tenses that consist of just one word. ne goes before the verb and the other half of the expression comes after the verb.

Il <u>ne</u> boit <u>jamais</u> d'alcool.	He never drinks alcohol.
Il <u>ne</u> pleuvait <u>pas</u>.	It wasn't raining.

➤ In the perfect tense and other tenses that consist of two or more words such as the pluperfect, there are two possibilities:

- ne … pas, ne … rien, ne … plus and ne … jamais follow the pattern:
  ne (n') + avoir or être + pas + past participle

Elle n'a pas fait ses devoirs.	She hasn't done her homework.
Je n'ai rien dit.	I didn't say anything.
Pierre n'est pas encore arrivé.	Pierre isn't here yet.

- ne … personne follows the pattern:
  ne (n') + avoir or être + past participle + personne

Je n'ai vu personne.	I didn't see anybody.

⇨ *For more information on the **Perfect tense**, see page 111.*

➤ A negative sentence may also contain a pronoun such as te, le, lui and so on that is the direct or indirect object of the verb, or a reflexive pronoun. If so, ne comes before the pronoun.

Je ne t'entends pas.	I can't hear you.
Ne lui parle pas!	Don't speak to him/her!
Tu ne te rappelles pas de lui?	Don't you remember him?
Il ne se lève jamais avant midi.	He never gets up before midday.

⇨ *For more information on **Direct** and **Indirect object pronouns** and on **Reflexive pronouns**, see pages 47, 49 and 89.*

➤ When a verb is in the infinitive, ne … pas, ne … rien, ne … plus and ne .. jamais come together before the infinitive.

Il essayait de ne pas rire.	He was trying not to laugh.
J'ai peur de ne pas réussir.	I'm afraid of not succeeding.

Tip

After these negative expressions, un, une and des (the <u>indefinite article</u>) and du, de la, de l' and des (the <u>partitive article</u>) change to de.

⇨ *For more information on the **Indefinite article** and the **Partitive article**, see pages 19 and 22.*

---

non **and** pas

▸ non (meaning *no*) is the usual negative answer to a question. It can also correspond to *not* in English.

'**Tu veux nous accompagner?'** – '<u>Non</u>, merci.'	'Do you want to come with us?' – '<u>No</u> thanks.'
Tu viens ou <u>non</u>?	Are you coming or <u>not</u>?
J'espère que <u>non</u>.	I hope <u>not</u>.

▸ pas is generally used when a distinction is being made, or for emphasis. It, too, often corresponds to *not* in English.

'Qui veut m'aider?' – '<u>Pas</u> moi!'	'Who wants to help me?' – '<u>Not</u> me!'
'Est-il de retour?' – '<u>Pas</u> encore.'	'Is he back?' – '<u>Not</u> yet.'
'Tu as froid?' – '<u>Pas</u> du tout.'	'Are you cold?' – '<u>Not</u> at all.'
<u>Pas</u> question!	<u>No</u> way!

Key points

✔ Negatives indicate when something is not happening or is not true. French uses set expressions or word pairs to indicate this.

✔ The two parts of these negative expressions 'sandwich' the verb in tenses consisting of only one word.

✔ ne comes before any object pronouns or reflexive pronouns.

✔ Before infinitives, ne ... pas, ne ... rien, ne ... plus and ne ... jamais come together.

✔ The articles un, une, des, du, de la and de l' change to de after negatives.

QUESTIONS

How to ask a question in French

1 The basic rules

➤ There are four ways of asking questions in French:

- by making your voice go up at the end of the sentence
- by using the phrase est-ce que
- by changing round the order of words in a sentence
- by using a question word

2 Asking a question by making your voice go up

➤ If you are expecting the answer *yes* or *no*, there is a very straightforward way of asking a question. You can keep word order just as it would be in a normal sentence (subject then verb), but turn it into a question by making your voice go up at the end of the sentence. So to turn the sentence Vous aimez la France (meaning *You like France)* into a question, all you need to do is to add a question mark and make your voice go up at the end.

Vous (*subject*) **aimez** (*verb*) **la France?**	Do you like France?
On part tout de suite.	We're leaving right away.
On part tout de suite?	Are we leaving right away?
C'est vrai.	That's true.
C'est vrai?	Is that true?
Tes parents sont en vacances.	Your parents on holiday.
Tes parents sont en vacances?	Are your parents on holiday?

Tip

French speakers use this way of asking a question in ordinary, everyday conversations.

3 Asking a question by using est-ce que

▶ The phrase est-ce que is used to ask a question. Word order stays just the same as it would in an ordinary sentence. Est-ce que comes before the subject, and the verb comes after the subject. So to turn the sentence Tu connais Marie (meaning *You know Marie*) into a question, all you need to do is to add est-ce que.

Est-ce que tu *(subject)* **connais** *(verb)* **Marie?**	Do you know Marie?
Est-ce que vous allez en ville?	Are you going into town?
Est-ce que ta sœur est vraiment heureuse?	Is your sister really happy?

4 Asking a question by changing word order

▶ In ordinary sentences, the verb comes AFTER its subject. In this type of question, the verb is put BEFORE the subject. This change to normal word order is called inversion. You can do this when the subject is a pronoun such as vous or il. When you change the word order (or invert) in this way, you add a hyphen (-) between the verb and the pronoun.

Vous *(subject)* **aimez** *(verb)* **la France.**	You like France.
Aimez *(verb)***-vous** *(subject)* **la France?**	Do you like France?
Il écrit bien.	He writes well.
Écrit-il bien?	Does he write well?
On part tout de suite.	We're leaving right away.
Part-on tout de suite?	Are we leaving right away?

⟹ *For more information on **Pronouns**, see page 42.*

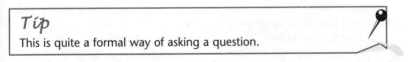

Tip
This is quite a formal way of asking a question.

▶ In the perfect tense and other tenses that consist of two or more words such as the pluperfect, the part of the verb that comes from avoir or être is the one that goes before the pronoun.

As-tu vu mon sac?	Have you seen my bag?
Est-elle restée longtemps?	Did she stay long?

⟹ *For more information on the **Perfect tense**, see page 111.*

➤ When the verb ends in a vowel in the **il/elle** form, -t- is inserted before the pronoun to make the words easier to say.

Aime-t-il les chiens?	Does he like dogs?
A-t-elle assez d'argent?	Does she have enough money?

Tip

Unlike English there are two ways in French of answering *yes* to a question or statement. **oui** is the word you use to reply to an ordinary question.

'Tu l'as fait?' – 'Oui.'	'Have you done it?' – 'Yes.'
'Elle est belle, n'est-ce pas?' – 'Oui.'	'She's beautiful, isn't she?' – 'Yes.'

si is the word you use to reply to a question or statement that contains a negative expression like **ne ... pas**.

'Tu ne l'as pas fait?' – 'Si.'	'Haven't you done it?' – 'Yes (I have).'
'Elle n'est pas très belle.' – 'Mais si!'	'She isn't very beautiful.' – 'Yes, she is!'

⤷ *For more information on **Negatives**, see page 138.*

Grammar Extra!

You can also form a question in this way with a noun or a person's name. If you do this, the noun or name comes first, then you add an extra pronoun after the verb and link them with a hyphen.

Jean-Pierre *(subject)* **est***(verb)***-il** *(pronoun)* **là?**	Is Jean-Pierre there?
La pièce dure-t-elle longtemps?	Does the play last long?

In less formal French, the pronoun may come before the verb, and the noun or name may come at the end of the sentence.

Il est là, Jean-Pierre?	Is Jean-Pierre there?
Elle dure longtemps, la pièce?	Does the play last long?

---

5 Asking a question by using a question word

➤ A question word is a word like *when* or *how* that is used to ask for information. The most common French question words are listed on pages 146-150.

You can use a question word with one of the methods described above:

- you can make your voice go up at the end of the sentence. If you do this, the question word goes at the <u>END</u> of the sentence.
- you can use est-ce que. If you do this, the question word goes at the <u>START</u> of the sentence.
- you can change word order so that the verb comes before the subject. If you do this, the question word goes at the <u>START</u> of the sentence.

Vous arrivez <u>quand</u>?	
<u>Quand</u> est-ce que vous arrivez?	<u>When</u> do you arrive?
<u>Quand</u> arrivez-vous?	
Tu prends <u>quel</u> train?	
<u>Quel</u> train est-ce que tu prends?	<u>What</u> train are you getting?
<u>Quel</u> train prends-tu?	
Ils vont <u>où</u>?	
<u>Où</u> est-ce qu'ils vont?	<u>Where</u> are they going?
<u>Où</u> vont-ils?	

Key points

✔ You ask a question in French by making your voice go up at the end of the sentence, by using est-ce que, by changing normal word order, or by using a question word.

✔ When you put the verb in front of the subject, you join the two words with a hyphen. A -t- is used in the il/elle form if the verb ends in a vowel.

✔ You use oui to answer *yes* to an ordinary question, but si if there is a negative in the question or statement.

Question words

1 Common question words

➤ Listed below are some very common question words. que, quel, qui, quoi and lequel, are explained on pages 147–150.

- combien + *verb?* how much?, how many?
  combien de + *noun?* how much?, how many?

Combien coûte cet ordinateur?	How much does this computer cost?
C'est **combien**, ce pantalon?	How much are these trousers?
Tu en veux **combien**? Deux?	How many do you want? Two?
Combien de personnes vas-tu inviter?	How many people are you going to invite?

- comment? how?

Comment va-t-elle?	How is she?
Comment tu t'appelles?	What's your name?

> ## Tip
> pardon is also used to ask someone to repeat something, and is the same as *Pardon?* in English. comment and quoi can mean the same thing, but are informal, and are the same as *What?* in English.

- où? where?

Où allez-vous?	Where are you going?
D'où viens-tu?	Where are you from?

> ## Tip
> Be careful not to mix up où, which means *where*, and ou (without an accent), which means *or*.

- pourquoi? why?

Pourquoi est-ce qu'il ne vient pas avec nous?	Why isn't he coming with us?

- quand? when?

Quand est-ce que tu pars en vacances?	When are you going on holiday?
Depuis quand est-ce que vous le connaissez?	How long have you known him?

2 **qui?, que? and quoi?**

➤ In questions, qui, que and quoi are all pronouns. Which of them you choose depends on:

- whether you are referring to people or to things
- whether you are referring to the subject or object of the verb (the subject is the person or thing that is carrying out the action described by the verb; the object is the person or thing that 'receives' the action)
- whether the word you use will come after a preposition such as à, de or en

➪ *For more information on **Pronouns** and **Prepositions**, see pages 42 and 62.*

➤ qui? and que? have longer forms, as shown in the table below. There is a difference in word order between the longer and shorter forms.

➤ qui? is used for talking about people, and means *who?* or *whom?* in English. You can use *whom?* in formal English to refer to the object of verb, (though most people use *who?*). qui? can be used after a preposition.

Who? Whom?	Referring to people	Meaning	Examples	Meaning
Subject	qui? qui est-ce qui?	who?	Qui vient? Qui est-ce qui vient?	Who's coming?
Object	qui? qui est-ce que?	who? whom?	Qui vois-tu? Qui est-ce que tu vois?	Who/Whom can you see?
After prepositions	qui? qui est-ce que?	who? whom?	De qui est-ce qu'il parle? Pour qui est ce livre? À qui avez-vous écrit?	Who's he talking about? Who's this book for? Who did you write to?, To whom did you write?

Tip

que changes to qu' before a vowel, most words beginning with h, and the French word y.

➪ *For more information on **que** and **qui**, see page 62.*

➤ à qui is the usual way of saying *whose* in questions.

> <u>À qui</u> est ce sac?   Whose is this bag?

⇨ *For more information on using à to show possession, see page 165.*

➤ que? and quoi? are used for talking about things, and mean *what?* in English. que? <u>cannot</u> be used after a preposition; you have to use quoi? instead.

What?	Referring to things	Meaning	Examples	Meaning
Subject	qu'est-ce qui?	what?	Qu'est-ce qui se passe? Qu'est-ce qui t'inquiète?	What's happening? What's worrying you?
Object	qu'est-ce que? que?	what?	Qu'est-ce que vous faites? Que faites-vous?	What are you doing?
After prepositions	quoi?	what?	À quoi penses-tu? De quoi parlez-vous?	What are you thinking about? What are you talking about?

> *Tip*
>
> It is possible to finish an English sentence with a preposition such as *about* or *of*.
> *Who did you write <u>to</u>?*
> *What are you talking <u>about</u>?*
> It is <u>NEVER</u> possible to end a French sentence with a preposition.

3 | quel?, quelle?, quels? **and** quelles?

➤ quel? (meaning *who?*, *which?* or *what?*) can be used with a noun (as an <u>adjective</u>) or can replace a noun (as a <u>pronoun</u>). Compare this with que? (and its longer forms) and quoi?, which also mean *what?*, but are <u>NEVER</u> used with nouns.

⇨ *For more information on **Adjectives** and **Pronouns**, see pages 25 and 42.*

➤ quel, quelle, quels and quelles are all forms of the same word. The form that you choose depends on whether you are referring to something that is masculine or feminine, singular or plural.

	Masculine	Feminine	Meaning
Singular	quel?	quelle?	who? what? which?
Plural	quels?	quelles?	who? what? which?

<u>Quel</u> est ton chanteur préféré?	Who's your favourite singer?
<u>Quel</u> vin recommandez-vous?	Which wine do you recommend?
<u>Quelle</u> est ta couleur préférée?	What's your favourite colour?
<u>Quelle</u> heure est-il?	What time is it?
<u>Quels</u> sont tes chanteurs préférés?	Who are your favourite singers?
Vous jouez de <u>quels</u> instruments?	What instruments do you play?
<u>Quelles</u> sont tes couleurs préférées?	What are your favourite colours?
<u>Quelles</u> chaussures te plaisent le plus?	Which shoes do you like best?

➪ *For more information on how **quel** in used in exclamations, see page 21.*

4 lequel?, laquelle?, lesquels? and lesquelles?

➤ In questions lequel, laquelle, lesquels and lesquelles (meaning *which one/ones?*) are all forms of the same pronoun, and are used to replace nouns. The form that you choose depends on whether you are referring to something that is masculine or feminine, singular or plural.

	Masculine	Feminine	Meaning
Singular	lequel?	laquelle?	which? which one?
Plural	lesquels?	lesquelles?	which? which ones?

'J'ai choisi un livre.' – '<u>Lequel</u>?'	'I've chosen a book.' – 'Which one?'
<u>Laquelle</u> de ces valises est à Bruno?	Which of these cases is Bruno's?

| 'Tu te souviens de mes amis?' – 'Lesquels?' | 'Do you remember my friends?' – 'Which ones?' |
| Lesquelles de vos sœurs sont mariées? | Which of your sisters are married? |

⇨ *For more information on **lequel**, see page 63.*

5 n'est-ce pas? **and** non?

➤ English-speakers often use an expression like *isn't it?*, *don't they?*, *weren't we?* or *will you?* tagged on to the end of a sentence to turn it into a question. French uses n'est-ce pas? instead. This useful little phrase never changes, so is very easy to use. You use it in questions when you expect the person you are talking to to agree with you.

Il fait chaud, n'est-ce pas?	It's warm, isn't it?
Tu parles français, n'est-ce pas?	You speak French, don't you?
Vous n'oublierez pas, n'est-ce pas?	You won't forget, will you?

➤ It is very common to use non (meaning *no*) in the same way in spoken French. hein? means the same as *eh?* in English, and is only used in very informal conversations.

| Il fait chaud, non? | It's warm, isn't it? |
| Il fait chaud, hein? | It's warm, eh? |

Key points

✔ In questions qui? means *who?*; que? and quoi? mean *what?*

✔ qui est-ce qui? (*subject*) and qui est-ce que? (*object*) are longer forms of qui? Both mean *who?* The word order is different from qui.

✔ qu'est-ce qui? (*subject*) and qu'est-ce que? (*object*) are longer forms of que? Both mean *what?* The word order is different from que.

✔ qui? (for people) and quoi? (for things) are used after prepositions.

✔ quel? is both an adjective and a pronoun. It means *who?*, *what?* or *which?* in questions, and is used with a noun or replaces a noun.

✔ lequel? is a pronoun; it means *which?*, *which one?* or *which ones?* in questions.

✔ n'est-ce pas? or non? can be tagged on to the end of sentences to turn them into questions.

Grammar Extra!

All the questions in the previous section are the actual words that someone uses when they are asking a question, and so they all end with a question mark. These are called <u>direct</u> questions. When you are telling someone else about a question that is being asked, you use an <u>indirect</u> question. Indirect questions never end with a question mark, and they are always introduced by a verb such as *to ask, to tell, to wonder, to know* and so on.

> He asked me what the time was. (His actual question was *What is the time?*)
> Tell me which way to go. (Your actual question was *Which way do I go?*)

Word order in indirect questions is generally the same as in English:
question word + subject + verb.

Dites-moi quel *(question word)* **autobus** *(subject)* **va** *(verb)* **à la gare.**	Tell me which bus goes to the station.
Il m'a demandé combien d'argent j'avais.	He asked me how much money I had.
Je me demande s'il viendra ou pas.	I wonder if he'll come or not.
Demande-lui qui est venu.	Ask him who came.

When the subject of the question is a noun and <u>NOT</u> a pronoun like je or il, the subject and verb that come after the question word are often swapped round.

Je me demande où *(question word)* **sont** *(verb)* **mes clés** *(subject)*.	I wonder where my keys are.

ADVERBS

What is an adverb?
An **adverb** is a word usually used with verbs, adjectives or other adverbs that gives more information about when, how, where, or in what circumstances something happens, for example, *quickly, happily, now.*

How adverbs are used

➤ In general, adverbs are used together with:

- verbs (*act <u>quickly</u>, speak <u>strangely</u>, smile <u>cheerfully</u>*)
- adjectives (*<u>rather</u> ill, <u>a lot</u> better, <u>deeply</u> sorry*)
- other adverbs (*<u>really</u> fast, <u>too</u> quickly, <u>very</u> well*)

➤ Adverbs can also relate to the whole sentence; they often tell you what the speaker is thinking or feeling.

> <u>Fortunately</u>, Jan had already left.
> <u>Actually</u>, I don't think I'll come.

How adverbs are formed

1 The basic rules

➤ Adverbs in French <u>NEVER</u> change their form, no matter what they refer to.

Il est <u>très</u> beau.	He's very handsome.
Elles sont <u>très</u> belles.	They're very beautiful.
J'y vais <u>souvent</u>.	I often go there.
Nous y allons <u>souvent</u>.	We often go there.

i Note that there is one exception to this rule. The word tout changes in certain phrases, for example, tout seul (meaning *all alone*).

Il est arrivé <u>tout seul</u>.	He arrived on his own.
Elle est souvent <u>toute seule</u>.	She's often on her own.

➤ Many English adverbs end in *-ly*, which is added to the end of the adjective (*quick → quickly; sad → sadly; frequent → frequently*). In French, many adverbs end in *-ment*. This is usually added to the end of the <u>feminine singular</u> form of the adjective.

Masculine adjective	Feminine adjective	Adverb	Meaning
heureux	heureuse	heureusement	fortunately
doux	douce	doucement	gently, slowly
seul	seule	seulement	only

➤ The adverb ending -ment is added to the <u>masculine</u> not the feminine form of the adjective if the masculine ends in -é, -i or -u.

Masculine adjective	Feminine adjective	Adverb	Meaning
désespéré	désespérée	désespérément	desperately
vrai	vraie	vraiment	truly
absolu	absolue	absolument	absolutely

➤ If the adjective ends in -ant, the adverb ends in -amment. If the adjective ends in -ent, the adverb ends in -emment. The first vowel in the -emment and -amment endings is pronounced in the same way in both – like the *a* in the English word *cat*.

> courant → couramment (*fluently*)
> récent → récemment (*recently*)

[i] Note that an exception to this rule is the adverb lentement (meaning *slowly*), which comes from the adjective lent (meaning *slow*).

2 Irregular adverbs

➤ There are a number of common irregular adverbs.

Adjective	Meaning	Adverb	Meaning
bon	good	bien	well
gentil	nice, kind	gentiment	nicely, kindly
mauvais	bad	mal	badly
meilleur	better, best	mieux	better
petit	small	peu	little
pire	worse	pis	worse

> Elle travaille <u>bien</u>.   She works well.
> C'est un emploi très <u>mal</u> payé.   It's a very badly paid job.

3 Adjectives used as adverbs

➤ Certain adjectives are used as adverbs, mostly in set phrases:

• bon good
  sentir bon to smell nice

- cher expensive
  coûter cher to be expensive
  payer cher to pay a lot

- droit straight
  aller tout droit to go straight on

- dur hard
  travailler dur to work hard

- fort loud
  parler plus fort to speak up

- mauvais bad
  sentir mauvais to smell

4 Adverbs made up of more than one word

➤ Adverbs can be made up of several words instead of just one. Here are some common ones:

bien sûr	of course
c'est-à-dire	that is
d'abord	first
d'habitude	usually
de temps en temps	from time to time
en général	usually
en retard	late
tout de suite	straight away

Key points

✔ With the exception of tout, French adverbs do not change their form.

✔ The ending -ment is usually added to the feminine singular form of the corresponding adjective.

✔ If the masculine singular adjective ends in -é, -i or -u, the -ment ending is added to that.

✔ If the adjective ends in -ant or -ent, the adverb ends in -amment or -emment (apart from lentement).

Comparatives and superlatives of adverbs

1 Comparative adverbs

> **What is a comparative adverb?**
> A **comparative adverb** is one which, in English, has *-er* on the end of it or *more* or *less* in front of it, for example, *earlier, later, sooner, more/less frequently.*

➤ Adverbs can be used to make comparisons in French, just as they can in English. The comparative (*more often, faster*) of adverbs is formed using the same phrases as for adjectives.

- plus ... (que)   more ... (than)

  Tu marches <u>plus</u> vite <u>que</u> moi.   You walk faster than me.

  Elle chante <u>plus</u> fort <u>que</u> les autres.   She's singing louder than the others.

- moins ... (que)   less ... (than)

  Parle <u>moins</u> vite!   Don't speak so fast! (*literally*: *Speak less fast!*)

  Nous nous voyons <u>moins</u> souvent <u>qu'</u>avant.   We see each other less often than before.

- aussi ... que   as ... as

  Je parle français <u>aussi</u> bien <u>que</u> toi!   I can speak French as well as you!

  Viens <u>aussi</u> vite <u>que</u> possible.   Come as quickly as possible.

➩ *For more information on **Comparative adjectives**, see page 34.*

2 Superlative adverbs

> **What is a superlative adverb?**
> A **superlative adverb** is one which, in English, has *-est* on the end of it or *most* or *least* in front of it, for example, *soonest, fastest, most/least frequently.*

➤ The superlative of adverbs (*the most, the fastest*) is formed using the same phrases as for adjectives, except that le <u>NEVER</u> changes to la or les in the feminine and plural with adverbs as it does with adjectives.

- le plus ... (que) the most ... (that)

  Marianne parle <u>le plus</u> vite.   Marianne speaks fastest.

- le moins ... (que) the least ... (that)

  C'est Gordon qui a mangé <u>le moins</u>.   Gordon ate the least.

➩ *For more information on **Superlative adjectives**, see page 34.*

3 Adverbs with irregular comparatives and superlatives

➤ Some of the most common adverbs have irregular comparative and superlative forms.

Adverb	Meaning	Comparative	Meaning	Superlative	Meaning
beaucoup	a lot	plus	more	le plus	(the) most
bien	well	mieux	better	le mieux	(the) best
mal	badly	pis plus mal	worse	le pis le plus mal	(the) worst
peu	little	moins	less	le moins	(the) least

C'est lui qui danse <u>le mieux</u>.   He dances best.

Key points
- ✔ Comparatives of adverbs are formed in the same way as comparatives of adjectives, using plus … (que), moins … (que) and aussi … que.
- ✔ Superlatives of adverbs are formed in the same way as superlatives of adjectives, using le plus … (que) and le moins … (que). le never changes in the feminine and plural.
- ✔ Unlike adjectives, adverbs do not change their form to agree with the verb, adjective or other adverb they relate to.

Some common adverbs

➤ Here are some common adverbs that do not end in -ment:

alors	then, so, at that time
après	afterwards
après-demain	the day after tomorrow
aujourd'hui	today
assez	enough, quite
aussi	also, too, as
avant-hier	the day before yesterday
beaucoup	a lot, much
bientôt	soon
cependant	however
dedans	inside
dehors	outside
déjà	already, before
demain	tomorrow
depuis	since
derrière	behind
devant	in front
encore	still, even, again
enfin	at last
ensemble	together
ensuite	then
environ	about
hier	yesterday
ici	here
jamais	never, ever

Tip

jamais can sometimes be used without ne to mean *never* or *ever*.

'Est-ce que tu vas souvent au cinema?' – 'Non, <u>jamais</u>.'

'Do you go to the cinema a lot?' – 'No, <u>never</u>.'

As-tu <u>jamais</u> revu ton père?

Did you <u>ever</u> see your father again?

➡ For more information on **Negatives**, see page 138.

là	there, here
là-bas	over there
loin	far, far off, a long time ago

longtemps	a long time
maintenant	now, nowadays
même	even
moins	less
où	where
parfois	sometimes
partout	everywhere
peu	not much, not very

Tip

Be careful not to confuse peu, which means *not much* or *not very*, with un peu, which means *a little* or *a bit*.

| Il voyage <u>peu</u>. | He doesn<u>'t</u> travel <u>much</u>. |
| Elle est <u>un peu</u> timide. | She's <u>a bit</u> shy. |

peut-être	perhaps
plus	more
presque	nearly
puis	then
quelquefois	sometimes
si	so
soudain	suddenly
souvent	often
surtout	especially, above all
tard	late
tôt	early
toujours	always, still
tout	all, very
très	very
trop	too much, too
vite	quick, fast, soon

Tip

vite and rapide can both mean *fast* or *quick*. Remember, though, that vite is an <u>adverb</u> and rapide is an <u>adjective</u>.

| une voiture <u>rapide</u> | a fast car |
| Il roule trop <u>vite</u>. | He drives too fast. |

For further explanation of grammatical terms, please see pages viii-xii.

➤ Some of the adverbs listed on pages 157 and 158 can be followed by **de** and used in front of a noun to talk about quantities or numbers of things or people:

- **assez de** enough

  | **Nous n'avons pas assez de temps.** | We don't have enough time. |

- **beaucoup de** a lot of

  | **Elle fait beaucoup de fautes.** | She makes a lot of mistakes. |

- **trop de** too much, too many

  | **J'ai mangé trop de fromage.** | I've eaten too much cheese. |

➤ Several of the adverbs listed on pages 157 and 158 can also be used as prepositions: **après, avant, devant, derrière** and **depuis**.

🡆 *For more information on* **Prepositions***, see page 162.*

➤ The question words **combien** (meaning *how much, how many*), **comment** (meaning *how*), **pourquoi** (meaning *why*) and **quand** (meaning *when*) are described on page 146.

➤ **pas, plus** and **jamais** are used in negative word pairs.

🡆 *For more information on* **Negatives***, see page 138.*

> **Key points**
> ✔ Many very common adverbs do not end in **-ment**. They are worth learning.
> ✔ Several adverbs can be followed by **de** + noun and used to talk about quantities and numbers.

Word order with adverbs

1 Adverbs with verbs

➤ In English, adverbs can come in different places in a sentence.

I'm <u>never</u> coming back.

See you <u>soon</u>!

<u>Suddenly</u> the phone rang.

I'd <u>really</u> like to come.

➤ In French, the rules are more fixed. When an adverb goes with a verb that consists of just one word, such as a verb in the <u>present tense</u> or the <u>imperfect tense</u>, it generally goes AFTER that verb.

Il neige <u>toujours</u> en janvier.	It always snows in January.
Je pensais <u>souvent</u> à toi.	I often used to think about you.

➤ When an adverb goes with a verb that consists of more than one word, such as a verb in the <u>perfect tense</u>, it generally comes BETWEEN the part of the verb that comes from avoir or être and the past participle.

Il a <u>trop</u> mangé.	He's eaten too much.
Ils sont <u>déjà</u> partis.	They've already gone.

⇨ *For more information on the **Perfect tense**, see page 111.*

➤ The rule above covers most adverbs that tell you about quantity or time (apart from a few listed later), and some very common ones telling you how something is done.

beaucoup	a lot, much
bien	well
bientôt	soon
déjà	already, before
encore	still, even, again
enfin	at last
mal	badly
mieux	better
peu	not much, not very
rarement	rarely
souvent	often
toujours	always, still
trop	too much, too
vraiment	really

For further explanation of grammatical terms, please see pages viii-xii.

➤ Some adverbs <u>FOLLOW</u> the past participle of verbs that consist of more than one word. This rule covers most adverbs that tell you how or where something is done, and a few adverbs that tell you about time.

aujourd'hui	today
demain	tomorrow
hier	yesterday
loin	far, far off, a long time ago
longtemps	a long time
partout	everywhere
quelquefois	sometimes
tôt	early
tard	late
vite	quick, fast, soon

On les a vus <u>partout</u>.	We saw them everywhere.
Elle est revenue <u>hier</u>.	She came back yesterday.

2 | Adverbs with adjectives and other adverbs

➤ When an adverb goes with an <u>adjective</u>, it generally comes just <u>BEFORE</u> that adjective.

Ils ont une <u>très</u> belle maison.	They have a very nice house.
une femme <u>bien</u> habillée	a well-dressed woman

➤ When an adverb goes with another <u>adverb</u>, it generally comes just <u>BEFORE</u> that adverb.

C'est <u>trop</u> tard.	It's too late.
Fatima travaille <u>beaucoup</u> plus vite.	Fatima works much faster.

Key points
- ✔ Adverbs follow verbs that consist of just one word.
- ✔ They generally go before the past participle of verbs that consist of two words when they relate to quantity or time.
- ✔ They generally go after the past participle of verbs that consist of two words when they relate to how or where something is done.
- ✔ When used with an adjective or another adverb, they generally come just before it.

PREPOSITIONS

What is a preposition?
A **preposition** is a word such as *at, for, with, into* or *from*, which is usually followed by a noun, pronoun or, in English, a word ending in *-ing*. Prepositions show how people and things relate to the rest of the sentence, for example, *She's <u>at</u> home.; a tool <u>for</u> cutting grass; it's <u>from</u> David.*

Using prepositions

➤ Prepositions are used in front of nouns and pronouns (such as *me, him, the man* and so on), and show the relationship between the noun or pronoun and the rest of the sentence. Some prepositions can be used before verb forms ending in *-ing* in English.

I showed my ticket <u>to</u> the inspector.
Come <u>with</u> me.
This brush is really good <u>for</u> cleaning shoes.

➪ *For more information on **Nouns** and **Pronouns**, see pages 1 and 42.*

➤ Prepositions are also used after certain adjectives and verbs and link them to the rest of the sentence.

Je suis très contente <u>de</u> te voir.	I'm very happy to see you.
Tu aimes jouer <u>au</u> tennis?	Do you like playing tennis?

➤ In English it is possible to finish a sentence with a preposition such as *for, about* or *on*, even though some people think this is not good grammar. You can <u>NEVER</u> end a French sentence with a preposition.

Le café au lait, c'est <u>pour</u> qui?	Who's the white coffee <u>for</u>?
<u>De</u> quoi parlez-vous?	What are you talking <u>about</u>?

> *Tip*
> The French preposition is not always the direct equivalent of the preposition that is used in English. It is often difficult to give just one English equivalent for French prepositions, as the way they are used varies so much between the two languages.

à, de and en

1 **à**

➤ Be careful not to confuse the preposition à with the il/elle/on form of the verb avoir: il a (meaning *he has*) and so on.

> ### Tip
> When à is followed by le, the two words become au. Similarly, when à is followed by les, the two words become aux.
>
> ⟴ *For more information on **Articles**, see page 12.*

➤ à can mean *at*.

Les melons se vendent à 2 euros pièce.	Melons are selling <u>at</u> 2 euros each.
Nous roulions à 100 km à l'heure.	We were driving <u>at</u> 100 km an hour
J'ai lancé une pierre à Chantal.	I threw a stone <u>at</u> Chantal.
Je suis à la maison.	I'm <u>at</u> home.

i Note that à la maison can also mean *to the house*.

Je rentre à la maison.	I'm going back to the house *or* back home.

➤ à can mean *in*.

Nous habitons à la campagne.	We live <u>in</u> the country.
Mon père est à Londres.	My father is <u>in</u> London.
Restez au lit.	Stay <u>in</u> bed.
Jean est entré, un livre à la main.	Jean came in with a book <u>in</u> his hand.

> ### Tip
> à is used to mean *in* with the names of towns and cities, and au (*singular*) or aux (*plural*) are used to mean *in* with the names of countries that are masculine in French.
>
> | | |
> |---|---|
> | J'habite <u>au</u> Mexique. | I live <u>in</u> Mexico. |
> | Elle est <u>aux</u> États-Unis. | She's <u>in</u> the States. |

➤ à can mean *to*.

Je vais au cinéma ce soir.	I'm going <u>to</u> the cinema tonight.
Donne le ballon à ton frère.	Give the ball <u>to</u> your brother.

> **Tip**
>
> à is used to mean *to* with the names of towns and cities, and au (*singular*) or aux (*plural*) are used to mean *to* with the names of countries that are masculine in French.
>
> | | |
> |---|---|
> | Je vais assez souvent <u>à</u> Paris. | I go <u>to</u> Paris quite often. |
> | Il va <u>aux</u> États-Unis la semaine prochaine. | He's going <u>to</u> the States next week. |

➤ à is also used with de to mean *from ... to ...*

le trajet <u>de</u> Londres <u>à</u> Paris	the journey <u>from</u> London <u>to</u> Paris
La banque est ouverte <u>de</u> 9 heures <u>à</u> midi.	The bank is open <u>from</u> 9 <u>to</u> 12.
Je suis en vacances <u>du</u> 21 juin <u>au</u> 5 juillet.	I'm on holiday <u>from</u> 21 June <u>to</u> 5 July.

➤ à can mean *on.*

Il y a deux beaux tableaux <u>au</u> mur.	There are two beautiful paintings <u>on</u> the wall.
Le bureau se trouve <u>au</u> premier étage.	The office is <u>on</u> the first floor.
Qu'est-ce qu'il y a <u>à la</u> télé ce soir?	What's <u>on</u> TV tonight?

[i] Note that à and sur can both mean *on* in English. sur usually means *on the top of something.* sur la télé means *on top of the TV set,* but à la télé means *broadcast on TV.* sur le mur means *on top of the wall,* but au mur means *hanging on the wall.*

➤ à is often used to describe:

- what someone looks like or is wearing

la femme <u>au</u> chapeau vert	the woman in the green hat
un garçon <u>aux</u> yeux bleus	a boy with blue eyes

- how something is done

fait <u>à la</u> main	hand-made
laver <u>à la</u> machine	to machine-wash

- what a type of food is made of

une tarte <u>aux</u> poires	a pear tart
un sandwich <u>au</u> jambon	a ham sandwich

- how you travel

On y va à pied?	Shall we walk?
Il est venu à vélo.	He came on his bike.

> *Tip*
>
> Apart from à vélo and à cheval (meaning *on horseback*), the prepositions en and par are used with most other means of transport.

➤ à can also show what something is used for.

une boîte aux lettres	a letter box
une machine à laver	a washing machine
une tasse à café	a coffee cup

[*i*] Note that une tasse à café means a *coffee cup*, but une tasse de café means *a cup of coffee*. In the same way, un verre à vin means *a wine glass* but un verre de vin means *a glass of wine*.

➤ à is used with times, centuries and the names of festivals.

à trois heures	at three o'clock
au vingtième siècle	in the twentieth century
à Noël	at Christmas
à Pâques	at Easter

➤ à is used to talk about distances and rates.

La maison est à 6 kilomètres d'ici.	The house is 6 kilometres from here.
C'est à deux minutes de chez moi.	It's two minutes from my place.
Je suis payé à l'heure.	I'm paid by the hour.

➤ à shows who owns something, or whose turn it is.

Ce cahier est à Paul.	This notebook is Paul's.
C'est à toi?	Is this yours?
C'est à qui de nettoyer la salle de bains?	Whose turn is it to clean the bathroom?

➤ If you want to say where something hurts, you use à.

J'ai mal à la tête.	I've got a headache.
J'ai mal aux jambes.	My legs ache.
J'ai mal à la gorge.	I've got a sore throat.

➤ à is used with certain adjectives.

Son écriture est difficile à lire.	His/Her writing is difficult to read.
Je suis prêt à tout.	I'm ready for anything.

⇨ *For more information about **Prepositions after adjectives**, see page 183.*

➤ à is used with certain verbs.

s'intéresser à quelque chose	to be interested in something
penser à quelque chose	to think about something

⇨ *For more information about **Prepositions after verbs**, see page 178.*

➤ Finally, some common ways of saying goodbye contain à.

À bientôt!	See you soon!
À demain!	See you tomorrow!
À samedi!	See you Saturday!
À tout à l'heure!	See you later!

2 de

➤ de is used as part of the <u>partitive article</u>, which is usually the equivalent of *some* or *any* in English.

⇨ *For more information on the **Partitive article**, see page 22.*

> *Tip*
>
> When de is followed by le, the two words become du. Similarly, when de is followed by les, the two words become des.
>
> ⇨ *For more information on **Articles**, see page 12.*

➤ de can mean *from*.

Je viens <u>d'</u>Édimbourg.	I'm <u>from</u> Edinburgh.
une lettre <u>de</u> Rachid	a letter from Rachid
Je la vois <u>de</u> temps en temps.	I see her <u>from</u> time to time.

> *Tip*
>
> de changes to d' in front of a word starting with a vowel, most words starting with h, and the French word y.

For further explanation of grammatical terms, please see pages viii-xii.

➤ de is also used with à to mean *from ... to ...*

le trajet **de** Londres **à** Paris	the journey <u>from</u> London <u>to</u> Paris
La banque est ouverte de 9 **heures à midi.**	The bank is open <u>from</u> 9 <u>to</u> 12.
Je suis en vacances du 21 juin **au** 5 juillet.	I'm on holiday <u>from</u> 21 June <u>to</u> 5 July.

➤ de often shows who or what something belongs to.

un ami **de** la famille	a friend of the family
les fenêtres **de** la maison	the windows of the house
la voiture **de** Marie-Pierre	Marie-Pierre's car

➤ de can indicate what something contains, when it usually corresponds to *of* in English.

une boîte **d'**allumettes	a box <u>of</u> matches
deux bouteilles **de** vin	two bottles <u>of</u> wine
une tasse **de** café	a cup <u>of</u> coffee

i Note that une tasse **de** café means *a cup of coffee* but une tasse **à** café means *a coffee cup*. In the same way, un verre **à** vin means *a wine glass* but un verre **de** vin means *a glass of wine*.

➤ de can describe what material something is made of.

une robe **de** coton	a cotton dress
une porte **de** bois	a wooden door

Tip

en can also be used to say what something is made of, and is used when it is important to stress the material.

un bracelet **en** or	a gold bracelet

➤ You can use de to say what something is used for.

un sac **de** couchage	a sleeping bag
un terrain **de** foot	a football pitch
un arrêt **de** bus	a bus stop

➤ de is found after superlatives *(the most..., the biggest, the least ... and so on)*.

la plus belle ville **du** monde	the most beautiful city in the world
le film le moins intéressant **du** festival	the least interesting film in the festival

➱ *For more information on **Superlative adjectives**, see page 34.*

➤ de is used in phrases to talk about quantities.

| Elle fait <u>beaucoup de</u> fautes. | She makes a lot of mistakes. |
| <u>Combien de</u> personnes as-tu invitées? | How many people have you invited? |

➤ de is used with certain adjectives.

| Je suis très surpris <u>de</u> te voir. | I'm very surprised to see you. |
| Il est triste <u>de</u> partir. | He's sad to be leaving. |

⇨ *For more information on **Prepositions after adjectives**, see page 183.*

Grammar Extra!

If you want to use an adjective after quelque chose, rien, quelqu'un and personne, you link the words with de.

quelqu'un <u>d</u>'important	someone important
quelque chose <u>d</u>'intéressant	something interesting
rien <u>d</u>'amusant	nothing funny

➤ de is found after certain verbs.

| dépendre <u>de</u> quelque chose | to depend on something |
| parler <u>de</u> quelque chose | to talk about something |

⇨ *For more information on **Prepositions after verbs**, see page 178.*

3 en

i Note that en is never followed by an article such as le, du or des.

➤ en is used to talk about a place. It can be the equivalent of the English *to* or *in*.

Je vais <u>en</u> ville.	I'm going <u>to</u> town.
Il a un appartement <u>en</u> ville.	He has a flat <u>in</u> town.
Nous allons <u>en</u> France cet été.	We're going <u>to</u> France this summer.
Nous habitons <u>en</u> France.	We live <u>in</u> France.

Tip

en is used with the names of countries that are feminine in French. Use à with the names of towns and cities, and au or aux with masculine countries.

➤ en is used to talk about years and months, and to say how long something will take, when it is the equivalent of *in/within*:

en 1923	<u>in</u> 1923
en janvier	<u>in</u> January
Je le ferai en trois jours.	I'll do it <u>in</u> three days.

Grammar Extra!

en and dans can both be used in French to talk about a length of time, but the meaning is very different.

Je le ferai dans trois jours.	I'll do it in three days.
Je le ferai en trois jours.	I'll do it in three days.

Though both can be translated in the same way, the first sentence means that you'll do it in three days' time; the second means that it will take three days for you to do it.

➤ en is used with the names of the seasons, except for spring.

en été	in summer
en automne	in autumn
en hiver	in winter
BUT: **au printemps**	in spring

➤ en is used for most means of transport.

Je suis venu en voiture.	I came by car.
C'est plus rapide en train.	It's quicker by train.
Il est allé en Italie en avion.	He flew to Italy.

Tip
The prepositions à and par are also used with means of transport.

➤ Use en to say what language something is in.

une lettre écrite en espagnol	a letter written in Spanish
Dis-le en anglais.	Say it in English.

➤ en can be used to say what something is made of when you particularly want to stress the material.

un bracelet en or	a bracelet made of gold, a gold bracelet
un manteau en cuir	a coat made of leather, a leather coat

> *Tip*
> de can also be used to say what something is made of.
>
> **une porte <u>de</u> bois**   a wooden door

➤ en often describes the situation or state that something or someone is in.

Je suis <u>en</u> vacances.	I'm on holiday.
La voiture est <u>en</u> panne.	The car's broken down.
Tu es toujours <u>en</u> retard!	You're always late!

➤ en is found before <u>present participles</u>, the form of the verb that ends in *-ing* in English and *-ant* in French.

Je fais mes devoirs <u>en regardant</u> la télé.	I do my homework while watching TV.
Il m'a vu <u>en passant</u> devant la porte.	He saw me as he came past the door.

⇨ *For more information on the **Present participle**, see page 125.*

> **Key points**
> ✔ à, de and en are very frequent prepositions which you will use all the time.
> ✔ Each of them has several possible meanings, which depend on the context they are used in.

Some other common prepositions

🛈 Note that some of these words are also adverbs, for example, avant, depuis.

⇨ *For more information on the Adverbs, see page 152.*

➤ The following prepositions are also frequently used in French:

- après after

<u>après</u> le déjeuner	after lunch
<u>après</u> son départ	after he had left
la troisième maison <u>après</u> la mairie	the third house after the town hall
<u>Après</u> vous!	After you!

🛈 Note that where English uses a verb in the perfect tense following *after*, French uses the infinitive avoir or être and a past participle.

Nous viendrons <u>après avoir fait</u> la vaisselle.	We'll come after we'<u>ve done</u> the dishes.

- avant before

Il est arrivé <u>avant</u> toi.	He arrived before you.
Tournez à gauche <u>avant</u> la poste.	Turn left before the post office.

🛈 Note that where English uses a verb ending in *-ing* after *before*, French uses de followed by the infinitive.

Je préfère finir mes devoirs <u>avant de manger</u>.	I prefer to finish my homework <u>before eating</u>.

- avec with

<u>avec</u> mon père	with my father
une chambre <u>avec</u> salle de bain	a room with its own bathroom
Ouvre-la <u>avec</u> un couteau.	Open it with a knife.

- chez

Elle est <u>chez</u> Pierre.	She's at Pierre's house.
Elle va <u>chez</u> Pierre.	She's going to Pierre's house.
Je reste <u>chez</u> moi ce weekend.	I'm staying at home this weekend.
Je vais rentrer <u>chez</u> moi.	I'm going home.
Ils habitent près de <u>chez</u> moi.	They live near my house.

> ## Tip
>
> chez is also used with the name of jobs or professions to indicate a shop or place of business.
>
> Je vais <u>chez le médecin</u>.   I'm going to the doctor's.

- contre against

  Ne mets pas ton vélo <u>contre</u> le mur.   Don't put your bike against the wall.

- dans in, into

  Il est <u>dans</u> sa chambre.   He's in his bedroom.

  Nous passons une semaine <u>dans</u> les Alpes.   We're spending a week in the Alps.

  <u>dans</u> deux mois   in two months' time

  Il est entré <u>dans</u> mon bureau.   He came into my office.

Grammar Extra!

dans and en can both be used in French to talk about a length of time, but the meaning is very different.

     Je le ferai <u>dans</u> trois jours.   I'll do it in three days.

     Je le ferai <u>en</u> trois jours.   I'll do it in three days.

Though both can be translated in the same way, the first sentence means that you'll do it in three days' time; the second means that it will take three days for you to do it.

- depuis since, for

  Elle habite Paris <u>depuis</u> 1998.   She's been living in Paris since 1998.

  Elle habite Paris <u>depuis</u> cinq ans.   She's been living in Paris for five years.

[*i*] Note that French uses the <u>present tense</u> with depuis to talk about actions that started in the past and are still going on.

     Il <u>est</u> en France <u>depuis</u> le mois de septembre.   He's been in France since September. (*and he is still there*)

If you are saying how long something has <u>NOT</u> happened for, you use the <u>perfect tense</u> with depuis.

     Nous ne l'<u>avons</u> pas <u>vu</u> depuis un mois.   We haven't seen him for a month.

⇨ For more information on the **Present tense** and the **Perfect tense**, see pages 71 and 111.

- derrière behind

    derrière la porte   behind the door

- devant in front of

    Il est assis devant moi.   He's sitting in front of me.

- entre ... et between ... and

    Il est assis entre son père et   He's sitting between his father and
    son oncle.   his uncle.

    Le bureau est fermé entre 13   The office is closed between 1 and
    et 14 heures.   2 p.m.

- jusque as far as, until

    Je te raccompagne jusque   I'll go with you as far as your house.
    chez toi.

    Jusqu'où vas-tu?   How far are you going?

    Jusqu'ici nous n'avons pas eu   Up to now we've had no problems.
    de problèmes.

    Je reste jusqu'à la fin du mois.   I'm staying until the end of the
                                                 month.

Tip

jusque changes to jusqu' before a word beginning with a vowel,
most words starting with h, and the French word y.

- par by, with, per

    deux par deux   two by two

    par le train   by train

    par la poste   by post

    par email   by email

    Son nom commence par un H.   His name begins with H.

    Prenez trois cachets par jour.   Take three tablets per day.

    Le voyage coûte quatre cents   The trip costs four hundred euros
    euros par personne.   per person.

    Nous nous voyons une fois par   We see each other once a month.
    mois.

    Il est tombé par terre.   He fell down.

    Il y a beaucoup de touristes   There are a lot of tourists around
    par ici.   here.

Tip

The prepositions à and en are also used with means of transport.

- pendant *during, for*

  Ça s'est passé <u>pendant</u> l'été.   It happened during the summer.
  Il n'a pas pu travailler <u>pendant</u>   He couldn't work for several
  plusieurs mois.   months.

Tip

French uses the <u>perfect tense</u> with pendant to talk about actions
in the past that are completed.

Nous <u>avons habité pendant</u> dix   We lived in Scotland for ten
ans en Écosse.   years. (*but don't any more*)

You can also miss out pendant.

Nous avons habité dix ans en   We lived in Scotland for ten
Écosse.   years.

pendant is also used to talk about something that will happen in the
future.

Je <u>serai</u> à New York <u>pendant</u>   I'll be in New York for a month.
un mois.

⇨ *For more information on the **Perfect tense**, see page 111.*

- pour *for (who or what something is for, and where something or someone is going)*

  C'est un cadeau <u>pour</u> toi.   It's a present for you.
  Nous voudrions une chambre   We'd like a room for two nights.
  <u>pour</u> deux nuits.
  le train <u>pour</u> Bordeaux   the train for Bordeaux

[*i*] Note that pour can also be used with infinitives, when it has the
meaning of *in order to*.

  Elle téléphone <u>pour savoir</u> à   She's ringing to find out what time
  quelle heure on arrivera.   we'll get there.
  <u>Pour aller</u> à Nice, s'il vous plaît? Which way is it to Nice, please?

- sans without

Elle est venue <u>sans</u> son frère.	She came without her brother.
un café <u>sans</u> sucre	a coffee without sugar
un pull <u>sans</u> manches	a sleeveless sweater

i Note that sans can also be used before infinitives in French. In English a verb form ending in -ing is used after *without*.

Elle est partie <u>sans dire</u> au revoir.	She left <u>without saying</u> goodbye.

- sauf except

Tout le monde vient <u>sauf</u> lui.	Everyone's coming except him.

- sous under

<u>sous</u> la table	under the table
<u>sous</u> terre	underground

- sur on

Pose-le <u>sur</u> le bureau.	Put it down on the desk.
Ton sac est <u>sur</u> la table.	Your bag is on the table.
Vous verrez l'hôpital <u>sur</u> votre gauche.	You'll see the hospital on your left.
un livre <u>sur</u> la politique	a book on politics

i Note that à and sur can both mean *on* in English. sur usually means on the top of something. sur la télé means *on top of the TV set*, but à la télé means *broadcast on TV*. sur le mur means *on top of the wall*, but au mur means *hanging on the wall*.

Tip

With numbers and measurements sur can also mean *in*, *out of* and *by*.

une personne <u>sur</u> dix	one person <u>in</u> ten
J'ai eu quatorze <u>sur</u> vingt en maths.	I got 14 <u>out of</u> 20 in maths.
La pièce fait quatre mètres <u>sur</u> deux.	The room measures four metres <u>by</u> two.

- vers towards (*a place*), at about

Il allait <u>vers</u> la gare.	He was going towards the station.
Je rentre chez moi <u>vers</u> cinq heures.	I go home at about 5 o'clock.

➤ voici (meaning *this is, here is*) and voilà (meaning *there is, that is*) are two very useful prepositions that French speakers often use to point things out.

<u>Voici</u> mon frère et <u>voilà</u> ma sœur.	This is my brother and that's my sister.
<u>Voici</u> ton sac.	Here's your bag.
Le <u>voici</u>!	Here he/it is!
Tiens! <u>Voilà</u> Paul.	Look! There's Paul.
Tu as perdu ton stylo? En <u>voilà</u> un autre.	Have you lost your pen? Here's another one.
Les <u>voilà</u>!	There they are!

Prepositions consisting of more than one word

➤ Prepositions can also be made up of several words instead of just one.

au bord de	at the edge of, at the side of
au bout de	after, at the end of
à cause de	because of
au-dessous de	below
au-dessus de	above
au fond de	at the bottom of, at the end of
au milieu de	in the middle of

Au bout d'un moment, il s'est endormi.	After a while, he fell asleep.
Nous ne pouvons pas sortir à cause du mauvais temps.	We can't go out because of the bad weather.
J'ai garé la voiture au bord de la route.	I parked the car by the side of the road.
Mon porte-monnaie est au fond de mon sac.	My purse is at the bottom of my bag.
Place le vase au milieu de la table.	Put the vase in the middle of the table.

Prepositions after verbs

➤ Some French verbs can be followed by an <u>infinitive</u> (the *to* form of the verb) and linked to it by either de or à, or no preposition at all. This is also true of verbs and their <u>objects</u>: the person or thing that the verb 'happens' to.

➪ *For more information on* **Verbs followed by an infinitive**, *see page 133.*

> ### Tip
>
> The preposition that is used in French is not always the same as the one that is used in English. Whenever you learn a new verb, try to learn which preposition can be used after it too.

➤ The lists in this section concentrate on those French verbs that involve a different construction from the one that is used in English.

1 Verbs that are followed by à + object

➤ à is often the equivalent of the English word *to* when it is used with an indirect object after verbs like *send*, *give* and *say*.

dire quelque chose <u>à</u> quelqu'un	to say something <u>to</u> someone
donner quelque chose <u>à</u> quelqu'un	to give something <u>to</u> someone
écrire quelque chose <u>à</u> quelqu'un	to write something <u>to</u> someone
envoyer quelque chose <u>à</u> quelqu'un	to send something <u>to</u> someone
montrer quelque chose <u>à</u> quelqu'un	to show something <u>to</u> someone

➪ *For more information on* **Indirect objects**, *see page 49.*

> ### Tip
>
> There is an important difference between French and English with this type of verb. In English, you can say either *to give something* <u>*to*</u> *someone* or *to give someone something*; to *show something* <u>*to*</u> *someone* or *to show someone something*.
> You can <u>NEVER</u> miss out à in French in the way that you can sometimes miss out *to* in English.

➤ Here are some verbs taking à in French that have a different construction in English.

croire **à** quelque chose	to believe <u>in</u> something
s'intéresser **à** quelqu'un/quelque chose	to be interested <u>in</u> someone/something
jouer **à** quelque chose	to play something (*sports, games*)
obéir **à** quelqu'un	to obey someone
penser **à** quelqu'un/quelque chose	to think <u>about</u> someone/something
répondre **à** quelqu'un	to answer someone
téléphoner **à** quelqu'un	to phone someone

Tip

When you are using jouer to talk about sports and games, you use à. When you are using jouer to talk about musical instruments, you use de.

jouer <u>au</u> tennis	to play tennis
jouer <u>aux</u> échecs	to play chess
jouer <u>de</u> la guitare	to play the guitar
jouer <u>du</u> piano	to play the piano

➤ plaire followed by à is a common way of saying you like something.

plaire **à** quelqu'un	to please someone (*literally*)
Ton cadeau me plaît beaucoup.	I like your present a lot.
Ce film plaît beaucoup aux jeunes.	This film is very popular with young people.

Grammar Extra!

manquer à works quite differently from its English equivalent, *to miss*. The English object is the French subject, and the English subject is the French object.

manquer **à** quelqu'un	to be missed by someone (*literally*)
Tu (*subject*) **me** (*object*) **manques.**	I (*subject*) miss you (*object*).
Mon pays (*subject*) **me** (*object*) **manque beaucoup.**	I (*subject*) miss my country (*object*) very much.

➤ There are also some verbs where you can put a direct object before à. The verb demander is the most common.

demander quelque chose **à** quelqu'un   to ask someone something, to ask someone for something

➪ *For more information on **Direct objects**, see page 47.*

[*i*] Note that demander in French does <u>NOT</u> mean *to demand*. It means *to ask something* or *to ask for something*. If you want to say *demand* in French, use exiger.

Nous avons demandé notre chemin à un chauffeur de taxi.	We asked a taxi driver the way.
J'exige des excuses!	I demand an apology!

2 Verbs that are followed by de + object

➤ Here are some verbs taking de in French that have a different construction in English.

changer <u>de</u> quelque chose	to change something (*one's shoes and so on*)
dépendre <u>de</u> quelqu'un/ quelque chose	to depend <u>on</u> someone/something
s'excuser <u>de</u> quelque chose	to apologize <u>for</u> something
jouer <u>de</u> quelque chose	to play something
parler <u>de</u> quelque chose	to talk <u>about</u> something
se servir <u>de</u> quelque chose	to use something
se souvenir <u>de</u> quelqu'un/ quelque chose	to remember someone/something

> ### Tip
>
> When you are using jouer to talk about sports and games, you use à. When you are using jouer to talk about musical instruments, you use de.
>
> | | |
> |---|---|
> | jouer <u>au</u> tennis | to play tennis |
> | jouer <u>aux</u> échecs | to play chess |
> | jouer <u>de</u> la guitare | to play the guitar |
> | jouer <u>du</u> piano | to play the piano |

➤ Some common phrases using avoir also contain de.

<u>avoir</u> besoin <u>de</u> quelque chose	to need something
<u>avoir</u> envie <u>de</u> quelque chose	to want something
<u>avoir</u> peur <u>de</u> quelque chose	to be afraid of something

➤ There are also some verbs where you can put a direct object before de. remercier is the most common.

remercier quelqu'un <u>de</u> quelque chose   to thank someone for something

➨ *For more information on* **Direct objects**, *see page 47.*

Grammar Extra!

The verb se tromper de quelque chose is often the equivalent of *to get the wrong …*

Je me suis trompé de numéro.	I got the wrong number.
Je me suis trompé de maison.	I got the wrong house.

---

3 Verbs taking a direct object in French but not in English

➤ In English there are a few verbs that are followed by *for, on, in, to* or *at* which, in French, are not followed by a preposition such as à or de. Here are the most common:

attendre quelqu'un/quelque chose	to wait <u>for</u> sb/sth
chercher quelqu'un/quelque chose	to look <u>for</u> sb/sth
demander quelqu'un/quelque chose	to ask <u>for</u> sb/sth
écouter quelqu'un/quelque chose	to listen <u>to</u> sb/sth
espérer quelque chose	to hope <u>for</u> sth
payer quelque chose	to pay <u>for</u> sth
regarder quelqu'un/quelque chose	to look <u>at</u> sb/sth

[*i*] Note that attendre does <u>NOT</u> mean *to attend* in English. It means *to wait for*. If you want to say that you attend something, use assister à quelque chose.

Je t'attends devant la gare.	I'll wait for you in front of the station.
Vous allez assister au concert?	Are you going to attend the concert?

➤ habiter can be used with or without a preposition:

- habiter is mostly used <u>without a preposition</u> when you are talking about living in a house, a flat and so on

Nous habitons un petit appartement en ville.	We live in a small flat in town.

- use habiter <u>with à</u> when you are talking about a town or city, and au (*singular*) or aux (*plural*) with the names of countries that are masculine in French

Nous habitons à Liverpool.	We live in Liverpool.
Nous habitons aux États-Unis.	We live in the United States.

- use habiter <u>with en</u> when you are talking about feminine countries

Nous habitons en Espagne.	We live in Spain.

Key points

✔ French prepositions after verbs are often not the ones that are used in English. French verbs often have a different construction from English verbs.

✔ French verbs are usually linked to their objects by de, à or nothing at all.

✔ You can never miss out à in French in the way that you can miss out *to* in English constructions like *to give someone something*.

Prepositions after adjectives

➤ Just like verbs, some French adjectives can be linked to what follows by either à or de.

➤ An adjective followed by de or à can be followed by a noun, a pronoun or an infinitive..

➤ Some adjectives that can be followed by de are used to say how you feel, that you are certain about something, or that it is necessary or important to do something. These are the most common:

certain	certain
content	happy
désolé	sorry
enchanté	delighted
heureux	happy
important	important
malheureux	unhappy
nécessaire	necessary
sûr	sure
triste	sad

Tu es <u>sûr de</u> pouvoir venir?	Are you sure you can come?
<u>Enchanté de</u> faire votre connaissance.	Delighted to meet you.
Il est <u>nécessaire de</u> réserver.	You have to book.

Grammar Extra!

➤ Some adjectives, such as facile (meaning *easy*), intéressant (meaning *interesting*) or impossible (meaning *impossible*), can be followed by either à or de. de tends to be used when you are saying something that is generally true. à tends to be used when you are saying something about someone or something in particular.

Il est difficile <u>de</u> prendre une décision.	It's difficult to make a decision.
<u>Il</u> est difficile <u>à</u> connaître.	He's difficult to get to know.
<u>Son accent</u> est difficile <u>à</u> comprendre.	His accent is difficult to understand.

CONJUNCTIONS

What is a conjunction?
A **conjunction** is a word such as *and*, *but*, *or*, *so*, *if* and *because*, that links two words or phrases of a similar type, or two parts of a sentence, for example, *Diane <u>and</u> I have been friends for years; I left <u>because</u> I was bored.*

et, mais, ou, parce que **and** si

➤ et, mais, ou, parce que and si are the most common conjunctions that you need to know in French.

- et and

  toi <u>et</u> moi   you <u>and</u> me
  Il pleut <u>et</u> il fait très froid.   It's raining <u>and</u> it's very cold.

- mais but

  C'est cher <u>mais</u> de très bonne   It's expensive, <u>but</u> very good quality.
  qualité.

📖 Note that mais is also commonly found in front of oui and si.

  'Tu viens ce soir?' – '<u>Mais oui</u>!'   'Are you coming tonight?' –
                                                'Definitely!'

  'Il n'a pas encore fini?' –   'Hasn't he finished yet?' – 'He
  '<u>Mais si</u>!'   certainly has!'

- ou or

  Tu préfères le vert <u>ou</u> le bleu?   Do you like the green one <u>or</u> the
                                                blue one?

  Donne-moi ça <u>ou</u> je me fâche!   Give me that <u>or</u> I'll get cross!

Tip
Be careful not to confuse ou (meaning *or*) with où (meaning *where*).

- parce que because

  Je ne peux pas sortir <u>parce que</u>   I can't go out <u>because</u> I've still got
  j'ai encore du travail à faire.   work to do.

> **Tip**
>
> parce que changes to parce qu' before a word beginning with a vowel, most words starting with h, and the French word y.
>
> **Il ne vient pas <u>parce qu</u>'il n'a pas de voiture.**   He isn't coming <u>because</u> he doesn't have a car.

- si if

  Je me demande <u>si</u> elle ment.   I wonder <u>if</u> she's lying.
  <u>Si</u> j'étais à ta place, je ne l'inviterais pas.   <u>If</u> I were you, I wouldn't invite him.

> **Tip**
>
> si changes to s' before il or ils.
>
> **<u>S'</u>il ne pleut pas, on mangera dehors.**   <u>If</u> it doesn't rain, we'll eat outside.

Some other common conjunctions

➤ Here are some other common French conjunctions:

- car because

  | Il faut prendre un bus pour y accéder <u>car</u> il est interdit d'y monter en voiture. | You need to take a bus to get there because cars are prohibited. |

[i] Note that car is used in formal language or in writing. The normal way of saying *because* is parce que.

- comme as

  | <u>Comme</u> il pleut, je prends la voiture. | <u>As</u> it's raining, I'm taking the car. |

- donc so

  | J'ai raté le train, <u>donc</u> je serai en retard. | I missed the train, <u>so</u> I'll be late. |

- lorsque when

  | J'allais composer ton numéro <u>lorsque</u> tu as appelé. | I was about to dial your number <u>when</u> you called. |

- quand when

  | Je ne sors pas <u>quand</u> il pleut. | I don't go out <u>when</u> it rains. |

[i] Note that when quand and lorsque are used to talk about something that will happen in the future, the French verb has to be in the <u>future tense</u> even though English uses a verb in the <u>present tense</u>.

| Quand je <u>serai</u> riche, j'achèterai une belle maison. | When I'<u>m</u> rich, I'll buy a nice house. |

➪ *For more information on the **Present tense** and the **Future tense**, see pages 71 and 98.*

➤ French, like English, also has conjunctions which have more than one part. Here are the most common:

- ne ... ni ... ni neither ... nor

  | Je n'aime <u>ni</u> les lentilles <u>ni</u> les épinards. | I like <u>neither</u> lentils <u>nor</u> spinach. |

[i] Note that the ne part of this expression goes just before the verb.

- ou ... ou, ou bien ... ou bien either ... or

  | <u>Ou</u> il est malade <u>ou</u> il ment. | <u>Either</u> he's sick <u>or</u> he's lying. |
  | <u>Ou bien</u> il m'évite <u>ou bien</u> il ne me reconnaît pas. | <u>Either</u> he's avoiding me <u>or</u> he doesn't recognize me. |

The conjunction que

➤ When que is used to join two parts of a sentence, it means *that*.

Il dit qu'il m'aime.	He says <u>that</u> he loves me.
Elle sait que vous êtes là.	She knows <u>that</u> you're here.

> **Tip**
>
> In English you could say both *He says he loves me* and *He says <u>that</u> he loves me*, or *She knows you're here* and *She knows <u>that</u> you're here*. You can <u>NEVER</u> leave out que in French in the same way.

➤ que is also used when you are comparing two things or two people. In this case, it means *as* or *than*.

Ils n'y vont pas aussi souvent que nous.	They don't go as often <u>as</u> us.
Les melons sont plus chers que les bananes.	Melons are more expensive <u>than</u> bananas.

⇨ *For more information on **Comparative adjectives**, see page 34.*

➤ Some prepositions which give you information about when something happens, can also be conjunctions if you put que after them. pendant que (meaning *while*) is the most common of these.

Christian a téléphoné <u>pendant que</u> Chantal prenait son bain.	Christian phoned <u>while</u> Chantal was in the bath.

ⓘ Note that when pendant que (meaning *while*), quand (meaning *when*) and lorsque (meaning *when*) are used to talk about something that will happen in the future, the French verb has to be in the <u>future tense</u> even though English uses a verb in the <u>present tense</u>.

Pendant que je <u>serai</u> en France, j'irai les voir.	I'll go and visit them while I'<u>m</u> in France.

⇨ *For more information on the **Present tense** and the **Future tense**, see pages 71 and 98.*

Grammar Extra!

que can replace another conjunction to avoid having to repeat it.

<u>Quand</u> tu seras plus grand et <u>que</u> tu auras une maison à toi, ...	When you're older and you have a house of your own, ...
<u>Comme</u> il pleut et <u>que</u> je n'ai pas de parapluie, ...	As it's raining and I don't have an umbrella, ...

NUMBERS

1	un (une)
2	deux
3	trois
4	quatre
5	cinq
6	six
7	sept
8	huit
9	neuf
10	dix
11	onze
12	douze
13	treize
14	quatorze
15	quinze
16	seize
17	dix-sept
18	dix-huit
19	dix-neuf
20	vingt
21	vingt et un (une)
22	vingt-deux
30	trente
40	quarante
50	cinquante
60	soixante
70	soixante-dix
71	soixante et onze
72	soixante-douze
80	quatre-vingts
81	quatre-vingt-un (-une)
90	quatre-vingt-dix
91	quatre-vingt-onze
100	cent
101	cent un (une)
300	trois cents
301	trois cent un (une)
1000	mille
2000	deux mille
1,000,000	un million

1st	premier (1er), première (1re)
2nd	deuxième (2e or 2ème) or second(e) (2$^{nd(e)}$)
3rd	troisième (3e or 3ème)
4th	quatrième (4e or 4ème)
5th	cinquième (5e or 5ème)
6th	sixième (6e or 6ème)
7th	septième (7e or 7ème)
8th	huitième (8e or 8ème)
9th	neuvième (9e or 9ème)
10th	dixième (10e or 10ème)
11th	onzième (11e or 11ème)
12th	douzième (12e or 12ème)
13th	treizième (13e or 13ème)
14th	quatorzième (14e or 14ème)
15th	quinzième (15e or 15ème)
16th	seizième (16e or 16ème)
17th	dix-septième (17e or 17ème)
18th	dix-huitième (18e or 18ème)
19th	dix-neuvième (19e or 19ème)
20th	vingtième (20e or 20ème)
21st	vingt et unième (21e or 21ème)
22nd	vingt-deuxième (22e or 22ème)
30th	trentième (30e or 30ème)
100th	centième (100e or 100ème)
101st	cent unième (101e or 101ème)
1000th	millième (1000e or 1000ème)

1/2	un demi
1/3	un tiers
2/3	deux tiers
1/4	un quart
1/5	un cinquième
0.5	zéro virgule cinq (0,5)
3.4	trois virgule quatre (3,4)
10%	dix pour cent
100%	cent pour cent

EXEMPLES	**EXAMPLES**
Il habite au dix.	He lives at number ten.
à la page dix-neuf	on page nineteen
au chapitre sept	in chapter seven
Il habite au cinquième (étage).	He lives on the fifth floor.
Il est arrivé troisième.	He came in third.
échelle au vingt-cinq millième	scale one to twenty-five thousand

L'HEURE	THE TIME
Quelle heure est-il?	What time is it?
Il est...	It's...
une heure	one o'clock
une heure dix	ten past one
une heure et quart	quarter past one
une heure et demie	half past one
deux heures moins vingt	twenty to two
deux heures moins le quart	quarter to two

À quelle heure?	At what time?
à minuit	at midnight
à midi	at midday, at noon
à une heure (de l'après-midi)	at one o'clock (in the afternoon)
à huit heures (du soir)	at eight o'clock (in the evening)
à 11h15 or	at 11.15 or eleven fifteen
onze heures quinze	
à 20h45 or	at 20.45 or twenty forty-five
vingt heures quarante-cinq	

LA DATE	THE DATE
LES JOURS DE LA SEMAINE	**DAYS OF THE WEEK**
lundi	Monday
mardi	Tuesday
mercredi	Wednesday
jeudi	Thursday
vendredi	Friday
samedi	Saturday
dimanche	Sunday

Quand?	**When?**
lundi	on Monday
le lundi	on Mondays
tous les lundis	every Monday
mardi dernier	last Tuesday
vendredi prochain	next Friday
samedi en huit	a week on Saturday
samedi en quinze	two weeks on Saturday

[i] Note that days of the week are <u>NOT</u> written with a capital letter in French.

LES MOIS	MONTHS OF THE YEAR
janvier	January
février	February
mars	March
avril	April
mai	May
juin	June
juillet	July
août	August
septembre	September
octobre	October
novembre	November
décembre	December

Quand?	When?
en février	in February
le 1er décembre	on December 1st
le premier décembre	on December first
en 1998	in 1998
en mille neuf cent quatre-vingt-dix-huit	in nineteen ninety-eight

Quel jour sommes-nous?
Nous sommes le...

What day is it?
It's...

lundi 26 février *or*	Monday 26 February *or*
lundi vingt-six février	Monday twenty-sixth of February
dimanche 1er octobre *or*	Sunday 1st October *or*
dimanche premier octobre	Sunday the first of October

i Note that months of the year are <u>NOT</u> written with a capital letter in French.

VOCABULAIRE	USEFUL VOCABULARY
Quand?	**When?**
aujourd'hui	today
ce matin	this morning
cet après-midi	this afternoon
ce soir	this evening
Souvent?	**How often?**
tous les jours	every day
tous les deux jours	every other day
une fois par semaine	once a week
deux fois par semaine	twice a week
une fois par mois	once a month
Ça s'est passé quand?	**When did it happen?**
le matin	in the morning
le soir	in the evening
hier	yesterday
hier soir	yesterday evening
avant-hier	the day before yesterday
il y a une semaine	a week ago
il y a quinze jours	two weeks ago
l'an dernier or l'année dernière	last year
Ça va se passer quand?	**When is it going to happen?**
demain	tomorrow
demain matin	tomorrow morning
après-demain	the day after tomorrow
dans deux jours	in two days
dans une semaine	in a week
dans quinze jours	in two weeks
le mois prochain	next month
l'an prochain or l'année prochaine	next year

SOME COMMON DIFFICULTIES

General problems

➤ You can't always translate French into English and English into French word for word. While occasionally it is possible to do this, often it is not. For example:

- English <u>phrasal verbs</u> (verbs followed by a preposition or adverb), such as, *to run away, to fall down,* are often translated by ONE word in French.

continuer	to go on
tomber	to fall down
rendre	to give back

⇨ *For more information on **Verbs**, see pages 69–137.*

- Sentences which contain a verb and preposition in English, might NOT contain a preposition in French.

payer quelque chose	to pay <u>for</u> something
regarder quelqu'un/quelque chose	to look <u>at</u> somebody/something
écouter quelqu'un/quelque chose	to listen <u>to</u> somebody/something

- Similarly, sentences which contain a verb and preposition in French, might NOT contain a preposition in English.

obéir <u>à</u> quelqu'un/quelque chose	to obey somebody/something
changer <u>de</u> quelque chose	to change something
manquer <u>de</u> quelque chose	to lack something

- The same French preposition may be translated into English in different ways.

parler <u>de</u> quelque chose	to talk <u>about</u> something
sûr <u>de</u> quelque chose	sure <u>of</u> something
voler quelque chose <u>à</u> quelqu'un	to steal something <u>from</u> someone
croire <u>à</u> quelque chose	to believe <u>in</u> something

⇨ *For more information on **Prepositions**, see page 162.*

- A word which is singular in English may not be in French.

les bagages	luggage
ses cheveux	his/her hair

- Similarly, a word which is singular in French may not be in English.

un short	shorts
mon pantalon	my trousers

⇨ *For more information on **Nouns**, see page 1.*

- In English, you can use 's to show who or what something belongs to; in French, you have to use **de**.

la voiture de mon frère	my brother's car
la chambre des enfants	the children's bedroom

⇨ *For more information on the preposition de, see page 166.*

Specific problems

1 -ing

➤ The *-ing* ending in English is translated in a number of different ways in French:

- *to be …-ing* is translated by a verb consisting of one word.

Il part demain.	He's leaving tomorrow.
Je lisais un roman.	I was reading a book.

⇨ *For more information on **Verbs**, see pages 69–137.*

📖 Note that when you are talking about somebody's or something's physical position, you use a past participle.

Elle est assise là-bas	She's sitting over there.
Il était couché par terre.	He was lying on the ground.

⇨ *For more information on the **Past participle**, see page 111.*

➤ *-ing* can also be translated by:

- an infinitive

J'aime aller au cinéma	I like going to the cinema.
Arrêtez de vous disputer!	Stop arguing!
Avant de partir…	Before leaving…

⇨ *For more information on **Infinitives**, see page 133.*

For further explanation of grammatical terms, please see pages viii-xii.

• a present participle

<u>Étant</u> plus timide que moi, elle...	Being shyer than me, she...

⮕ *For more information on the **Present participle**, see page 125.*

• a noun

<u>Le ski</u> me maintient en forme.	<u>Skiing</u> keeps me fit.

⮕ *For more information on **Nouns**, see page 1.*

2 to be

➤ The verb *to be* is generally translated by être.

Il <u>est</u> tard.	It<u>'s</u> late.
Ce n'<u>est</u> pas possible!	It<u>'s</u> not possible!

➤ When you are talking about the physical position of something, se trouver may be used.

Où <u>se trouve</u> la gare?	Where<u>'s</u> the station?

➤ In certain set phrases which describe how you are feeling or a state you are in, the verb avoir is used.

avoir chaud	to be warm
avoir froid	to be cold
avoir faim	to be hungry
avoir soif	to be thirsty
avoir peur	to be afraid
avoir tort	to be wrong
avoir raison	to be right

➤ When you are describing what the weather is like, use the verb faire.

Quel temps <u>fait</u>-il?	What<u>'s</u> the weather like?
Il <u>fait</u> beau.	It<u>'s</u> lovely.
Il <u>fait</u> mauvais.	It<u>'s</u> miserable.
Il <u>fait</u> du vent.	It<u>'s</u> windy.

➤ When you are talking about someone's age, use the verb avoir.

Quel âge <u>as</u>-tu?	How old <u>are</u> you?
J'<u>ai</u> quinze ans.	I<u>'m</u> fifteen.

➤ When talking about your health, use the verb aller.

Comment <u>allez</u>-vous?	How <u>are</u> you?
Je <u>vais</u> très bien.	I<u>'m</u> very well.

3 | it is, it's

➤ *it is* and *it's* are usually translated by il est or elle est when referring to a noun.

'Où est mon parapluie?' – '<u>Il est</u> là, dans le coin.'	Where's my umbrella? <u>It's</u> there, in the corner.
Descends la valise si <u>elle</u> n'<u>est</u> pas trop lourde.	Bring the case down if <u>it is</u>n't too heavy.

➤ When you are talking about the time, use il est.

'Quelle heure <u>est-il</u>?' – '<u>Il est</u> sept heures et demie.'	What time <u>is it</u>? – <u>It's</u> half past seven.

➤ When you are describing what the weather is like, use the verb faire.

Il <u>fait</u> beau.	It's lovely.
Il <u>fait</u> mauvais.	It's miserable.
Il <u>fait</u> du vent.	It's windy.

➤ If you want to say, for example, *it is difficult to do something* or *it is easy to do something,* use il est.

<u>Il est</u> difficile de répondre à cette question.	<u>It is</u> difficult to answer this question.

➤ In <u>ALL</u> other phrases and constructions, use c'est.

<u>C'est</u> moi qui ne l'aime pas.	<u>It's</u> me who doesn't like him.
<u>C'est</u> Charles qui l'a dit.	<u>It's</u> Charles who said so.
<u>C'est</u> ici que je les ai achetés.	<u>It's</u> here that I bought them.
<u>C'est</u> parce que la poste est fermée que...	<u>It's</u> because the post office is closed that...

4 | there is, there are

➤ Both *there is* and *there are* are translated by il y a.

<u>Il y a</u> quelqu'un à la porte.	<u>There is</u> someone at the door.
<u>Il y a</u> cinq livres sur la table.	<u>There are</u> five books on the table.

5 | can, to be able

➤ If you want to talk about someone's physical ability to do something, use pouvoir.

<u>Pouvez</u>-vous faire dix kilomètres à pied?	<u>Can</u> you walk ten kilometres?

For further explanation of grammatical terms, please see pages viii-xii.

➤ If you want to say that *you know how to do something*, use savoir.

> Elle ne <u>sait</u> pas nager.   She <u>can</u>'t swim.

➤ When *can* is used with verbs to do with what you can see or hear, you do NOT use pouvoir in French.

> Je ne vois rien.   I <u>can't see</u> anything.
> Il les entendait.   He <u>could hear</u> them.

6 to

➤ The preposition *to* is generally translated by à.

> Donne le livre <u>à</u> Patrick.   Give the book <u>to</u> Patrick.

➪ *For more information on the preposition* à, *see page 163.*

➤ When you are talking about the time, use moins.

> dix heures <u>moins</u> cinq   five <u>to</u> ten
> à sept heures <u>moins</u> le quart   at a quarter <u>to</u> seven

➤ If you want to say *(in order) to*, use pour.

> Je l'ai fait <u>pour</u> vous aider.   I did it <u>to</u> help you.
> Il va en ville <u>pour</u> acheter un   He's going into town <u>to</u> buy a
> cadeau.   present.

THE ALPHABET

➤ The French alphabet is pronounced differently from the way it is pronounced in English. Use the list below to help you sound out the letters.

A, a	[ɑ]	(ah)	like 'a' in 'la'
B, b	[be]	(bay)	
C, c	[se]	(say)	
D, d	[de]	(day)	
E, e	[ə]	(uh)	like 'e' in 'le'
F, f	[ɛf]	(eff)	
G, g	[ʒe]	(jay)	
H, h	[aʃ]	(ash)	
I, i	[i]	(ee)	
J, j	[ʒi]	(jee)	
K, k	[ka]	(ka)	
L, l	[ɛl]	(ell)	
M, m	[ɛm]	(emm)	
N, n	[ɛn]	(enn)	
O, o	[o]	(oh)	
P, p	[pe]	(pay)	
Q, q	[ky]	(ku)	like 'u' in 'une'
R, r	[ɛr]	(air)	
S, s	[ɛs]	(ess)	
T, t	[te]	(tay)	
U, u	[y]	(u)	like 'u' in 'une'
V, v	[ve]	(vay)	
W, w	[dubləve]	(doobla-vay)	
X, x	[iks]	(eex)	
Y, y	[igrɛk]	(ee-grek)	
Z, z	[zɛd]	(zed)	

For further explanation of grammatical terms, please see pages viii-xii.

VERB TABLES

Introduction

The **Verb Tables** in the following section contain 93 tables of French verbs (some regular and some irregular) in alphabetical order. Each table shows you the following forms: **Present**, **Perfect**, **Future**, **Subjunctive**, **Imperfect**, **Conditional**, **Imperative** and the **Present** and **Past Participles**. For more information on these tenses, how they are formed, when they are used and so on, you should look at the section on **Verbs** in the main text on pages 69–137.

In order to help you use the verbs shown in the **Verb Tables** correctly, there are also a number of example phrases at the bottom of each page to show the verb as it is used in context.

In French there are both **regular** verbs (their forms follow the normal rules) and **irregular** verbs (their forms do not follow the normal rules). The regular verbs in these tables are:

donner (regular -er verb, Verb Table 29)
finir (regular -ir verb, Verb Table 39)
attendre (regular -re verb, Verb Table 8)

The irregular verbs are shown in full.

The **Verb Index** at the end of this section contains over 2000 verbs, each of which is cross-referred to one of the verbs given in the Verb Tables. The table shows the patterns that the verb listed in the index follows.

▶ **acheter** (to buy)

PRESENT

j'	achète
tu	achètes
il/elle/on	achète
nous	achetons
vous	achetez
ils/elles	achètent

PRESENT SUBJUNCTIVE

j'	achète
tu	achètes
il/elle/on	achète
nous	achetions
vous	achetiez
ils/elles	achètent

PERFECT

j'	ai acheté
tu	as acheté
il/elle/on	a acheté
nous	avons acheté
vous	avez acheté
ils/elles	ont acheté

IMPERFECT

j'	achetais
tu	achetais
il/elle/on	achetait
nous	achetions
vous	achetiez
ils/elles	achetaient

FUTURE

j'	achèterai
tu	achèteras
il/elle/on	achètera
nous	achèterons
vous	achèterez
ils/elles	achèteront

CONDITIONAL

j'	achèterais
tu	achèterais
il/elle/on	achèterait
nous	achèterions
vous	achèteriez
ils/elles	achèteraient

IMPERATIVE

achète / achetons / achetez

PAST PARTICIPLE

acheté

PRESENT PARTICIPLE

achetant

EXAMPLE PHRASES

J'ai acheté des gâteaux à la pâtisserie. I bought some cakes at the cake shop.
Qu'est-ce que tu lui as acheté pour son anniversaire? What did you buy him for his
  birthday?
Je n'achète jamais de chips. I never buy crisps.

---

je/j' = I **tu** = you **il** = he/it **elle** = she/it **on** = we/one **nous** = we **vous** = you **ils/elles** = they

▶ acquérir (to acquire)

PRESENT

j'	acquiers
tu	acquiers
il/elle/on	acquiert
nous	acquérons
vous	acquérez
ils/elles	acquièrent

PRESENT SUBJUNCTIVE

j'	acquière
tu	acquières
il/elle/on	acquière
nous	acquérions
vous	acquériez
ils/elles	acquièrent

PERFECT

j'	ai acquis
tu	as acquis
il/elle/on	a acquis
nous	avons acquis
vous	avez acquis
ils/elles	ont acquis

IMPERFECT

j'	acquérais
tu	acquérais
il/elle/on	acquérait
nous	acquérions
vous	acquériez
ils/elles	acquéraient

FUTURE

j'	acquerrai
tu	acquerras
il/elle/on	acquerra
nous	acquerrons
vous	acquerrez
ils/elles	acquerront

CONDITIONAL

j'	acquerrais
tu	acquerrais
il/elle/on	acquerrait
nous	acquerrions
vous	acquerriez
ils/elles	acquerraient

IMPERATIVE

acquiers / acquérons / acquérez

PAST PARTICIPLE

acquis

PRESENT PARTICIPLE

acquérant

EXAMPLE PHRASES

*Elle **a acquis** la nationalité française en 2003.* She acquired French nationality in 2003.

je/j' = I **tu** = you **il** = he/it **elle** = she/it **on** = we/one **nous** = we **vous** = you **ils/elles** = they

▶ aller (to go)

PRESENT

je	vais
tu	vas
il/elle/on	va
nous	allons
vous	allez
ils/elles	vont

PRESENT SUBJUNCTIVE

j'	aille
tu	ailles
il/elle/on	aille
nous	allions
vous	alliez
ils/elles	aillent

PERFECT

je	suis allé(e)
tu	es allé(e)
il/elle/on	est allé(e)
nous	sommes allé(e)s
vous	êtes allé(e)(s)
ils/elles	sont allé(e)s

IMPERFECT

j'	allais
tu	allais
il/elle/on	allait
nous	allions
vous	alliez
ils/elles	allaient

FUTURE

j'	irai
tu	iras
il/elle/on	ira
nous	irons
vous	irez
ils/elles	iront

CONDITIONAL

j'	irais
tu	irais
il/elle/on	irait
nous	irions
vous	iriez
ils/elles	iraient

IMPERATIVE

va / allons / allez

PAST PARTICIPLE

allé

PRESENT PARTICIPLE

allant

EXAMPLE PHRASES

*Vous **allez** au cinéma?* Are you going to the cinema?
*Je **suis allé** à Londres.* I went to London.
*Est-ce que tu **es** déjà **allé** en Allemagne?* Have you ever been to Germany?

je/j' = I **tu** = you **il** = he/it **elle** = she/it **on** = we/one **nous** = we **vous** = you **ils/elles** = they

▶ appeler (to call)

PRESENT

j'	appelle
tu	appelles
il/elle/on	appelle
nous	appelons
vous	appelez
ils/elles	appellent

PERFECT

j'	ai appelé
tu	as appelé
il/elle/on	a appelé
nous	avons appelé
vous	avez appelé
ils/elles	ont appelé

FUTURE

j'	appellerai
tu	appelleras
il/elle/on	appellera
nous	appellerons
vous	appellerez
ils/elles	appelleront

IMPERATIVE

appelle / appelons / appelez

PRESENT PARTICIPLE

appelant

PRESENT SUBJUNCTIVE

j'	appelle
tu	appelles
il/elle/on	appelle
nous	appelions
vous	appeliez
ils/elles	appellent

IMPERFECT

j'	appelais
tu	appelais
il/elle/on	appelait
nous	appelions
vous	appeliez
ils/elles	appelaient

CONDITIONAL

j'	appellerais
tu	appellerais
il/elle/on	appellerait
nous	appellerions
vous	appelleriez
ils/elles	appelleraient

PAST PARTICIPLE

appelé

EXAMPLE PHRASES

*Elle **a appelé** le médecin.* She phoned the doctor.
*J'**ai appelé** Richard à Londres.* I phoned Richard in London.
*Comment tu **t'appelles**?* What's your name?

⇨ *See pages 88–91 for information on how to form the reflexive verb **s'appeler**.*

je/j' = I **tu** = you **il** = he/it **elle** = she/it **on** = we/one **nous** = we **vous** = you **ils/elles** = they

▶ arriver (to arrive)

PRESENT

j'	arrive
tu	arrives
il/elle/on	arrive
nous	arrivons
vous	arrivez
ils/elles	arrivent

PRESENT SUBJUNCTIVE

j'	arrive
tu	arrives
il/elle/on	arrive
nous	arrivions
vous	arriviez
ils/elles	arrivent

PERFECT

je	suis arrivé(e)
tu	es arrivé(e)
il/elle/on	est arrivé(e)
nous	sommes arrivé(e)s
vous	êtes arrivé(e)(s)
ils/elles	sont arrivé(e)s

IMPERFECT

j'	arrivais
tu	arrivais
il/elle/on	arrivait
nous	arrivions
vous	arriviez
ils/elles	arrivaient

FUTURE

j'	arriverai
tu	arriveras
il/elle/on	arrivera
nous	arriverons
vous	arriverez
ils/elles	arriveront

CONDITIONAL

j'	arriverais
tu	arriverais
il/elle/on	arriverait
nous	arriverions
vous	arriveriez
ils/elles	arriveraient

IMPERATIVE

arrive / arrivons / arrivez

PAST PARTICIPLE

arrivé

PRESENT PARTICIPLE

arrivant

EXAMPLE PHRASES

*J'**arrive** à l'école à huit heures.* I arrive at school at 8 o'clock.
*Le prof n'**est** pas encore **arrivé**.* The teacher hasn't arrived yet.
*Qu'est-ce qui **est arrivé** à Aurélie?* What happened to Aurélie?

---

je/j' = I **tu** = you **il** = he/it **elle** = she/it **on** = we/one **nous** = we **vous** = you **ils/elles** = they

▶ s'asseoir (to sit down)

PRESENT

je	m'assieds/m'assois
tu	t'assieds/t'assois
il/elle/on	s'assied/s'assoit
nous	nous asseyons/nous assoyons
vous	vous asseyez/vous assoyez
ils/elles	s'asseyent/s'assoient

PRESENT SUBJUNCTIVE

je	m'asseye
tu	t'asseyes
il/elle/on	s'asseye
nous	nous asseyions
vous	vous asseyiez
ils/elles	s'asseyent

PERFECT

je	me suis assis(e)
tu	t'es assis(e)
il/elle/on	s'est assis(e)
nous	nous sommes assis(es)
vous	vous êtes assis(e) (es)
ils/elles	se sont assis(es)

IMPERFECT

je	m'asseyais
tu	t'asseyais
il/elle/on	s'asseyait
nous	nous asseyions
vous	vous asseyiez
ils/elles	s'asseyaient

FUTURE

je	m'assiérai
tu	t'assiéras
il/elle/on	s'assiéra
nous	nous assiérons
vous	vous assiérez
ils/elles	s'assiéront

CONDITIONAL

je	m'assiérais
tu	t'assiérais
il/elle/on	s'assiérait
nous	nous assiérions
vous	vous assiériez
ils/elles	s'assiéraient

IMPERATIVE

assieds-toi / asseyons-nous / asseyez-vous

PAST PARTICIPLE

assis

PRESENT PARTICIPLE

s'asseyant

EXAMPLE PHRASES

Assieds-toi, *Nicole.* Sit down Nicole.
Asseyez-vous, *les enfants.* Sit down children.
Je peux **m'asseoir?** May I sit down?
Je **me suis assise** *sur un chewing-gum!* I've sat on some chewing gum!

---

je/j' = I **tu** = you **il** = he/it **elle** = she/it **on** = we/one **nous** = we **vous** = you **ils/elles** = they

▶ **attendre** (to wait)

PRESENT

j'	attends
tu	attends
il/elle/on	attend
nous	attendons
vous	attendez
ils/elles	attendent

PRESENT SUBJUNCTIVE

j'	attende
tu	attendes
il/elle/on	attende
nous	attendions
vous	attendiez
ils/elles	attendent

PERFECT

j'	ai attendu
tu	as attendu
il/elle/on	a attendu
nous	avons attendu
vous	avez attendu
ils/elles	ont attendu

IMPERFECT

j'	attendais
tu	attendais
il/elle/on	attendait
nous	attendions
vous	attendiez
ils/elles	attendaient

FUTURE

j'	attendrai
tu	attendras
il/elle/on	attendra
nous	attendrons
vous	attendrez
ils/elles	attendront

CONDITIONAL

j'	attendrais
tu	attendrais
il/elle/on	attendrait
nous	attendrions
vous	attendriez
ils/elles	attendraient

IMPERATIVE

attends / attendons / attendez

PAST PARTICIPLE

attendu

PRESENT PARTICIPLE

attendant

EXAMPLE PHRASES

Attends-moi! Wait for me!
*Tu **attends** depuis longtemps?* Have you been waiting long?
*Je l'**ai attendu** à la poste.* I waited for him at the post office.
*Je **m'attends** à ce qu'il soit en retard.* I expect he'll be late.

⇨ *See pages 88–91 for information on how to form the reflexive verb **s'attendre**.*

je/j' = I **tu** = you **il** = he/it **elle** = she/it **on** = we/one **nous** = we **vous** = you **ils/elles** = they

▶ avoir (to have)

PRESENT

j'	ai
tu	as
il/elle/on	a
nous	avons
vous	avez
ils/elles	ont

PRESENT SUBJUNCTIVE

j'	aie
tu	aies
il/elle/on	ait
nous	ayons
vous	ayez
ils/elles	aient

PERFECT

j'	ai eu
tu	as eu
il/elle/on	a eu
nous	avons eu
vous	avez eu
ils/elles	ont eu

IMPERFECT

j'	avais
tu	avais
il/elle/on	avait
nous	avions
vous	aviez
ils/elles	avaient

FUTURE

j'	aurai
tu	auras
il/elle/on	aura
nous	aurons
vous	aurez
ils/elles	auront

CONDITIONAL

j'	aurais
tu	aurais
il/elle/on	aurait
nous	aurions
vous	auriez
ils/elles	auraient

IMPERATIVE

aie / ayons / ayez

PAST PARTICIPLE

eu

PRESENT PARTICIPLE

ayant

EXAMPLE PHRASES

*Il **a** les yeux bleus.* He's got blue eyes.
*Quel âge **as**-tu?* How old are you?
*Il **a eu** un accident.* He's had an accident.
*J'**avais** faim.* I was hungry.
*Il y **a** beaucoup de monde.* There are lots of people.

---

je/j' = I **tu** = you **il** = he/it **elle** = she/it **on** = we/one **nous** = we **vous** = you **ils/elles** = they

▶ battre (to beat)

PRESENT

je	bats
tu	bats
il/elle/on	bat
nous	battons
vous	battez
ils/elles	battent

PRESENT SUBJUNCTIVE

je	batte
tu	battes
il/elle/on	batte
nous	battions
vous	battiez
ils/elles	battent

PERFECT

j'	ai battu
tu	as battu
il/elle/on	a battu
nous	avons battu
vous	avez battu
ils/elles	ont battu

IMPERFECT

je	battais
tu	battais
il/elle/on	battait
nous	battions
vous	battiez
ils/elles	battaient

FUTURE

je	battrai
tu	battras
il/elle/on	battra
nous	battrons
vous	battrez
ils/elles	battront

CONDITIONAL

je	battrais
tu	battrais
il/elle/on	battrait
nous	battrions
vous	battriez
ils/elles	battraient

IMPERATIVE

bats / battons / battez

PAST PARTICIPLE

battu

PRESENT PARTICIPLE

battant

EXAMPLE PHRASES

*On les **a battus** deux à un.* We beat them 2-1.
*J'ai le cœur qui **bat**!* My heart's beating (fast)!
*Arrêtez de **vous battre**!* Stop fighting!

⇨ *See pages 88–91 for information on how to form the reflexive verb **se battre**.*

▶ boire (to drink)

PRESENT

je	bois
tu	bois
il/elle/on	boit
nous	buvons
vous	buvez
ils/elles	boivent

PRESENT SUBJUNCTIVE

je	boive
tu	boives
il/elle/on	boive
nous	buvions
vous	buviez
ils/elles	boivent

PERFECT

j'	ai bu
tu	as bu
il/elle/on	a bu
nous	avons bu
vous	avez bu
ils/elles	ont bu

IMPERFECT

je	buvais
tu	buvais
il/elle/on	buvait
nous	buvions
vous	buviez
ils/elles	buvaient

FUTURE

je	boirai
tu	boiras
il/elle/on	boira
nous	boirons
vous	boirez
ils/elles	boiront

CONDITIONAL

je	boirais
tu	boirais
il/elle/on	boirait
nous	boirions
vous	boiriez
ils/elles	boiraient

IMPERATIVE

bois / buvons / buvez

PAST PARTICIPLE

bu

PRESENT PARTICIPLE

buvant

EXAMPLE PHRASES

*Qu'est-ce que tu veux **boire**?* What would you like to drink?
*Il ne **boit** jamais d'alcool.* He never drinks alcohol.
*J'**ai bu** un litre d'eau.* I drank a litre of water.

▶ bouillir (to boil)

PRESENT

je	bous
tu	bous
il/elle/on	bout
nous	bouillons
vous	bouillez
ils/elles	bouillent

PRESENT SUBJUNCTIVE

je	bouille
tu	bouilles
il/elle/on	bouille
nous	bouillions
vous	bouilliez
ils/elles	bouillent

PERFECT

j'	ai bouilli
tu	as bouilli
il/elle/on	a bouilli
nous	avons bouilli
vous	avez bouilli
ils/elles	ont bouilli

IMPERFECT

je	bouillais
tu	bouillais
il/elle/on	bouillait
nous	bouillions
vous	bouilliez
ils/elles	bouillaient

FUTURE

je	bouillirai
tu	bouilliras
il/elle/on	bouillira
nous	bouillirons
vous	bouillirez
ils/elles	bouilliront

CONDITIONAL

je	bouillirais
tu	bouillirais
il/elle/on	bouillirait
nous	bouillirions
vous	bouilliriez
ils/elles	bouilliraient

IMPERATIVE

bous / bouillons / bouillez

PAST PARTICIPLE

bouilli

PRESENT PARTICIPLE

bouillant

EXAMPLE PHRASES

*L'eau **bout**.* The water's boiling.
*Tu peux mettre de l'eau à **bouillir**?* Can you boil some water?

---

je/j' = I **tu** = you **il** = he/it **elle** = she/it **on** = we/one **nous** = we **vous** = you **ils/elles** = they

▶ commencer (to begin)

PRESENT

je	commence
tu	commences
il/elle/on	commence
nous	commençons
vous	commencez
ils/elles	commencent

PRESENT SUBJUNCTIVE

je	commence
tu	commences
il/elle/on	commence
nous	commencions
vous	commenciez
ils/elles	commencent

PERFECT

j'	ai commencé
tu	as commencé
il/elle/on	a commencé
nous	avons commencé
vous	avez commencé
ils/elles	ont commencé

IMPERFECT

je	commençais
tu	commençais
il/elle/on	commençait
nous	commencions
vous	commenciez
ils/elles	commençaient

FUTURE

je	commencerai
tu	commenceras
il/elle/on	commencera
nous	commencerons
vous	commencerez
ils/elles	commenceront

CONDITIONAL

je	commencerais
tu	commencerais
il/elle/on	commencerait
nous	commencerions
vous	commenceriez
ils/elles	commenceraient

IMPERATIVE

commence / commençons / commencez

PAST PARTICIPLE

commencé

PRESENT PARTICIPLE

commençant

EXAMPLE PHRASES

Il a commencé à pleuvoir. It started to rain.
Les cours commencent à neuf heures. Lessons start at 9 o'clock.
Tu as déjà commencé de réviser pour les examens? Have you started revising for the exams?

---

je/j' = I **tu** = you **il** = he/it **elle** = she/it **on** = we/one **nous** = we **vous** = you **ils/elles** = they

▶ conclure (to conclude)

PRESENT

je	conclus
tu	conclus
il/elle/on	conclut
nous	concluons
vous	concluez
ils/elles	concluent

PRESENT SUBJUNCTIVE

je	conclue
tu	conclues
il/elle/on	conclue
nous	concluions
vous	concluiez
ils/elles	concluent

PERFECT

j'	ai conclu
tu	as conclu
il/elle/on	a conclu
nous	avons conclu
vous	avez conclu
ils/elles	ont conclu

IMPERFECT

je	concluais
tu	concluais
il/elle/on	concluait
nous	concluions
vous	concluiez
ils/elles	concluaient

FUTURE

je	conclurai
tu	concluras
il/elle/on	conclura
nous	conclurons
vous	conclurez
ils/elles	concluront

CONDITIONAL

je	conclurais
tu	conclurais
il/elle/on	conclurait
nous	conclurions
vous	concluriez
ils/elles	concluraient

IMPERATIVE

conclus / concluons / concluez

PAST PARTICIPLE

conclu

PRESENT PARTICIPLE

concluant

EXAMPLE PHRASES

*Ils **ont conclu** un marché.* They concluded a deal.
*J'en **ai conclu** qu'il était parti.* I concluded that he had gone.
*Je **conclurai** par ces mots…* I will conclude with these words…

---

je/j' = I **tu** = you **il** = he/it **elle** = she/it **on** = we/one **nous** = we **vous** = you **ils/elles** = they

connaître (to know)

PRESENT

je	connais
tu	connais
il/elle/on	connaît
nous	connaissons
vous	connaissez
ils/elles	connaissent

PRESENT SUBJUNCTIVE

je	connaisse
tu	connaisses
il/elle/on	connaisse
nous	connaissions
vous	connaissiez
ils/elles	connaissent

PERFECT

j'	ai connu
tu	as connu
il/elle/on	a connu
nous	avons connu
vous	avez connu
ils/elles	ont connu

IMPERFECT

je	connaissais
tu	connaissais
il/elle/on	connaissait
nous	connaissions
vous	connaissiez
ils/elles	connaissaient

FUTURE

je	connaîtrai
tu	connaîtras
il/elle/on	connaîtra
nous	connaîtrons
vous	connaîtrez
ils/elles	connaîtront

CONDITIONAL

je	connaîtrais
tu	connaîtrais
il/elle/on	connaîtrait
nous	connaîtrions
vous	connaîtriez
ils/elles	connaîtraient

IMPERATIVE

connais / connaissons / connaissez

PAST PARTICIPLE

connu

PRESENT PARTICIPLE

connaissant

EXAMPLE PHRASES

Je ne **connais** pas du tout cette région. I don't know the area at all.
Vous **connaissez** M Amiot? Do you know Mr Amiot?
Il n'a pas **connu** son grand-père. He never knew his granddad.
Ils **se sont connus** à Rouen. They first met in Rouen.

⇨ See pages 88–91 for information on how to form the reflexive verb **se connaître**.

je/j' = I **tu** = you **il** = he/it **elle** = she/it **on** = we/one **nous** = we **vous** = you **ils/elles** = they

▶ coudre (to sew)

PRESENT

je	couds
tu	couds
il/elle/on	coud
nous	cousons
vous	cousez
ils/elles	cousent

PRESENT SUBJUNCTIVE

je	couse
tu	couses
il/elle/on	couse
nous	cousions
vous	cousiez
ils/elles	cousent

PERFECT

j'	ai cousu
tu	as cousu
il/elle/on	a cousu
nous	avons cousu
vous	avez cousu
ils/elles	ont cousu

IMPERFECT

je	cousais
tu	cousais
il/elle/on	cousait
nous	cousions
vous	cousiez
ils/elles	cousaient

FUTURE

je	coudrai
tu	coudras
il/elle/on	coudra
nous	coudrons
vous	coudrez
ils/elles	coudront

CONDITIONAL

je	coudrais
tu	coudrais
il/elle/on	coudrait
nous	coudrions
vous	coudriez
ils/elles	coudraient

IMPERATIVE

couds / cousons / cousez

PAST PARTICIPLE

cousu

PRESENT PARTICIPLE

cousant

EXAMPLE PHRASES

*Tu sais **coudre**?* Can you sew?
*Elle **a cousu** elle-même son costume.* She made her costume herself.

je/j' = I   **tu** = you   **il** = he/it   **elle** = she/it   **on** = we/one   **nous** = we   **vous** = you   **ils/elles** = they

▶ **courir** (to run)

PRESENT

je	cours
tu	cours
il/elle/on	court
nous	courons
vous	courez
ils/elles	courent

PRESENT SUBJUNCTIVE

je	coure
tu	coures
il/elle/on	coure
nous	courions
vous	couriez
ils/elles	courent

PERFECT

j'	ai couru
tu	as couru
il/elle/on	a couru
nous	avons couru
vous	avez couru
ils/elles	ont couru

IMPERFECT

je	courais
tu	courais
il/elle/on	courait
nous	courions
vous	couriez
ils/elles	couraient

FUTURE

je	courrai
tu	courras
il/elle/on	courra
nous	courrons
vous	courrez
ils/elles	courront

CONDITIONAL

je	courrais
tu	courrais
il/elle/on	courrait
nous	courrions
vous	courriez
ils/elles	courraient

IMPERATIVE

cours / courons / courez

PAST PARTICIPLE

couru

PRESENT PARTICIPLE

courant

EXAMPLE PHRASES

*Je ne **cours** pas très vite.* I can't run very fast.
*Elle est sortie en **courant**.* She ran out.
*Ne **courez** pas dans le couloir.* Don't run in the corridor.
*J'**ai couru** jusqu'à l'école.* I ran all the way to school.

---

je/j' = I **tu** = you **il** = he/it **elle** = she/it **on** = we/one **nous** = we **vous** = you **ils/elles** = they

▶ **craindre** (to fear)

PRESENT

je	crains
tu	crains
il/elle/on	craint
nous	craignons
vous	craignez
ils/elles	craignent

PRESENT SUBJUNCTIVE

je	craigne
tu	craignes
il/elle/on	craigne
nous	craignions
vous	craigniez
ils/elles	craignent

PERFECT

j'	ai craint
tu	as craint
il/elle/on	a craint
nous	avons craint
vous	avez craint
ils/elles	ont craint

IMPERFECT

je	craignais
tu	craignais
il/elle/on	craignait
nous	craignions
vous	craigniez
ils/elles	craignaient

FUTURE

je	craindrai
tu	craindras
il/elle/on	craindra
nous	craindrons
vous	craindrez
ils/elles	craindront

CONDITIONAL

je	craindrais
tu	craindrais
il/elle/on	craindrait
nous	craindrions
vous	craindriez
ils/elles	craindraient

IMPERATIVE

crains / craignons / craignez

PAST PARTICIPLE

craint

PRESENT PARTICIPLE

craignant

EXAMPLE PHRASES

*Tu n'as rien à **craindre**.* You've got nothing to fear.
*Je **crains** le pire.* I fear the worst.

▶ créer (to create)

PRESENT

je	crée
tu	crées
il/elle/on	crée
nous	créons
vous	créez
ils/elles	créent

PRESENT SUBJUNCTIVE

je	crée
tu	crées
il/elle/on	crée
nous	créions
vous	créiez
ils/elles	créent

PERFECT

j'	ai créé
tu	as créé
il/elle/on	a créé
nous	avons créé
vous	avez créé
ils/elles	ont créé

IMPERFECT

je	créais
tu	créais
il/elle/on	créait
nous	créions
vous	créiez
ils/elles	créaient

FUTURE

je	créerai
tu	créeras
il/elle/on	créera
nous	créerons
vous	créerez
ils/elles	créeront

CONDITIONAL

je	créerais
tu	créerais
il/elle/on	créerait
nous	créerions
vous	créeriez
ils/elles	créeraient

IMPERATIVE

crée / créons / créez

PAST PARTICIPLE

créé

PRESENT PARTICIPLE

créant

EXAMPLE PHRASES

*Il **a créé** une nouvelle invention.* He's created a new invention.
*Ce virus **crée** des difficultés dans le monde entier.* This virus is creating difficulties all over the world.
*Le gouvernement **créera** deux mille emplois supplémentaires.* The government will create an extra 2000 jobs.

je/j' = I **tu** = you **il** = he/it **elle** = she/it **on** = we/one **nous** = we **vous** = you **ils/elles** = they

▶ crier (to shout)

PRESENT

je	crie
tu	cries
il/elle/on	crie
nous	crions
vous	criez
ils/elles	crient

PRESENT SUBJUNCTIVE

je	crie
tu	cries
il/elle/on	crie
nous	criions
vous	criiez
ils/elles	crient

PERFECT

j'	ai crié
tu	as crié
il/elle/on	a crié
nous	avons crié
vous	avez crié
ils/elles	ont crié

IMPERFECT

je	criais
tu	criais
il/elle/on	criait
nous	criions
vous	criiez
ils/elles	criaient

FUTURE

je	crierai
tu	crieras
il/elle/on	criera
nous	crierons
vous	crierez
ils/elles	crieront

CONDITIONAL

je	crierais
tu	crierais
il/elle/on	crierait
nous	crierions
vous	crieriez
ils/elles	crieraient

IMPERATIVE

crie / crions / criez

PAST PARTICIPLE

crié

PRESENT PARTICIPLE

criant

EXAMPLE PHRASES

*Ne **crie** pas comme ça!* Don't shout!
*Elle **a crié** au secours.* She cried for help.
*"Attention!", **a-t-il crié**.* "Watch out!" he shouted.

▶ **croire** (to believe)

PRESENT

je	crois
tu	crois
il/elle/on	croit
nous	croyons
vous	croyez
ils/elles	croient

PRESENT SUBJUNCTIVE

je	croie
tu	croies
il/elle/on	croie
nous	croyions
vous	croyiez
ils/elles	croient

PERFECT

j'	ai cru
tu	as cru
il/elle/on	a cru
nous	avons cru
vous	avez cru
ils/elles	ont cru

IMPERFECT

je	croyais
tu	croyais
il/elle/on	croyait
nous	croyions
vous	croyiez
ils/elles	croyaient

FUTURE

je	croirai
tu	croiras
il/elle/on	croira
nous	croirons
vous	croirez
ils/elles	croiront

CONDITIONAL

je	croirais
tu	croirais
il/elle/on	croirait
nous	croirions
vous	croiriez
ils/elles	croiraient

IMPERATIVE

crois / croyons / croyez

PAST PARTICIPLE

cru

PRESENT PARTICIPLE

croyant

EXAMPLE PHRASES

*Je ne te **crois** pas.* I don't believe you.
*J'**ai cru** que tu n'allais pas venir.* I thought you weren't going to come.
*Elle **croyait** encore au père Noël.* She still believed in Santa.

je/j' = I **tu** = you **il** = he/it **elle** = she/it **on** = we/one **nous** = we **vous** = you **ils/elles** = they

▶ croître (to grow)

PRESENT

je	croîs
tu	croîs
il/elle/on	croît
nous	croissons
vous	croissez
ils/elles	croissent

PRESENT SUBJUNCTIVE

je	croisse
tu	croisses
il/elle/on	croisse
nous	croissions
vous	croissiez
ils/elles	croissent

PERFECT

j'	ai crû
tu	as crû
il/elle/on	a crû
nous	avons crû
vous	avez crû
ils/elles	ont crû

IMPERFECT

je	croissais
tu	croissais
il/elle/on	croissait
nous	croissions
vous	croissiez
ils/elles	croissaient

FUTURE

je	croîtrai
tu	croîtras
il/elle/on	croîtra
nous	croîtrons
vous	croîtrez
ils/elles	croîtront

CONDITIONAL

je	croîtrais
tu	croîtrais
il/elle/on	croîtrait
nous	croîtrions
vous	croîtriez
ils/elles	croîtraient

IMPERATIVE

croîs / croissons / croissez

PAST PARTICIPLE

crû (*NB*: crue, crus, crues)

PRESENT PARTICIPLE

croissant

EXAMPLE PHRASES

*Les ventes **croissent** de 6% par an.* Sales are growing by 6% per year.
*C'est une plante qui **croît** dans les pays chauds.* This plant grows in hot countries.

---

je/j' = I **tu** = you **il** = he/it **elle** = she/it **on** = we/one **nous** = we **vous** = you **ils/elles** = they

▶ cueillir (to pick)

PRESENT

je	cueille
tu	cueilles
il/elle/on	cueille
nous	cueillons
vous	cueillez
ils/elles	cueillent

PRESENT SUBJUNCTIVE

je	cueille
tu	cueilles
il/elle/on	cueille
nous	cueillions
vous	cueilliez
ils/elles	cueillent

PERFECT

j'	ai cueilli
tu	as cueilli
il/elle/on	a cueilli
nous	avons cueilli
vous	avez cueilli
ils/elles	ont cueilli

IMPERFECT

je	cueillais
tu	cueillais
il/elle/on	cueillait
nous	cueillions
vous	cueilliez
ils/elles	cueillaient

FUTURE

je	cueillerai
tu	cueilleras
il/elle/on	cueillera
nous	cueillerons
vous	cueillerez
ils/elles	cueilleront

CONDITIONAL

je	cueillerais
tu	cueillerais
il/elle/on	cueillerait
nous	cueillerions
vous	cueilleriez
ils/elles	cueilleraient

IMPERATIVE

cueille / cueillons / cueillez

PAST PARTICIPLE

cueilli

PRESENT PARTICIPLE

cueillant

EXAMPLE PHRASES

J'ai cueilli quelques fraises dans le jardin. I've picked a few strawberries in the garden.
Il est interdit de cueillir des fleurs sauvages dans la montagne. It's forbidden to pick wild flowers in the mountains.

---

je/j' = I **tu** = you **il** = he/it **elle** = she/it **on** = we/one **nous** = we **vous** = you **ils/elles** = they

▶ **cuire** (to cook)

PRESENT

je	cuis
tu	cuis
il/elle/on	cuit
nous	cuisons
vous	cuisez
ils/elles	cuisent

PRESENT SUBJUNCTIVE

je	cuise
tu	cuises
il/elle/on	cuise
nous	cuisions
vous	cuisiez
ils/elles	cuisent

PERFECT

j'	ai cuit
tu	as cuit
il/elle/on	a cuit
nous	avons cuit
vous	avez cuit
ils/elles	ont cuit

IMPERFECT

je	cuisais
tu	cuisais
il/elle/on	cuisait
nous	cuisions
vous	cuisiez
ils/elles	cuisaient

FUTURE

je	cuirai
tu	cuiras
il/elle/on	cuira
nous	cuirons
vous	cuirez
ils/elles	cuiront

CONDITIONAL

je	cuirais
tu	cuirais
il/elle/on	cuirait
nous	cuirions
vous	cuiriez
ils/elles	cuiraient

IMPERATIVE

cuis / cuisons / cuisez

PAST PARTICIPLE

cuit

PRESENT PARTICIPLE

cuisant

EXAMPLE PHRASES

*Je les **ai cuits** au beurre.* I cooked them in butter.
*En général, je **cuis** les légumes à la vapeur.* I usually steam vegetables.
*Ce gâteau prend environ une heure à **cuire**.* This cake takes about an hour to bake.

▶ descendre (to go down)

PRESENT

je	descends
tu	descends
il/elle/on	descend
nous	descendons
vous	descendez
ils/elles	descendent

PRESENT SUBJUNCTIVE

je	descende
tu	descendes
il/elle/on	descende
nous	descendions
vous	descendiez
ils/elles	descendent

PERFECT

je	suis descendu(e)
tu	es descendu(e)
il/elle/on	est descendu(e)
nous	sommes descendu(e)s
vous	êtes descendu(e)(s)
ils/elles	sont descendu(e)s

IMPERFECT

je	descendais
tu	descendais
il/elle/on	descendait
nous	descendions
vous	descendiez
ils/elles	descendaient

FUTURE

je	descendrai
tu	descendras
il/elle/on	descendra
nous	descendrons
vous	descendrez
ils/elles	descendront

CONDITIONAL

je	descendrais
tu	descendrais
il/elle/on	descendrait
nous	descendrions
vous	descendriez
ils/elles	descendraient

IMPERATIVE

descends / descendons / descendez

PAST PARTICIPLE

descendu

PRESENT PARTICIPLE

descendant

EXAMPLE PHRASES

Descendez la rue jusqu'au rond-point. Go down the street to the roundabout.
Reste en bas: je descends! Stay downstairs – I'm coming down!
Nous sommes descendus à la station Trocadéro. We got off at the Trocadéro station.
Vous pouvez descendre ma valise, s'il vous plaît? Can you get my suitcase down, please?

ⓘ Note that **descendre** takes **avoir** in the perfect tense when it is used with a direct object; see page 114.

je/j' = I **tu** = you **il** = he/it **elle** = she/it **on** = we/one **nous** = we **vous** = you **ils/elles** = they

▶ **devenir** (to become)

PRESENT

je	deviens
tu	deviens
il/elle/on	devient
nous	devenons
vous	devenez
ils/elles	deviennent

PRESENT SUBJUNCTIVE

je	devienne
tu	deviennes
il/elle/on	devienne
nous	devenions
vous	deveniez
ils/elles	deviennent

PERFECT

je	suis devenu(e)
tu	es devenu(e)
il/elle/on	est devenu(e)
nous	sommes devenu(e)s
vous	êtes devenu(e)(s)
ils/elles	sont devenu(e)s

IMPERFECT

je	devenais
tu	devenais
il/elle/on	devenait
nous	devenions
vous	deveniez
ils/elles	devenaient

FUTURE

je	deviendrai
tu	deviendras
il/elle/on	deviendra
nous	deviendrons
vous	deviendrez
ils/elles	deviendront

CONDITIONAL

je	deviendrais
tu	deviendrais
il/elle/on	deviendrait
nous	deviendrions
vous	deviendriez
ils/elles	deviendraient

IMPERATIVE

deviens / devenons / devenez

PAST PARTICIPLE

devenu

PRESENT PARTICIPLE

devenant

EXAMPLE PHRASES

*Il **est devenu** médecin.* He became a doctor.
*Ça **devient** de plus en plus difficile.* It's becoming more and more difficult.
*Qu'est-ce qu'elle **est devenue**?* What has become of her?

---

je/j' = I **tu** = you **il** = he/it **elle** = she/it **on** = we/one **nous** = we **vous** = you **ils/elles** = they

▶ devoir (to have to; to owe)

PRESENT

je	dois
tu	dois
il/elle/on	doit
nous	devons
vous	devez
ils/elles	doivent

PRESENT SUBJUNCTIVE

je	doive
tu	doives
il/elle/on	doive
nous	devions
vous	deviez
ils/elles	doivent

PERFECT

j'	ai dû
tu	as dû
il/elle/on	a dû
nous	avons dû
vous	avez dû
ils/elles	ont dû

IMPERFECT

je	devais
tu	devais
il/elle/on	devait
nous	devions
vous	deviez
ils/elles	devaient

FUTURE

je	devrai
tu	devras
il/elle/on	devra
nous	devrons
vous	devrez
ils/elles	devront

CONDITIONAL

je	devrais
tu	devrais
il/elle/on	devrait
nous	devrions
vous	devriez
ils/elles	devraient

IMPERATIVE

dois / devons / devez

PAST PARTICIPLE

dû (*NB*: due, dus, dues)

PRESENT PARTICIPLE

devant

EXAMPLE PHRASES

*Je **dois** aller faire les courses ce matin.* I have to do the shopping this morning.
*À quelle heure est-ce que tu **dois** partir?* What time do you have to leave?
*Il **a dû** faire ses devoirs hier soir.* He had to do his homework last night.
*Il **devait** prendre le train pour aller travailler.* He had to go to work by train.

je/j' = I **tu** = you **il** = he/it **elle** = she/it **on** = we/one **nous** = we **vous** = you **ils/elles** = they

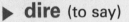

▶ **dire** (to say)

PRESENT

je	dis
tu	dis
il/elle/on	dit
nous	disons
vous	dites
ils/elles	disent

PRESENT SUBJUNCTIVE

je	dise
tu	dises
il/elle/on	dise
nous	disions
vous	disiez
ils/elles	disent

PERFECT

j'	ai dit
tu	as dit
il/elle/on	a dit
nous	avons dit
vous	avez dit
ils/elles	ont dit

IMPERFECT

je	disais
tu	disais
il/elle/on	disait
nous	disions
vous	disiez
ils/elles	disaient

FUTURE

je	dirai
tu	diras
il/elle/on	dira
nous	dirons
vous	direz
ils/elles	diront

CONDITIONAL

je	dirais
tu	dirais
il/elle/on	dirait
nous	dirions
vous	diriez
ils/elles	diraient

IMPERATIVE

dis / disons / dites

PAST PARTICIPLE

dit

PRESENT PARTICIPLE

disant

EXAMPLE PHRASES

*Qu'est-ce qu'elle **dit**?* What is she saying?
*"Bonjour!", a-t-il **dit**.* "Hello!" he said.
*Ils m'ont **dit** que le film était nul.* They told me that the film was rubbish.
*Comment ça **se dit** en anglais?* How do you say that in English?

⟹ *See pages 88–91 for information on how to form the reflexive verb **se dire**.*

---

je/j' = I **tu** = you **il** = he/it **elle** = she/it **on** = we/one **nous** = we **vous** = you **ils/elles** = they

▶ donner (to give)

PRESENT

je	donne
tu	donnes
il/elle/on	donne
nous	donnons
vous	donnez
ils/elles	donnent

PRESENT SUBJUNCTIVE

je	donne
tu	donnes
il/elle/on	donne
nous	donnions
vous	donniez
ils/elles	donnent

PERFECT

j'	ai donné
tu	as donné
il/elle/on	a donné
nous	avons donné
vous	avez donné
ils/elles	ont donné

IMPERFECT

je	donnais
tu	donnais
il/elle/on	donnait
nous	donnions
vous	donniez
ils/elles	donnaient

FUTURE

je	donnerai
tu	donneras
il/elle/on	donnera
nous	donnerons
vous	donnerez
ils/elles	donneront

CONDITIONAL

je	donnerais
tu	donnerais
il/elle/on	donnerait
nous	donnerions
vous	donneriez
ils/elles	donneraient

IMPERATIVE

donne / donnons / donnez

PAST PARTICIPLE

donné

PRESENT PARTICIPLE

donnant

EXAMPLE PHRASES

Donne-moi la main. Give me your hand.
Est-ce que je t'ai donné mon adresse? Did I give you my address?
L'appartement donne sur la place. The flat overlooks the square.

je/j' = I **tu** = you **il** = he/it **elle** = she/it **on** = we/one **nous** = we **vous** = you **ils/elles** = they

▶ dormir (to sleep)

PRESENT

je	dors
tu	dors
il/elle/on	dort
nous	dormons
vous	dormez
ils/elles	dorment

PERFECT

j'	ai dormi
tu	as dormi
il/elle/on	a dormi
nous	avons dormi
vous	avez dormi
ils/elles	ont dormi

FUTURE

je	dormirai
tu	dormiras
il/elle/on	dormira
nous	dormirons
vous	dormirez
ils/elles	dormiront

IMPERATIVE

dors / dormons / dormez

PRESENT PARTICIPLE

dormant

PRESENT SUBJUNCTIVE

je	dorme
tu	dormes
il/elle/on	dorme
nous	dormions
vous	dormiez
ils/elles	dorment

IMPERFECT

je	dormais
tu	dormais
il/elle/on	dormait
nous	dormions
vous	dormiez
ils/elles	dormaient

CONDITIONAL

je	dormirais
tu	dormirais
il/elle/on	dormirait
nous	dormirions
vous	dormiriez
ils/elles	dormiraient

PAST PARTICIPLE

dormi

EXAMPLE PHRASES

*Tu **as** bien **dormi**?* Did you sleep well?
*Nous **dormons** dans la même chambre.* We sleep in the same bedroom.
*À 9 heures, il **dormait** déjà.* He was already asleep by nine.

---

je/j' = I **tu** = you **il** = he/it **elle** = she/it **on** = we/one **nous** = we **vous** = you **ils/elles** = they

▶ écrire (to write)

PRESENT

j'	écris
tu	écris
il/elle/on	écrit
nous	écrivons
vous	écrivez
ils/elles	écrivent

PRESENT SUBJUNCTIVE

j'	écrive
tu	écrives
il/elle/on	écrive
nous	écrivions
vous	écriviez
ils/elles	écrivent

PERFECT

j'	ai écrit
tu	as écrit
il/elle/on	a écrit
nous	avons écrit
vous	avez écrit
ils/elles	ont écrit

IMPERFECT

j'	écrivais
tu	écrivais
il/elle/on	écrivait
nous	écrivions
vous	écriviez
ils/elles	écrivaient

FUTURE

j'	écrirai
tu	écriras
il/elle/on	écrira
nous	écrirons
vous	écrirez
ils/elles	écriront

CONDITIONAL

j'	écrirais
tu	écrirais
il/elle/on	écrirait
nous	écririons
vous	écririez
ils/elles	écriraient

IMPERATIVE

écris / écrivons / écrivez

PAST PARTICIPLE

écrit

PRESENT PARTICIPLE

écrivant

EXAMPLE PHRASES

Tu as écrit à ta correspondante récemment? Have you written to your penfriend lately?
Elle écrit des romans. She writes novels.
Comment ça s'écrit, "brouillard"? How do you spell "brouillard"?

⟹ See pages 88–91 for information on how to form the reflexive verb *s'écrire*.

---

je/j' = I **tu** = you **il** = he/it **elle** = she/it **on** = we/one **nous** = we **vous** = you **ils/elles** = they

▶ émouvoir (to move)

PRESENT

j'	émeus
tu	émeus
il/elle/on	émeut
nous	émouvons
vous	émouvez
ils/elles	émeuvent

PRESENT SUBJUNCTIVE

j'	émeuve
tu	émeuves
il/elle/on	émeuve
nous	émouvions
vous	émouviez
ils/elles	émeuvent

PERFECT

j'	ai ému
tu	as ému
il/elle/on	a ému
nous	avons ému
vous	avez ému
ils/elles	ont ému

IMPERFECT

j'	émouvais
tu	émouvais
il/elle/on	émouvait
nous	émouvions
vous	émouviez
ils/elles	émouvaient

FUTURE

j'	émouvrai
tu	émouvras
il/elle/on	émouvra
nous	émouvrons
vous	émouvrez
ils/elles	émouvront

CONDITIONAL

j'	émouvrais
tu	émouvrais
il/elle/on	émouvrait
nous	émouvrions
vous	émouvriez
ils/elles	émouvraient

IMPERATIVE

émeus / émouvons / émouvez

PAST PARTICIPLE

ému

PRESENT PARTICIPLE

émouvant

EXAMPLE PHRASES

*Ce film nous **a ému**.* This film moved us.
*Cette histoire m'**émeut** toujours beaucoup.* This story always moves me deeply.

je/j' = I **tu** = you **il** = he/it **elle** = she/it **on** = we/one **nous** = we **vous** = you **ils/elles** = they

▶ entrer (to enter)

PRESENT

j'	entre
tu	entres
il/elle/on	entre
nous	entrons
vous	entrez
ils/elles	entrent

PRESENT SUBJUNCTIVE

j'	entre
tu	entres
il/elle/on	entre
nous	entrions
vous	entriez
ils/elles	entrent

PERFECT

je	suis entré(e)
tu	es entré(e)
il/elle/on	est entré(e)
nous	sommes entré(e)s
vous	êtes entré(e)(s)
ils/elles	sont entré(e)s

IMPERFECT

j'	entrais
tu	entrais
il/elle/on	entrait
nous	entrions
vous	entriez
ils/elles	entraient

FUTURE

j'	entrerai
tu	entreras
il/elle/on	entrera
nous	entrerons
vous	entrerez
ils/elles	entreront

CONDITIONAL

j'	entrerais
tu	entrerais
il/elle/on	entrerait
nous	entrerions
vous	entreriez
ils/elles	entreraient

IMPERATIVE

entre / entrons / entrez

PAST PARTICIPLE

entré

PRESENT PARTICIPLE

entrant

EXAMPLE PHRASES

Je peux entrer? Can I come in?
Essuie-toi les pieds en entrant. Wipe your feet as you come in.
Ils sont tous entrés dans la maison. They all went into the house.

je/j' = I **tu** = you **il** = he/it **elle** = she/it **on** = we/one **nous** = we **vous** = you **ils/elles** = they

▶ **envoyer** (to send)

PRESENT

j'	envoie
tu	envoies
il/elle/on	envoie
nous	envoyons
vous	envoyez
ils/elles	envoient

PRESENT SUBJUNCTIVE

j'	envoie
tu	envoies
il/elle/on	envoie
nous	envoyions
vous	envoyiez
ils/elles	envoient

PERFECT

j'	ai envoyé
tu	as envoyé
il/elle/on	a envoyé
nous	avons envoyé
vous	avez envoyé
ils/elles	ont envoyé

IMPERFECT

j'	envoyais
tu	envoyais
il/elle/on	envoyait
nous	envoyions
vous	envoyiez
ils/elles	envoyaient

FUTURE

j'	enverrai
tu	enverras
il/elle/on	enverra
nous	enverrons
vous	enverrez
ils/elles	enverront

CONDITIONAL

j'	enverrais
tu	enverrais
il/elle/on	enverrait
nous	enverrions
vous	enverriez
ils/elles	enverraient

IMPERATIVE

envoie / envoyons / envoyez

PAST PARTICIPLE

envoyé

PRESENT PARTICIPLE

envoyant

EXAMPLE PHRASES

J'ai envoyé une carte postale à ma tante. I sent my aunt a postcard.
Envoie-moi un e-mail. Send me an email.
Je t'enverrai ton cadeau par la poste. I'll send you your present by post.

je/j' = I **tu** = you **il** = he/it **elle** = she/it **on** = we/one **nous** = we **vous** = you **ils/elles** = they

▶ espérer (to hope)

PRESENT

j'	espère
tu	espères
il/elle/on	espère
nous	espérons
vous	espérez
ils/elles	espèrent

PRESENT SUBJUNCTIVE

j'	espère
tu	espères
il/elle/on	espère
nous	espérions
vous	espériez
ils/elles	espèrent

PERFECT

j'	ai espéré
tu	as espéré
il/elle/on	a espéré
nous	avons espéré
vous	avez espéré
ils/elles	ont espéré

IMPERFECT

j'	espérais
tu	espérais
il/elle/on	espérait
nous	espérions
vous	espériez
ils/elles	espéraient

FUTURE

j'	espérerai
tu	espéreras
il/elle/on	espérera
nous	espérerons
vous	espérerez
ils/elles	espéreront

CONDITIONAL

j'	espérerais
tu	espérerais
il/elle/on	espérerait
nous	espérerions
vous	espéreriez
ils/elles	espéreraient

IMPERATIVE

espère / espérons / espérez

PAST PARTICIPLE

espéré

PRESENT PARTICIPLE

espérant

EXAMPLE PHRASES

J'espère que tu vas bien. I hope you're well.
Il espérait pouvoir venir. He was hoping he'd be able to come.
Tu penses réussir tes examens? – J'espère bien! Do you think you'll pass your exams?
– I hope so!

je/j' = I **tu** = you **il** = he/it **elle** = she/it **on** = we/one **nous** = we **vous** = you **ils/elles** = they

▶ être (to be)

PRESENT

je	suis
tu	es
il/elle/on	est
nous	sommes
vous	êtes
ils/elles	sont

PRESENT SUBJUNCTIVE

je	sois
tu	sois
il/elle/on	soit
nous	soyons
vous	soyez
ils/elles	soient

PERFECT

j'	ai été
tu	as été
il/elle/on	a été
nous	avons été
vous	avez été
ils/elles	ont été

IMPERFECT

j'	étais
tu	étais
il/elle/on	était
nous	étions
vous	étiez
ils/elles	étaient

FUTURE

je	serai
tu	seras
il/elle/on	sera
nous	serons
vous	serez
ils/elles	seront

CONDITIONAL

je	serais
tu	serais
il/elle/on	serait
nous	serions
vous	seriez
ils/elles	seraient

IMPERATIVE

sois / soyons / soyez

PAST PARTICIPLE

été

PRESENT PARTICIPLE

étant

EXAMPLE PHRASES

Mon père est professeur. My father's a teacher.
Quelle heure est-il? – Il est dix heures. What time is it? – It's 10 o'clock.
Ils ne sont pas encore arrivés. They haven't arrived yet.

▶ **faire** (to do; to make)

PRESENT

je	fais
tu	fais
il/elle/on	fait
nous	faisons
vous	faites
ils/elles	font

PRESENT SUBJUNCTIVE

je	fasse
tu	fasses
il/elle/on	fasse
nous	fassions
vous	fassiez
ils/elles	fassent

PERFECT

j'	ai fait
tu	as fait
il/elle/on	a fait
nous	avons fait
vous	avez fait
ils/elles	ont fait

IMPERFECT

je	faisais
tu	faisais
il/elle/on	faisait
nous	faisions
vous	faisiez
ils/elles	faisaient

FUTURE

je	ferai
tu	feras
il/elle/on	fera
nous	ferons
vous	ferez
ils/elles	feront

CONDITIONAL

je	ferais
tu	ferais
il/elle/on	ferait
nous	ferions
vous	feriez
ils/elles	feraient

IMPERATIVE

fais / faisons / faites

PAST PARTICIPLE

fait

PRESENT PARTICIPLE

faisant

EXAMPLE PHRASES

*Qu'est-ce que tu **fais**?* What are you doing?
*Qu'est-ce qu'il **a fait**?* What has he done? *or* What did he do?
*J'**ai fait** un gâteau.* I've made a cake *or* I made a cake.
*Il **s'est fait** couper les cheveux.* He's had his hair cut.

➪ *See pages 88–91 for information on how to form the reflexive verb **se faire**.*

falloir (to be necessary)

PRESENT

il faut

PRESENT SUBJUNCTIVE

il faille

PERFECT

il a fallu

IMPERFECT

il fallait

FUTURE

il faudra

CONDITIONAL

il faudrait

IMPERATIVE

not used

PAST PARTICIPLE

fallu

PRESENT PARTICIPLE

not used

EXAMPLE PHRASES

*Il **faut** se dépêcher!* We have to hurry up!
*Il me **fallait** de l'argent.* I needed money.
*Il **faudra** que tu sois là à 8 heures.* You'll have to be there at 8.

---

je/j' = I **tu** = you **il** = he/it **elle** = she/it **on** = we/one **nous** = we **vous** = you **ils/elles** = they

▶ **finir** (to finish)

PRESENT

je	finis
tu	finis
il/elle/on	finit
nous	finissons
vous	finissez
ils/elles	finissent

PRESENT SUBJUNCTIVE

je	finisse
tu	finisses
il/elle/on	finisse
nous	finissions
vous	finissiez
ils/elles	finissent

PERFECT

j'	ai fini
tu	as fini
il/elle/on	a fini
nous	avons fini
vous	avez fini
ils/elles	ont fini

IMPERFECT

je	finissais
tu	finissais
il/elle/on	finissait
nous	finissions
vous	finissiez
ils/elles	finissaient

FUTURE

je	finirai
tu	finiras
il/elle/on	finira
nous	finirons
vous	finirez
ils/elles	finiront

CONDITIONAL

je	finirais
tu	finirais
il/elle/on	finirait
nous	finirions
vous	finiriez
ils/elles	finiraient

IMPERATIVE

finis / finissons / finissez

PAST PARTICIPLE

fini

PRESENT PARTICIPLE

finissant

EXAMPLE PHRASES

Finis ta soupe! Finish your soup!
J'ai fini! I've finished!
Je finirai mes devoirs demain. I'll finish my homework tomorrow.

je/j' = I **tu** = you **il** = he/it **elle** = she/it **on** = we/one **nous** = we **vous** = you **ils/elles** = they

▶ **fuir** (to flee)

PRESENT

je	fuis
tu	fuis
il/elle/on	fuit
nous	fuyons
vous	fuyez
ils/elles	fuient

PRESENT SUBJUNCTIVE

je	fuie
tu	fuies
il/elle/on	fuie
nous	fuyions
vous	fuyiez
ils/elles	fuient

PERFECT

j'	ai fui
tu	as fui
il/elle/on	a fui
nous	avons fui
vous	avez fui
ils/elles	ont fui

IMPERFECT

je	fuyais
tu	fuyais
il/elle/on	fuyait
nous	fuyions
vous	fuyiez
ils/elles	fuyaient

FUTURE

je	fuirai
tu	fuiras
il/elle/on	fuira
nous	fuirons
vous	fuirez
ils/elles	fuiront

CONDITIONAL

je	fuirais
tu	fuirais
il/elle/on	fuirait
nous	fuirions
vous	fuiriez
ils/elles	fuiraient

IMPERATIVE

fuis / fuyons / fuyez

PAST PARTICIPLE

fui

PRESENT PARTICIPLE

fuyant

EXAMPLE PHRASES

*Ils **ont fui** leur pays.* They fled their country.
*Le robinet **fuit**.* The tap is dripping.

▶ haïr (to hate)

PRESENT

je	hais
tu	hais
il/elle/on	hait
nous	haïssons
vous	haïssez
ils/elles	haïssent

PRESENT SUBJUNCTIVE

je	haïsse
tu	haïsses
il/elle/on	haïsse
nous	haïssions
vous	haïssiez
ils/elles	haïssent

PERFECT

j'	ai haï
tu	as haï
il/elle/on	a haï
nous	avons haï
vous	avez haï
ils/elles	ont haï

IMPERFECT

je	haïssais
tu	haïssais
il/elle/on	haïssait
nous	haïssions
vous	haïssiez
ils/elles	haïssaient

FUTURE

je	haïrai
tu	haïras
il/elle/on	haïra
nous	haïrons
vous	haïrez
ils/elles	haïront

CONDITIONAL

je	haïrais
tu	haïrais
il/elle/on	haïrait
nous	haïrions
vous	haïriez
ils/elles	haïraient

IMPERATIVE

hais / haïssons / haïssez

PAST PARTICIPLE

haï

PRESENT PARTICIPLE

haïssant

EXAMPLE PHRASES

*Je te **hais**!* I hate you!
*Elle **haïssait** tout le monde.* She hated everyone.
*Ils **se haïssent**.* They hate each other.

je/j' = I **tu** = you **il** = he/it **elle** = she/it **on** = we/one **nous** = we **vous** = you **ils/elles** = they

▶ **jeter** (to throw)

PRESENT

je	jette
tu	jettes
il/elle/on	jette
nous	jetons
vous	jetez
ils/elles	jettent

PRESENT SUBJUNCTIVE

je	jette
tu	jettes
il/elle/on	jette
nous	jetions
vous	jetiez
ils/elles	jettent

PERFECT

j'	ai jeté
tu	as jeté
il/elle/on	a jeté
nous	avons jeté
vous	avez jeté
ils/elles	ont jeté

IMPERFECT

je	jetais
tu	jetais
il/elle/on	jetait
nous	jetions
vous	jetiez
ils/elles	jetaient

FUTURE

je	jetterai
tu	jetteras
il/elle/on	jettera
nous	jetterons
vous	jetterez
ils/elles	jetteront

CONDITIONAL

je	jetterais
tu	jetterais
il/elle/on	jetterait
nous	jetterions
vous	jetteriez
ils/elles	jetteraient

IMPERATIVE

jette / jetons / jetez

PAST PARTICIPLE

jeté

PRESENT PARTICIPLE

jetant

EXAMPLE PHRASES

*Ne **jette** pas tes vêtements par terre.* Don't throw your clothes on the floor.
*Elle **a jeté** son chewing-gum par la fenêtre.* She threw her chewing gum out of the window.
*Ils ne **jettent** jamais rien.* They never throw anything away.

---

je/j' = I **tu** = you **il** = he/it **elle** = she/it **on** = we/one **nous** = we **vous** = you **ils/elles** = they

▶ joindre (to join)

PRESENT

je	joins
tu	joins
il/elle/on	joint
nous	joignons
vous	joignez
ils/elles	joignent

PRESENT SUBJUNCTIVE

je	joigne
tu	joignes
il/elle/on	joigne
nous	joignions
vous	joigniez
ils/elles	joignent

PERFECT

j'	ai joint
tu	as joint
il/elle/on	a joint
nous	avons joint
vous	avez joint
ils/elles	ont joint

IMPERFECT

je	joignais
tu	joignais
il/elle/on	joignait
nous	joignions
vous	joigniez
ils/elles	joignaient

FUTURE

je	joindrai
tu	joindras
il/elle/on	joindra
nous	joindrons
vous	joindrez
ils/elles	joindront

CONDITIONAL

je	joindrais
tu	joindrais
il/elle/on	joindrait
nous	joindrions
vous	joindriez
ils/elles	joindraient

IMPERATIVE

joins / joignons / joignez

PAST PARTICIPLE

joint

PRESENT PARTICIPLE

joignant

EXAMPLE PHRASES

*Où est-ce qu'on peut te **joindre** ce week-end?* Where can we contact you this weekend?
*On **a joint** les deux tables.* We put the two tables together.

je/j' = I **tu** = you **il** = he/it **elle** = she/it **on** = we/one **nous** = we **vous** = you **ils/elles** = they

▶ lever (to lift)

PRESENT

je	lève
tu	lèves
il/elle/on	lève
nous	levons
vous	levez
ils/elles	lèvent

PRESENT SUBJUNCTIVE

je	lève
tu	lèves
il/elle/on	lève
nous	levions
vous	leviez
ils/elles	lèvent

PERFECT

j'	ai levé
tu	as levé
il/elle/on	a levé
nous	avons levé
vous	avez levé
ils/elles	ont levé

IMPERFECT

je	levais
tu	levais
il/elle/on	levait
nous	levions
vous	leviez
ils/elles	levaient

FUTURE

je	lèverai
tu	lèveras
il/elle/on	lèvera
nous	lèverons
vous	lèverez
ils/elles	lèveront

CONDITIONAL

je	lèverais
tu	lèverais
il/elle/on	lèverait
nous	lèverions
vous	lèveriez
ils/elles	lèveraient

IMPERATIVE

lève / levons / levez

PAST PARTICIPLE

levé

PRESENT PARTICIPLE

levant

EXAMPLE PHRASES

Lève la tête. Lift your head up.
Levez la main! Put your hand up!
Je me lève tous les jours à sept heures. I get up at 7 every day.

⇨ *See pages 88–91 for information on how to form the reflexive verb se lever.*

---

je/j' = I **tu** = you **il** = he/it **elle** = she/it **on** = we/one **nous** = we **vous** = you **ils/elles** = they

▶ **lire** (to read)

PRESENT

je	lis
tu	lis
il/elle/on	lit
nous	lisons
vous	lisez
ils/elles	lisent

PRESENT SUBJUNCTIVE

je	lise
tu	lises
il/elle/on	lise
nous	lisions
vous	lisiez
ils/elles	lisent

PERFECT

j'	ai lu
tu	as lu
il/elle/on	a lu
nous	avons lu
vous	avez lu
ils/elles	ont lu

IMPERFECT

je	lisais
tu	lisais
il/elle/on	lisait
nous	lisions
vous	lisiez
ils/elles	lisaient

FUTURE

je	lirai
tu	liras
il/elle/on	lira
nous	lirons
vous	lirez
ils/elles	liront

CONDITIONAL

je	lirais
tu	lirais
il/elle/on	lirait
nous	lirions
vous	liriez
ils/elles	liraient

IMPERATIVE

lis / lisons / lisez

PAST PARTICIPLE

lu

PRESENT PARTICIPLE

lisant

EXAMPLE PHRASES

*Vous **avez lu** "Madame Bovary"?* Have you read "Madame Bovary"?
*Je le **lirai** dans l'avion.* I'll read it on the plane.
*Elle lui **lisait** une histoire.* She was reading him a story.

---

je/j' = I **tu** = you **il** = he/it **elle** = she/it **on** = we/one **nous** = we **vous** = you **ils/elles** = they

▶ **manger** (to eat)

PRESENT

je	mange
tu	manges
il/elle/on	mange
nous	mangeons
vous	mangez
ils/elles	mangent

PRESENT SUBJUNCTIVE

je	mange
tu	manges
il/elle/on	mange
nous	mangions
vous	mangiez
ils/elles	mangent

PERFECT

j'	ai mangé
tu	as mangé
il/elle/on	a mangé
nous	avons mangé
vous	avez mangé
ils/elles	ont mangé

IMPERFECT

je	mangeais
tu	mangeais
il/elle/on	mangeait
nous	mangions
vous	mangiez
ils/elles	mangeaient

FUTURE

je	mangerai
tu	mangeras
il/elle/on	mangera
nous	mangerons
vous	mangerez
ils/elles	mangeront

CONDITIONAL

je	mangerais
tu	mangerais
il/elle/on	mangerait
nous	mangerions
vous	mangeriez
ils/elles	mangeraient

IMPERATIVE

mange / mangeons / mangez

PAST PARTICIPLE

mangé

PRESENT PARTICIPLE

mangeant

EXAMPLE PHRASES

*Nous ne **mangeons** pas souvent ensemble.* We don't often eat together.
*Tu **as** assez **mangé**?* Have you had enough to eat?
*Je **mangerai** plus tard.* I'll eat later on.

je/j' = I **tu** = you **il** = he/it **elle** = she/it **on** = we/one **nous** = we **vous** = you **ils/elles** = they

▶ **maudire** (to curse)

PRESENT

je	maudis
tu	maudis
il/elle/on	maudit
nous	maudissons
vous	maudissez
ils/elles	maudissent

PRESENT SUBJUNCTIVE

je	maudisse
tu	maudisses
il/elle/on	maudisse
nous	maudissions
vous	maudissiez
ils/elles	maudissent

PERFECT

j'	ai maudit
tu	as maudit
il/elle/on	a maudit
nous	avons maudit
vous	avez maudit
ils/elles	ont maudit

IMPERFECT

je	maudissais
tu	maudissais
il/elle/on	maudissait
nous	maudissions
vous	maudissiez
ils/elles	maudissaient

FUTURE

je	maudirai
tu	maudiras
il/elle/on	maudira
nous	maudirons
vous	maudirez
ils/elles	maudiront

CONDITIONAL

je	maudirais
tu	maudirais
il/elle/on	maudirait
nous	maudirions
vous	maudiriez
ils/elles	maudiraient

IMPERATIVE

maudis / maudissons / maudissez

PAST PARTICIPLE

maudit

PRESENT PARTICIPLE

maudissant

EXAMPLE PHRASES

*Ils **maudissent** leurs ennemis.* They curse their enemies.
*Ce **maudit** stylo ne marche pas!* This blasted pen doesn't work!

▶ **mettre** (to put)

PRESENT

je	mets
tu	mets
il/elle/on	met
nous	mettons
vous	mettez
ils/elles	mettent

PRESENT SUBJUNCTIVE

je	mette
tu	mettes
il/elle/on	mette
nous	mettions
vous	mettiez
ils/elles	mettent

PERFECT

j'	ai mis
tu	as mis
il/elle/on	a mis
nous	avons mis
vous	avez mis
ils/elles	ont mis

IMPERFECT

je	mettais
tu	mettais
il/elle/on	mettait
nous	mettions
vous	mettiez
ils/elles	mettaient

FUTURE

je	mettrai
tu	mettras
il/elle/on	mettra
nous	mettrons
vous	mettrez
ils/elles	mettront

CONDITIONAL

je	mettrais
tu	mettrais
il/elle/on	mettrait
nous	mettrions
vous	mettriez
ils/elles	mettraient

IMPERATIVE

mets / mettons / mettez

PAST PARTICIPLE

mis

PRESENT PARTICIPLE

mettant

EXAMPLE PHRASES

Mets ton manteau! Put your coat on!
Où est-ce que tu as mis les clés? Where have you put the keys?
J'ai mis le livre sur la table. I put the book on the table.
Elle s'est mise à pleurer. She started crying.

⇨ *See pages 88–91 for information on how to form the reflexive verb se mettre.*

---

je/j' = I **tu** = you **il** = he/it **elle** = she/it **on** = we/one **nous** = we **vous** = you **ils/elles** = they

▶ **monter** (to go up)

PRESENT

je	monte
tu	montes
il/elle/on	monte
nous	montons
vous	montez
ils/elles	montent

PERFECT

je	suis monté(e)
tu	es monté(e)
il/elle/on	est monté(e)
nous	sommes monté(e)s
vous	êtes monté(e)(s)
ils/elles	sont monté(e)s

FUTURE

je	monterai
tu	monteras
il/elle/on	montera
nous	monterons
vous	monterez
ils/elles	monteront

IMPERATIVE

monte / montons / montez

PRESENT PARTICIPLE

montant

PRESENT SUBJUNCTIVE

je	monte
tu	montes
il/elle/on	monte
nous	montions
vous	montiez
ils/elles	montent

IMPERFECT

je	montais
tu	montais
il/elle/on	montait
nous	montions
vous	montiez
ils/elles	montaient

CONDITIONAL

je	monterais
tu	monterais
il/elle/on	monterait
nous	monterions
vous	monteriez
ils/elles	monteraient

PAST PARTICIPLE

monté

EXAMPLE PHRASES

Je suis montée tout en haut de la tour. I went all the way up the tower.
Monte dans la voiture, je t'emmène. Get into the car, I'll take you there.
Il s'est tordu la cheville en montant à une échelle. He twisted his ankle going up
a ladder.

i Note that **monter** takes **avoir** in the perfect tense when it is used with a direct
object; see page 114.

je/j' = I **tu** = you **il** = he/it **elle** = she/it **on** = we/one **nous** = we **vous** = you **ils/elles** = they

▶ **mordre** (to bite)

PRESENT

je	mords
tu	mords
il/elle/on	mord
nous	mordons
vous	mordez
ils/elles	mordent

PRESENT SUBJUNCTIVE

je	morde
tu	mordes
il/elle/on	morde
nous	mordions
vous	mordiez
ils/elles	mordent

PERFECT

j'	ai mordu
tu	as mordu
il/elle/on	a mordu
nous	avons mordu
vous	avez mordu
ils/elles	ont mordu

IMPERFECT

je	mordais
tu	mordais
il/elle/on	mordait
nous	mordions
vous	mordiez
ils/elles	mordaient

FUTURE

je	mordrai
tu	mordras
il/elle/on	mordra
nous	mordrons
vous	mordrez
ils/elles	mordront

CONDITIONAL

je	mordrais
tu	mordrais
il/elle/on	mordrait
nous	mordrions
vous	mordriez
ils/elles	mordraient

IMPERATIVE

mords / mordons / mordez

PAST PARTICIPLE

mordu

PRESENT PARTICIPLE

mordant

EXAMPLE PHRASES

Le chien m'a mordue. The dog bit me.
*Il ne va pas te **mordre**!* He won't bite!

---

je/j' = I **tu** = you **il** = he/it **elle** = she/it **on** = we/one **nous** = we **vous** = you **ils/elles** = they

▶ **moudre** (to grind)

PRESENT

je	mouds
tu	mouds
il/elle/on	moud
nous	moulons
vous	moulez
ils/elles	moulent

PRESENT SUBJUNCTIVE

je	moule
tu	moules
il/elle/on	moule
nous	moulions
vous	mouliez
ils/elles	moulent

PERFECT

j'	ai moulu
tu	as moulu
il/elle/on	a moulu
nous	avons moulu
vous	avez moulu
ils/elles	ont moulu

IMPERFECT

je	moulais
tu	moulais
il/elle/on	moulait
nous	moulions
vous	mouliez
ils/elles	moulaient

FUTURE

je	moudrai
tu	moudras
il/elle/on	moudra
nous	moudrons
vous	moudrez
ils/elles	moudront

CONDITIONAL

je	moudrais
tu	moudrais
il/elle/on	moudrait
nous	moudrions
vous	moudriez
ils/elles	moudraient

IMPERATIVE

mouds / moulons / moulez

PAST PARTICIPLE

moulu

PRESENT PARTICIPLE

moulant

EXAMPLE PHRASES

J'ai moulu du café pour demain matin. I've ground some coffee for tomorrow morning.

▶ **mourir** (to die)

PRESENT

je	meurs
tu	meurs
il/elle/on	meurt
nous	mourons
vous	mourez
ils/elles	meurent

PRESENT SUBJUNCTIVE

je	meure
tu	meures
il/elle/on	meure
nous	mourions
vous	mouriez
ils/elles	meurent

PERFECT

je	suis mort(e)
tu	es mort(e)
il/elle/on	est mort(e)
nous	sommes mort(e)s
vous	êtes mort(e)(s)
ils/elles	sont mort(e)s

IMPERFECT

je	mourais
tu	mourais
il/elle/on	mourait
nous	mourions
vous	mouriez
ils/elles	mouraient

FUTURE

je	mourrai
tu	mourras
il/elle/on	mourra
nous	mourrons
vous	mourrez
ils/elles	mourront

CONDITIONAL

je	mourrais
tu	mourrais
il/elle/on	mourrait
nous	mourrions
vous	mourriez
ils/elles	mourraient

IMPERATIVE

meurs / mourons / mourez

PAST PARTICIPLE

mort

PRESENT PARTICIPLE

mourant

EXAMPLE PHRASES

*Elle **est morte** en 1998.* She died in 1998.
*Ils **sont morts**.* They're dead.
*On **meurt** de froid ici!* We're freezing to death in here!

je/j' = I **tu** = you **il** = he/it **elle** = she/it **on** = we/one **nous** = we **vous** = you **ils/elles** = they

▶ naître (to be born)

PRESENT

je	nais
tu	nais
il/elle/on	naît
nous	naissons
vous	naissez
ils/elles	naissent

PRESENT SUBJUNCTIVE

je	naisse
tu	naisses
il/elle/on	naisse
nous	naissions
vous	naissiez
ils/elles	naissent

PERFECT

je	suis né(e)
tu	es né(e)
il/elle/on	est né(e)
nous	sommes né(e)s
vous	êtes né(e)(s)
ils/elles	sont né(e)s

IMPERFECT

je	naissais
tu	naissais
il/elle/on	naissait
nous	naissions
vous	naissiez
ils/elles	naissaient

FUTURE

je	naîtrai
tu	naîtras
il/elle/on	naîtra
nous	naîtrons
vous	naîtrez
ils/elles	naîtront

CONDITIONAL

je	naîtrais
tu	naîtrais
il/elle/on	naîtrait
nous	naîtrions
vous	naîtriez
ils/elles	naîtraient

IMPERATIVE

nais / naissons / naissez

PAST PARTICIPLE

né

PRESENT PARTICIPLE

naissant

EXAMPLE PHRASES

Je suis née le 12 février. I was born on 12 February.
Le bébé de Delphine naîtra en mars. Delphine is going to have a baby in March.
Quand est-ce que tu es né? When were you born?

je/j' = I **tu** = you **il** = he/it **elle** = she/it **on** = we/one **nous** = we **vous** = you **ils/elles** = they

▶ **nettoyer** (to clean)

PRESENT

je	nettoie
tu	nettoies
il/elle/on	nettoie
nous	nettoyons
vous	nettoyez
ils/elles	nettoient

PERFECT

j'	ai nettoyé
tu	as nettoyé
il/elle/on	a nettoyé
nous	avons nettoyé
vous	avez nettoyé
ils/elles	ont nettoyé

FUTURE

je	nettoierai
tu	nettoieras
il/elle/on	nettoiera
nous	nettoierons
vous	nettoierez
ils/elles	nettoieront

IMPERATIVE

nettoie / nettoyons / nettoyez

PRESENT PARTICIPLE

nettoyant

PRESENT SUBJUNCTIVE

je	nettoie
tu	nettoies
il/elle/on	nettoie
nous	nettoyions
vous	nettoyiez
ils/elles	nettoient

IMPERFECT

je	nettoyais
tu	nettoyais
il/elle/on	nettoyait
nous	nettoyions
vous	nettoyiez
ils/elles	nettoyaient

CONDITIONAL

je	nettoierais
tu	nettoierais
il/elle/on	nettoierait
nous	nettoierions
vous	nettoieriez
ils/elles	nettoieraient

PAST PARTICIPLE

nettoyé

EXAMPLE PHRASES

*Richard **a nettoyé** tout l'appartement.* Richard has cleaned the whole flat.
*Elle **nettoyait** le sol en écoutant la radio.* She was cleaning the floor while listening to the radio.
*Je ne **nettoie** pas souvent mes lunettes.* I don't clean my glasses very often.

---

je/j' = I **tu** = you **il** = he/it **elle** = she/it **on** = we/one **nous** = we **vous** = you **ils/elles** = they

▶ **offrir** (to offer; to give)

PRESENT

j'	offre
tu	offres
il/elle/on	offre
nous	offrons
vous	offrez
ils/elles	offrent

PRESENT SUBJUNCTIVE

j'	offre
tu	offres
il/elle/on	offre
nous	offrions
vous	offriez
ils/elles	offrent

PERFECT

j'	ai offert
tu	as offert
il/elle/on	a offert
nous	avons offert
vous	avez offert
ils/elles	ont offert

IMPERFECT

j'	offrais
tu	offrais
il/elle/on	offrait
nous	offrions
vous	offriez
ils/elles	offraient

FUTURE

j'	offrirai
tu	offriras
il/elle/on	offrira
nous	offrirons
vous	offrirez
ils/elles	offriront

CONDITIONAL

j'	offrirais
tu	offrirais
il/elle/on	offrirait
nous	offririons
vous	offririez
ils/elles	offriraient

IMPERATIVE

offre / offrons / offrez

PAST PARTICIPLE

offert

PRESENT PARTICIPLE

offrant

EXAMPLE PHRASES

*On lui **a offert** un poste de secrétaire.* They offered her a secreterial post.
***Offre**-lui des fleurs.* Give her some flowers.
*Viens, je t'**offre** à boire.* Come on, I'll buy you a drink.
*Je **me suis offert** un nouveau stylo.* I treated myself to a new pen.

⇨ *See pages 88–91 for information on how to form the reflexive verb **s'offrir**.*

je/j' = I **tu** = you **il** = he/it **elle** = she/it **on** = we/one **nous** = we **vous** = you **ils/elles** = they

▶ ouvrir (to open)

PRESENT		PRESENT SUBJUNCTIVE	
j'	ouvre	j'	ouvre
tu	ouvres	tu	ouvres
il/elle/on	ouvre	il/elle/on	ouvre
nous	ouvrons	nous	ouvrions
vous	ouvrez	vous	ouvriez
ils/elles	ouvrent	ils/elles	ouvrent

PERFECT		IMPERFECT	
j'	ai ouvert	j'	ouvrais
tu	as ouvert	tu	ouvrais
il/elle/on	a ouvert	il/elle/on	ouvrait
nous	avons ouvert	nous	ouvrions
vous	avez ouvert	vous	ouvriez
ils/elles	ont ouvert	ils/elles	ouvraient

FUTURE		CONDITIONAL	
j'	ouvrirai	j'	ouvrirais
tu	ouvriras	tu	ouvrirais
il/elle/on	ouvrira	il/elle/on	ouvrirait
nous	ouvrirons	nous	ouvririons
vous	ouvrirez	vous	ouvririez
ils/elles	ouvriront	ils/elles	ouvriraient

IMPERATIVE

ouvre / ouvrons / ouvrez

PAST PARTICIPLE

ouvert

PRESENT PARTICIPLE

ouvrant

EXAMPLE PHRASES

*Elle **a ouvert** la porte.* She opened the door.
*Est-ce que tu pourrais **ouvrir** la fenêtre?* Could you open the window?
*Je me suis coupé en **ouvrant** une boîte de conserve.* I cut myself opening a tin.
La porte s'est ouverte. The door opened.

⇨ *See pages 88–91 for information on how to form the reflexive verb s'ouvrir.*

---

je/j' = I **tu** = you **il** = he/it **elle** = she/it **on** = we/one **nous** = we **vous** = you **ils/elles** = they

▶ **paraître** (to appear)

PRESENT

je	parais
tu	parais
il/elle/on	paraît
nous	paraissons
vous	paraissez
ils/elles	paraissent

PRESENT SUBJUNCTIVE

je	paraisse
tu	paraisses
il/elle/on	paraisse
nous	paraissions
vous	paraissiez
ils/elles	paraissent

PERFECT

j'	ai paru
tu	as paru
il/elle/on	a paru
nous	avons paru
vous	avez paru
ils/elles	ont paru

IMPERFECT

je	paraissais
tu	paraissais
il/elle/on	paraissait
nous	paraissions
vous	paraissiez
ils/elles	paraissaient

FUTURE

je	paraîtrai
tu	paraîtras
il/elle/on	paraîtra
nous	paraîtrons
vous	paraîtrez
ils/elles	paraîtront

CONDITIONAL

je	paraîtrais
tu	paraîtrais
il/elle/on	paraîtrait
nous	paraîtrions
vous	paraîtriez
ils/elles	paraîtraient

IMPERATIVE

parais / paraissons / paraissez

PAST PARTICIPLE

paru

PRESENT PARTICIPLE

paraissant

EXAMPLE PHRASES

*Elle **paraissait** fatiguée.* She seemed tired.
*Gisèle **paraît** plus jeune que son âge.* Gisèle doesn't look her age.
*Il **paraît** qu'il fait chaud toute l'année là-bas.* Apparently it's hot all year round over there.

---

je/j' = I **tu** = you **il** = he/it **elle** = she/it **on** = we/one **nous** = we **vous** = you **ils/elles** = they

▶ partir (to go; to leave)

PRESENT		PRESENT SUBJUNCTIVE	
je	pars	je	parte
tu	pars	tu	partes
il/elle/on	part	il/elle/on	parte
nous	partons	nous	partions
vous	partez	vous	partiez
ils/elles	partent	ils/elles	partent

PERFECT		IMPERFECT	
je	suis parti(e)	je	partais
tu	es parti(e)	tu	partais
il/elle/on	est parti(e)	il/elle/on	partait
nous	sommes parti(e)s	nous	partions
vous	êtes parti(e)(s)	vous	partiez
ils/elles	sont parti(e)s	ils/elles	partaient

FUTURE		CONDITIONAL	
je	partirai	je	partirais
tu	partiras	tu	partirais
il/elle/on	partira	il/elle/on	partirait
nous	partirons	nous	partirions
vous	partirez	vous	partiriez
ils/elles	partiront	ils/elles	partiraient

IMPERATIVE

pars / partons / partez

PAST PARTICIPLE

parti

PRESENT PARTICIPLE

partant

EXAMPLE PHRASES

*On **part** en vacances le 15 août.* We're going on holiday on 15 August.
*Ne **partez** pas sans moi!* Don't leave without me!
*Elle **est partie** tôt ce matin.* She left early this morning.

---

je/j' = I **tu** = you **il** = he/it **elle** = she/it **on** = we/one **nous** = we **vous** = you **ils/elles** = they

▶ **passer** (to pass)

PRESENT

je	passe
tu	passes
il/elle/on	passe
nous	passons
vous	passez
ils/elles	passent

PRESENT SUBJUNCTIVE

je	passe
tu	passes
il/elle/on	passe
nous	passions
vous	passiez
ils/elles	passent

PERFECT

j'	ai passé
tu	as passé
il/elle/on	a passé
nous	avons passé
vous	avez passé
ils/elles	ont passé

IMPERFECT

je	passais
tu	passais
il/elle/on	passait
nous	passions
vous	passiez
ils/elles	passaient

FUTURE

je	passerai
tu	passeras
il/elle/on	passera
nous	passerons
vous	passerez
ils/elles	passeront

CONDITIONAL

je	passerais
tu	passerais
il/elle/on	passerait
nous	passerions
vous	passeriez
ils/elles	passeraient

IMPERATIVE

passe / passons / passez

PAST PARTICIPLE

passé

PRESENT PARTICIPLE

passant

EXAMPLE PHRASES

*Les mois **ont passé**.* Months passed.
*Il **a passé** son examen en juin.* He took his exam in June.
*Je vais **passer** les vacances chez mes grands-parents.* I'm going to spend the holidays at my grandparents' house.
*Elle **est passée** me dire bonjour.* She came by to say hello.
*L'histoire **se passe** au Mexique.* The story takes place in Mexico.

ⓘ Note that **passer** can also take **être** in the perfect tense; see page 114.

⇨ *See pages 88–91 for information on how to form the reflexive verb se passer.*

je/j' = I **tu** = you **il** = he/it **elle** = she/it **on** = we/one **nous** = we **vous** = you **ils/elles** = they

▶ payer (to pay)

PRESENT

je	paye
tu	payes
il/elle/on	paye
nous	payons
vous	payez
ils/elles	payent

PRESENT SUBJUNCTIVE

je	paye
tu	payes
il/elle/on	paye
nous	payions
vous	payiez
ils/elles	payent

PERFECT

j'	ai payé
tu	as payé
il/elle/on	a payé
nous	avons payé
vous	avez payé
ils/elles	ont payé

IMPERFECT

je	payais
tu	payais
il/elle/on	payait
nous	payions
vous	payiez
ils/elles	payaient

FUTURE

je	payerai
tu	payeras
il/elle/on	payera
nous	payerons
vous	payerez
ils/elles	payeront

CONDITIONAL

je	payerais
tu	payerais
il/elle/on	payerait
nous	payerions
vous	payeriez
ils/elles	payeraient

IMPERATIVE

paye / payons / payez

PAST PARTICIPLE

payé

PRESENT PARTICIPLE

payant

EXAMPLE PHRASES

*Tu l'**as payé** combien?* How much did you pay for it?
*Ma patronne me **payera** demain.* My boss will pay me tomorrow.
*Les étudiants **payent** moitié prix.* Students pay half price.

▶ **peindre** (to paint)

PRESENT

je	peins
tu	peins
il/elle/on	peint
nous	peignons
vous	peignez
ils/elles	peignent

PRESENT SUBJUNCTIVE

je	peigne
tu	peignes
il/elle/on	peigne
nous	peignions
vous	peigniez
ils/elles	peignent

PERFECT

j'	ai peint
tu	as peint
il/elle/on	a peint
nous	avons peint
vous	avez peint
ils/elles	ont peint

IMPERFECT

je	peignais
tu	peignais
il/elle/on	peignait
nous	peignions
vous	peigniez
ils/elles	peignaient

FUTURE

je	peindrai
tu	peindras
il/elle/on	peindra
nous	peindrons
vous	peindrez
ils/elles	peindront

CONDITIONAL

je	peindrais
tu	peindrais
il/elle/on	peindrait
nous	peindrions
vous	peindriez
ils/elles	peindraient

IMPERATIVE

peins / peignons / peignez

PAST PARTICIPLE

peint

PRESENT PARTICIPLE

peignant

EXAMPLE PHRASES

*On **a peint** l'entrée en bleu clair.* We painted the hall light blue.
*Ce tableau **a été peint** en 1913.* This picture was painted in 1913.

---

je/j' = I **tu** = you **il** = he/it **elle** = she/it **on** = we/one **nous** = we **vous** = you **ils/elles** = they

▶ **perdre** (to lose)

PRESENT

je	perds
tu	perds
il/elle/on	perd
nous	perdons
vous	perdez
ils/elles	perdent

PRESENT SUBJUNCTIVE

je	perde
tu	perdes
il/elle/on	perde
nous	perdions
vous	perdiez
ils/elles	perdent

PERFECT

j'	ai perdu
tu	as perdu
il/elle/on	a perdu
nous	avons perdu
vous	avez perdu
ils/elles	ont perdu

IMPERFECT

je	perdais
tu	perdais
il/elle/on	perdait
nous	perdions
vous	perdiez
ils/elles	perdaient

FUTURE

je	perdrai
tu	perdras
il/elle/on	perdra
nous	perdrons
vous	perdrez
ils/elles	perdront

CONDITIONAL

je	perdrais
tu	perdrais
il/elle/on	perdrait
nous	perdrions
vous	perdriez
ils/elles	perdraient

IMPERATIVE

perds / perdons / perdez

PAST PARTICIPLE

perdu

PRESENT PARTICIPLE

perdant

EXAMPLE PHRASES

*J'**ai perdu** mon porte-monnaie dans le métro.* I lost my purse on the underground.
*L'Italie **a perdu** un à zéro.* Italy lost one-nil.
*Si tu **te perds**, appelle-moi.* Call me if you get lost.

⇨ *See pages 88–91 for information on how to form the reflexive verb **se perdre**.*

je/j' = I **tu** = you **il** = he/it **elle** = she/it **on** = we/one **nous** = we **vous** = you **ils/elles** = they

▶ plaire (to please)

PRESENT

je	plais
tu	plais
il/elle/on	plaît
nous	plaisons
vous	plaisez
ils/elles	plaisent

PRESENT SUBJUNCTIVE

je	plaise
tu	plaises
il/elle/on	plaise
nous	plaisions
vous	plaisiez
ils/elles	plaisent

PERFECT

j'	ai plu
tu	as plu
il/elle/on	a plu
nous	avons plu
vous	avez plu
ils/elles	ont plu

IMPERFECT

je	plaisais
tu	plaisais
il/elle/on	plaisait
nous	plaisions
vous	plaisiez
ils/elles	plaisaient

FUTURE

je	plairai
tu	plairas
il/elle/on	plaira
nous	plairons
vous	plairez
ils/elles	plairont

CONDITIONAL

je	plairais
tu	plairais
il/elle/on	plairait
nous	plairions
vous	plairiez
ils/elles	plairaient

IMPERATIVE

plais / plaisons / plaisez

PAST PARTICIPLE

plu

PRESENT PARTICIPLE

plaisant

EXAMPLE PHRASES

*Le menu ne me **plaît** pas.* I don't like the menu.
*Ça te **plairait** d'aller à la mer?* Would you like to go to the seaside?
*Ça t'**a plu**, le film?* Did you like the film?
*s'il te **plaît*** please
*s'il vous **plaît*** please

je/j' = I **tu** = you **il** = he/it **elle** = she/it **on** = we/one **nous** = we **vous** = you **ils/elles** = they

▶ **pleuvoir** (to rain)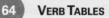

PRESENT

il pleut

PRESENT SUBJUNCTIVE

il pleuve

PERFECT

il a plu

IMPERFECT

il pleuvait

FUTURE

il pleuvra

CONDITIONAL

il pleuvrait

IMPERATIVE

not used

PAST PARTICIPLE

plu

PRESENT PARTICIPLE

pleuvant

EXAMPLE PHRASES

*Il **a plu** toute la journée.* It rained all day long.
*Il **pleut** beaucoup à Glasgow.* It rains a lot in Glasgow.
*J'espère qu'il ne **pleuvra** pas demain.* I hope it won't rain tomorrow.

je/j' = I **tu** = you **il** = he/it **elle** = she/it **on** = we/one **nous** = we **vous** = you **ils/elles** = they

▶ **pouvoir** (to be able)

PRESENT

je	peux
tu	peux
il/elle/on	peut
nous	pouvons
vous	pouvez
ils/elles	peuvent

PRESENT SUBJUNCTIVE

je	puisse
tu	puisses
il/elle/on	puisse
nous	puissions
vous	puissiez
ils/elles	puissent

PERFECT

j'	ai pu
tu	as pu
il/elle/on	a pu
nous	avons pu
vous	avez pu
ils/elles	ont pu

IMPERFECT

je	pouvais
tu	pouvais
il/elle/on	pouvait
nous	pouvions
vous	pouviez
ils/elles	pouvaient

FUTURE

je	pourrai
tu	pourras
il/elle/on	pourra
nous	pourrons
vous	pourrez
ils/elles	pourront

CONDITIONAL

je	pourrais
tu	pourrais
il/elle/on	pourrait
nous	pourrions
vous	pourriez
ils/elles	pourraient

IMPERATIVE

not used

PAST PARTICIPLE

pu

PRESENT PARTICIPLE

pouvant

EXAMPLE PHRASES

*Je **peux** t'aider, si tu veux.* I can help you if you like.
*J'ai fait tout ce que j'**ai pu**.* I did all I could.
*Je ne **pourrai** pas venir samedi.* I won't be able to come on Saturday.

je/j' = I **tu** = you **il** = he/it **elle** = she/it **on** = we/one **nous** = we **vous** = you **ils/elles** = they

▶ **prendre** (to take)

PRESENT

je	prends
tu	prends
il/elle/on	prend
nous	prenons
vous	prenez
ils/elles	prennent

PRESENT SUBJUNCTIVE

je	prenne
tu	prennes
il/elle/on	prenne
nous	prenions
vous	preniez
ils/elles	prennent

PERFECT

j'	ai pris
tu	as pris
il/elle/on	a pris
nous	avons pris
vous	avez pris
ils/elles	ont pris

IMPERFECT

je	prenais
tu	prenais
il/elle/on	prenait
nous	prenions
vous	preniez
ils/elles	prenaient

FUTURE

je	prendrai
tu	prendras
il/elle/on	prendra
nous	prendrons
vous	prendrez
ils/elles	prendront

CONDITIONAL

je	prendrais
tu	prendrais
il/elle/on	prendrait
nous	prendrions
vous	prendriez
ils/elles	prendraient

IMPERATIVE

prends / prenons / prenez

PAST PARTICIPLE

pris

PRESENT PARTICIPLE

prenant

EXAMPLE PHRASES

J'ai pris plein de photos. I took lots of pictures.
*N'oublie pas de **prendre** ton passeport.* Don't forget to take your passport.
*Il **prendra** le train de 8h20.* He'll take the 8.20 train.
*Pour qui est-ce qu'il **se prend**?* Who does he think he is?

⇨ *See pages 88–91 for information on how to form the reflexive verb **se prendre**.*

---

je/j' = I **tu** = you **il** = he/it **elle** = she/it **on** = we/one **nous** = we **vous** = you **ils/elles** = they

▶ protéger (to protect)

PRESENT

je	protège
tu	protèges
il/elle/on	protège
nous	protégeons
vous	protégez
ils/elles	protègent

PRESENT SUBJUNCTIVE

je	protège
tu	protèges
il/elle/on	protège
nous	protégions
vous	protégiez
ils/elles	protègent

PERFECT

j'	ai protégé
tu	as protégé
il/elle/on	a protégé
nous	avons protégé
vous	avez protégé
ils/elles	ont protégé

IMPERFECT

je	protégeais
tu	protégeais
il/elle/on	protégeait
nous	protégions
vous	protégiez
ils/elles	protégeaient

FUTURE

je	protégerai
tu	protégeras
il/elle/on	protégera
nous	protégerons
vous	protégerez
ils/elles	protégeront

CONDITIONAL

je	protégerais
tu	protégerais
il/elle/on	protégerait
nous	protégerions
vous	protégeriez
ils/elles	protégeraient

IMPERATIVE

protège / protégeons / protégez

PAST PARTICIPLE

protégé

PRESENT PARTICIPLE

protégeant

EXAMPLE PHRASES

Il protège sa petite sœur à l'école. He protects his little sister at school.
Protège ton livre de la pluie. Protect your book from the rain.
Le champ est protégé du vent par la colline. The field is sheltered from the wind
  by the hill.

je/j' = I **tu** = you **il** = he/it **elle** = she/it **on** = we/one **nous** = we **vous** = you **ils/elles** = they

▶ **recevoir** (to receive)

PRESENT

je	reçois
tu	reçois
il/elle/on	reçoit
nous	recevons
vous	recevez
ils/elles	reçoivent

PRESENT SUBJUNCTIVE

je	reçoive
tu	reçoives
il/elle/on	reçoive
nous	recevions
vous	receviez
ils/elles	reçoivent

PERFECT

j'	ai reçu
tu	as reçu
il/elle/on	a reçu
nous	avons reçu
vous	avez reçu
ils/elles	ont reçu

IMPERFECT

je	recevais
tu	recevais
il/elle/on	recevait
nous	recevions
vous	receviez
ils/elles	recevaient

FUTURE

je	recevrai
tu	recevras
il/elle/on	recevra
nous	recevrons
vous	recevrez
ils/elles	recevront

CONDITIONAL

je	recevrais
tu	recevrais
il/elle/on	recevrait
nous	recevrions
vous	recevriez
ils/elles	recevraient

IMPERATIVE

reçois / recevons / recevez

PAST PARTICIPLE

reçu

PRESENT PARTICIPLE

recevant

EXAMPLE PHRASES

*Elle **a reçu** une lettre de Charlotte.* She received a letter from Charlotte.
*Je ne **reçois** jamais de courrier.* I never get any mail.
*Elle **recevra** une réponse la semaine prochaine.* She'll get an answer next week.

---

je/j' = I **tu** = you **il** = he/it **elle** = she/it **on** = we/one **nous** = we **vous** = you **ils/elles** = they

▶ rentrer (to go back; to go in)

PRESENT

je	rentre
tu	rentres
il/elle/on	rentre
nous	rentrons
vous	rentrez
ils/elles	rentrent

PRESENT SUBJUNCTIVE

je	rentre
tu	rentres
il/elle/on	rentre
nous	rentrions
vous	rentriez
ils/elles	rentrent

PERFECT

je	suis rentré(e)
tu	es rentré(e)
il/elle/on	est rentré(e)
nous	sommes rentré(e)s
vous	êtes rentré(e)(s)
ils/elles	sont rentré(e)s

IMPERFECT

je	rentrais
tu	rentrais
il/elle/on	rentrait
nous	rentrions
vous	rentriez
ils/elles	rentraient

FUTURE

je	rentrerai
tu	rentreras
il/elle/on	rentrera
nous	rentrerons
vous	rentrerez
ils/elles	rentreront

CONDITIONAL

je	rentrerais
tu	rentrerais
il/elle/on	rentrerait
nous	rentrerions
vous	rentreriez
ils/elles	rentreraient

IMPERATIVE

rentre / rentrons / rentrez

PAST PARTICIPLE

rentré

PRESENT PARTICIPLE

rentrant

EXAMPLE PHRASES

Ne rentre pas trop tard. Don't come home too late.
Ils sont rentrés dans le magasin. They went into the shop.
À quelle heure est-ce qu'elle est rentrée? What time did she get in?
Je rentre déjeuner à midi. I go home for lunch.
Il a déjà rentré la voiture dans le garage. He's already put the car in the garage.

[i] Note that **rentrer** takes **avoir** in the perfect tense when it is used with a direct object; see page 114.

je/j' = I **tu** = you **il** = he/it **elle** = she/it **on** = we/one **nous** = we **vous** = you **ils/elles** = they

▶ répondre (to answer)

PRESENT

je	réponds
tu	réponds
il/elle/on	répond
nous	répondons
vous	répondez
ils/elles	répondent

PRESENT SUBJUNCTIVE

je	réponde
tu	répondes
il/elle/on	réponde
nous	répondions
vous	répondiez
ils/elles	répondent

PERFECT

j'	ai répondu
tu	as répondu
il/elle/on	a répondu
nous	avons répondu
vous	avez répondu
ils/elles	ont répondu

IMPERFECT

je	répondais
tu	répondais
il/elle/on	répondait
nous	répondions
vous	répondiez
ils/elles	répondaient

FUTURE

je	répondrai
tu	répondras
il/elle/on	répondra
nous	répondrons
vous	répondrez
ils/elles	répondront

CONDITIONAL

je	répondrais
tu	répondrais
il/elle/on	répondrait
nous	répondrions
vous	répondriez
ils/elles	répondraient

IMPERATIVE

réponds / répondons / répondez

PAST PARTICIPLE

répondu

PRESENT PARTICIPLE

répondant

EXAMPLE PHRASES

*Lisez le texte et **répondez** aux questions.* Read the passage and answer the questions.
*C'est elle qui **a répondu** au téléphone.* She answered the phone.
*Ça ne **répond** pas.* There's no reply.

je/j' = I **tu** = you **il** = he/it **elle** = she/it **on** = we/one **nous** = we **vous** = you **ils/elles** = they

▶ résoudre (to solve)

PRESENT

je	résous
tu	résous
il/elle/on	résout
nous	résolvons
vous	résolvez
ils/elles	résolvent

PRESENT SUBJUNCTIVE

je	résolve
tu	résolves
il/elle/on	résolve
nous	résolvions
vous	résolviez
ils/elles	résolvent

PERFECT

j'	ai résolu
tu	as résolu
il/elle/on	a résolu
nous	avons résolu
vous	avez résolu
ils/elles	ont résolu

IMPERFECT

je	résolvais
tu	résolvais
il/elle/on	résolvait
nous	résolvions
vous	résolviez
ils/elles	résolvaient

FUTURE

je	résoudrai
tu	résoudras
il/elle/on	résoudra
nous	résoudrons
vous	résoudrez
ils/elles	résoudront

CONDITIONAL

je	résoudrais
tu	résoudrais
il/elle/on	résoudrait
nous	résoudrions
vous	résoudriez
ils/elles	résoudraient

IMPERATIVE

résous / résolvons / résolvez

PAST PARTICIPLE

résolu

PRESENT PARTICIPLE

résolvant

EXAMPLE PHRASES

J'ai résolu le problème. I've solved the problem.
La violence ne résout rien. Violence doesn't solve anything.

---

je/j' = I **tu** = you **il** = he/it **elle** = she/it **on** = we/one **nous** = we **vous** = you **ils/elles** = they

▶ **rester** (to remain)

PRESENT

je	reste
tu	restes
il/elle/on	reste
nous	restons
vous	restez
ils/elles	restent

PRESENT SUBJUNCTIVE

je	reste
tu	restes
il/elle/on	reste
nous	restions
vous	restiez
ils/elles	restent

PERFECT

je	suis resté(e)
tu	es resté(e)
il/elle/on	est resté(e)
nous	sommes resté(e)s
vous	êtes resté(e)(s)
ils/elles	sont resté(e)s

IMPERFECT

je	restais
tu	restais
il/elle/on	restait
nous	restions
vous	restiez
ils/elles	restaient

FUTURE

je	resterai
tu	resteras
il/elle/on	restera
nous	resterons
vous	resterez
ils/elles	resteront

CONDITIONAL

je	resterais
tu	resterais
il/elle/on	resterait
nous	resterions
vous	resteriez
ils/elles	resteraient

IMPERATIVE

reste / restons / restez

PAST PARTICIPLE

resté

PRESENT PARTICIPLE

restant

EXAMPLE PHRASES

Cet été, je reste en Écosse. I'm staying in Scotland this summer.
Ils ne sont pas restés très longtemps. They didn't stay very long.
Il leur restait encore un peu d'argent. They still had some money left.

---

je/j' = I **tu** = you **il** = he/it **elle** = she/it **on** = we/one **nous** = we **vous** = you **ils/elles** = they

▶ retourner (to return)

PRESENT

je	retourne
tu	retournes
il/elle/on	retourne
nous	retournons
vous	retournez
ils/elles	retournent

PRESENT SUBJUNCTIVE

je	retourne
tu	retournes
il/elle/on	retourne
nous	retournions
vous	retourniez
ils/elles	retournent

PERFECT

je	suis retourné(e)
tu	es retourné(e)
il/elle/on	est retourné(e)
nous	sommes retourné(e)s
vous	êtes retourné(e)(s)
ils/elles	sont retourné(e)s

IMPERFECT

je	retournais
tu	retournais
il/elle/on	retournait
nous	retournions
vous	retourniez
ils/elles	retournaient

FUTURE

je	retournerai
tu	retourneras
il/elle/on	retournera
nous	retournerons
vous	retournerez
ils/elles	retourneront

CONDITIONAL

je	retournerais
tu	retournerais
il/elle/on	retournerait
nous	retournerions
vous	retourneriez
ils/elles	retourneraient

IMPERATIVE

retourne / retournons / retournez

PAST PARTICIPLE

retourné

PRESENT PARTICIPLE

retournant

EXAMPLE PHRASES

Est-ce que tu es retournée à Londres? Have you been back to London?
J'aimerais bien retourner en Italie un jour. I'd like to go back to Italy one day.
Elle a retourné la carte pour vérifier. She turned the card over to check.
Zoë, retourne-toi! Turn around Zoë!

ⓘ Note that **retourner** takes **avoir** in the perfect tense when it is used with a direct object; see page 114.

⇨ *See pages 88–91 for information on how to form the reflexive verb se retourner.*

je/j' = I **tu** = you **il** = he/it **elle** = she/it **on** = we/one **nous** = we **vous** = you **ils/elles** = they

▶ revenir (to come back)

PRESENT

je	reviens
tu	reviens
il/elle/on	revient
nous	revenons
vous	revenez
ils/elles	reviennent

PRESENT SUBJUNCTIVE

je	revienne
tu	reviennes
il/elle/on	revienne
nous	revenions
vous	reveniez
ils/elles	reviennent

PERFECT

je	suis revenu(e)
tu	es revenu(e)
il/elle/on	est revenu(e)
nous	sommes revenu(e)s
vous	êtes revenu(e)(s)
ils/elles	sont revenu(e)s

IMPERFECT

je	revenais
tu	revenais
il/elle/on	revenait
nous	revenions
vous	reveniez
ils/elles	revenaient

FUTURE

je	reviendrai
tu	reviendras
il/elle/on	reviendra
nous	reviendrons
vous	reviendrez
ils/elles	reviendront

CONDITIONAL

je	reviendrais
tu	reviendrais
il/elle/on	reviendrait
nous	reviendrions
vous	reviendriez
ils/elles	reviendraient

IMPERATIVE

reviens / revenons / revenez

PAST PARTICIPLE

revenu

PRESENT PARTICIPLE

revenant

EXAMPLE PHRASES

Mon chat n'est toujours pas revenu. My cat still hasn't come back.
Je reviens dans cinq minutes! I'll be back in five minutes!
Ça me revient! It's coming back to me now!

---

je/j' = I **tu** = you **il** = he/it **elle** = she/it **on** = we/one **nous** = we **vous** = you **ils/elles** = they

▶ **rire** (to laugh)

PRESENT

je	ris
tu	ris
il/elle/on	rit
nous	rions
vous	riez
ils/elles	rient

PRESENT SUBJUNCTIVE

je	rie
tu	ries
il/elle/on	rie
nous	riions
vous	riiez
ils/elles	rient

PERFECT

j'	ai ri
tu	as ri
il/elle/on	a ri
nous	avons ri
vous	avez ri
ils/elles	ont ri

IMPERFECT

je	riais
tu	riais
il/elle/on	riait
nous	riions
vous	riiez
ils/elles	riaient

FUTURE

je	rirai
tu	riras
il/elle/on	rira
nous	rirons
vous	rirez
ils/elles	riront

CONDITIONAL

je	rirais
tu	rirais
il/elle/on	rirait
nous	ririons
vous	ririez
ils/elles	riraient

IMPERATIVE

ris / rions / riez

PAST PARTICIPLE

ri

PRESENT PARTICIPLE

riant

EXAMPLE PHRASES

On a bien ri. We had a good laugh.
Ne ris pas, ce n'est pas drôle! Don't laugh, it's not funny!
C'était juste pour rire. It was only for a laugh.

je/j' = I **tu** = you **il** = he/it **elle** = she/it **on** = we/one **nous** = we **vous** = you **ils/elles** = they

▶ **rompre** (to break)

PRESENT

je	romps
tu	romps
il/elle/on	rompt
nous	rompons
vous	rompez
ils/elles	rompent

PRESENT SUBJUNCTIVE

je	rompe
tu	rompes
il/elle/on	rompe
nous	rompions
vous	rompiez
ils/elles	rompent

PERFECT

j'	ai rompu
tu	as rompu
il/elle/on	a rompu
nous	avons rompu
vous	avez rompu
ils/elles	ont rompu

IMPERFECT

je	rompais
tu	rompais
il/elle/on	rompait
nous	rompions
vous	rompiez
ils/elles	rompaient

FUTURE

je	romprai
tu	rompras
il/elle/on	rompra
nous	romprons
vous	romprez
ils/elles	rompront

CONDITIONAL

je	romprais
tu	romprais
il/elle/on	romprait
nous	romprions
vous	rompriez
ils/elles	rompraient

IMPERATIVE

romps / rompons / rompez

PAST PARTICIPLE

rompu

PRESENT PARTICIPLE

rompant

EXAMPLE PHRASES

*Elle **a rompu** le silence.* She broke the silence.
*Paul et Jo **ont rompu**.* Paul and Jo have split up.

---

je/j' = I **tu** = you **il** = he/it **elle** = she/it **on** = we/one **nous** = we **vous** = you **ils/elles** = they

▶ **savoir** (to know)

PRESENT

je	sais
tu	sais
il/elle/on	sait
nous	savons
vous	savez
ils/elles	savent

PRESENT SUBJUNCTIVE

je	sache
tu	saches
il/elle/on	sache
nous	sachions
vous	sachiez
ils/elles	sachent

PERFECT

j'	ai su
tu	as su
il/elle/on	a su
nous	avons su
vous	avez su
ils/elles	ont su

IMPERFECT

je	savais
tu	savais
il/elle/on	savait
nous	savions
vous	saviez
ils/elles	savaient

FUTURE

je	saurai
tu	sauras
il/elle/on	saura
nous	saurons
vous	saurez
ils/elles	sauront

CONDITIONAL

je	saurais
tu	saurais
il/elle/on	saurait
nous	saurions
vous	sauriez
ils/elles	sauraient

IMPERATIVE

sache / sachons / sachez

PAST PARTICIPLE

su

PRESENT PARTICIPLE

sachant

EXAMPLE PHRASES

Tu sais ce que tu vas faire l'année prochaine? Do you know what you're doing next year?

Je ne **sais** pas. I don't know.

Elle ne **sait** pas nager. She can't swim.

Tu savais que son père était pakistanais? Did you know her father was Pakistani?

---

je/j' = I **tu** = you **il** = he/it **elle** = she/it **on** = we/one **nous** = we **vous** = you **ils/elles** = they

▶ sentir (to smell; to feel)

PRESENT		PRESENT SUBJUNCTIVE	
je	sens	je	sente
tu	sens	tu	sentes
il/elle/on	sent	il/elle/on	sente
nous	sentons	nous	sentions
vous	sentez	vous	sentiez
ils/elles	sentent	ils/elles	sentent

PERFECT		IMPERFECT	
j'	ai senti	je	sentais
tu	as senti	tu	sentais
il/elle/on	a senti	il/elle/on	sentait
nous	avons senti	nous	sentions
vous	avez senti	vous	sentiez
ils/elles	ont senti	ils/elles	sentaient

FUTURE		CONDITIONAL	
je	sentirai	je	sentirais
tu	sentiras	tu	sentirais
il/elle/on	sentira	il/elle/on	sentirait
nous	sentirons	nous	sentirions
vous	sentirez	vous	sentiriez
ils/elles	sentiront	ils/elles	sentiraient

IMPERATIVE

sens / sentons / sentez

PAST PARTICIPLE

senti

PRESENT PARTICIPLE

sentant

EXAMPLE PHRASES

*Ça **sentait** mauvais.* It smelt bad.
*Je n'ai rien **senti**.* I didn't feel a thing.
*Elle ne **se sent** pas bien.* She's not feeling well.

⇨ *See pages 88–91 for information on how to form the reflexive verb **se sentir.***

je/j' = I **tu** = you **il** = he/it **elle** = she/it **on** = we/one **nous** = we **vous** = you **ils/elles** = they

▶ **servir** (to serve)

PRESENT

je	sers
tu	sers
il/elle/on	sert
nous	servons
vous	servez
ils/elles	servent

PRESENT SUBJUNCTIVE

je	serve
tu	serves
il/elle/on	serve
nous	servions
vous	serviez
ils/elles	servent

PERFECT

j'	ai servi
tu	as servi
il/elle/on	a servi
nous	avons servi
vous	avez servi
ils/elles	ont servi

IMPERFECT

je	servais
tu	servais
il/elle/on	servait
nous	servions
vous	serviez
ils/elles	servaient

FUTURE

je	servirai
tu	serviras
il/elle/on	servira
nous	servirons
vous	servirez
ils/elles	serviront

CONDITIONAL

je	servirais
tu	servirais
il/elle/on	servirait
nous	servirions
vous	serviriez
ils/elles	serviraient

IMPERATIVE

sers / servons / servez

PAST PARTICIPLE

servi

PRESENT PARTICIPLE

servant

EXAMPLE PHRASES

*On vous **sert**?* Are you being served?
*Ça **sert** à quoi ce bouton?* What is this button for?
***Servez-vous** en viande.* Help yourself to meat.

⟹ *See pages 88–91 for information on how to form the reflexive verb **se servir**.*

---

je/j' = I **tu** = you **il** = he/it **elle** = she/it **on** = we/one **nous** = we **vous** = you **ils/elles** = they

▶ sortir (to go out)

PRESENT

je	sors
tu	sors
il/elle/on	sort
nous	sortons
vous	sortez
ils/elles	sortent

PRESENT SUBJUNCTIVE

je	sorte
tu	sortes
il/elle/on	sorte
nous	sortions
vous	sortiez
ils/elles	sortent

PERFECT

je	suis sorti(e)
tu	es sorti(e)
il/elle/on	est sorti(e)
nous	sommes sorti(e)s
vous	êtes sorti(e)(s)
ils/elles	sont sorti(e)s

IMPERFECT

je	sortais
tu	sortais
il/elle/on	sortait
nous	sortions
vous	sortiez
ils/elles	sortaient

FUTURE

je	sortirai
tu	sortiras
il/elle/on	sortira
nous	sortirons
vous	sortirez
ils/elles	sortiront

CONDITIONAL

je	sortirais
tu	sortirais
il/elle/on	sortirait
nous	sortirions
vous	sortiriez
ils/elles	sortiraient

IMPERATIVE

sors / sortons / sortez

PAST PARTICIPLE

sorti

PRESENT PARTICIPLE

sortant

EXAMPLE PHRASES

*Je ne **suis** pas **sortie** ce week-end.* I didn't go out this weekend.
*Aurélie **sort** avec Bruno.* Aurélie is going out with Bruno.
*Elle **est sortie** de l'hôpital hier.* She came out of hospital yesterday.
*Je n'**ai** pas **sorti** le chien parce qu'il pleuvait.* I didn't take the dog out for a walk
  because it was raining.

ⓘ Note that **sortir** takes **avoir** in the perfect tense when it is used with a direct
  object; see page 114.

je/j' = I **tu** = you **il** = he/it **elle** = she/it **on** = we/one **nous** = we **vous** = you **ils/elles** = they

▶ suffire (to be enough)

PRESENT

je	suffis
tu	suffis
il/elle/on	suffit
nous	suffisons
vous	suffisez
ils/elles	suffisent

PRESENT SUBJUNCTIVE

je	suffise
tu	suffises
il/elle/on	suffise
nous	suffisions
vous	suffisiez
ils/elles	suffisent

PERFECT

j'	ai suffi
tu	as suffi
il/elle/on	a suffi
nous	avons suffi
vous	avez suffi
ils/elles	ont suffi

IMPERFECT

je	suffisais
tu	suffisais
il/elle/on	suffisait
nous	suffisions
vous	suffisiez
ils/elles	suffisaient

FUTURE

je	suffirai
tu	suffiras
il/elle/on	suffira
nous	suffirons
vous	suffirez
ils/elles	suffiront

CONDITIONAL

je	suffirais
tu	suffirais
il/elle/on	suffirait
nous	suffirions
vous	suffiriez
ils/elles	suffiraient

IMPERATIVE

suffis / suffisons / suffisez

PAST PARTICIPLE

suffi

PRESENT PARTICIPLE

suffisant

EXAMPLE PHRASES

Ça te suffira, 10 euros? Will 10 euros be enough?
Ça suffit! That's enough!
Il suffisait de me le demander. You only had to ask.

je/j' = I **tu** = you **il** = he/it **elle** = she/it **on** = we/one **nous** = we **vous** = you **ils/elles** = they

▶ **suivre** (to follow)

PRESENT

je	suis
tu	suis
il/elle/on	suit
nous	suivons
vous	suivez
ils/elles	suivent

PRESENT SUBJUNCTIVE

je	suive
tu	suives
il/elle/on	suive
nous	suivions
vous	suiviez
ils/elles	suivent

PERFECT

j'	ai suivi
tu	as suivi
il/elle/on	a suivi
nous	avons suivi
vous	avez suivi
ils/elles	ont suivi

IMPERFECT

je	suivais
tu	suivais
il/elle/on	suivait
nous	suivions
vous	suiviez
ils/elles	suivaient

FUTURE

je	suivrai
tu	suivras
il/elle/on	suivra
nous	suivrons
vous	suivrez
ils/elles	suivront

CONDITIONAL

je	suivrais
tu	suivrais
il/elle/on	suivrait
nous	suivrions
vous	suivriez
ils/elles	suivraient

IMPERATIVE

suis / suivons / suivez

PAST PARTICIPLE

suivi

PRESENT PARTICIPLE

suivant

EXAMPLE PHRASES

*Mon chat me **suit** partout dans la maison.* My cat follows me everywhere around the house.
*Il **a suivi** un cours d'allemand pendant six mois.* He did a German course for 6 months.
*Elles n'arrivent pas à **suivre** en maths.* They can't keep up in maths.

▶ **se taire** (to stop talking)

PRESENT

je	me tais
tu	te tais
il/elle/on	se tait
nous	nous taisons
vous	vous taisez
ils/elles	se taisent

PERFECT

je	me suis tu(e)
tu	t'es tu(e)
il/elle/on	s'est tu(e)
nous	nous sommes tu(e)s
vous	vous êtes tu(e)(s)
ils/elles	se sont tu(e)s

FUTURE

je	me tairai
tu	te tairas
il/elle/on	se taira
nous	nous tairons
vous	vous tairez
ils/elles	se tairont

IMPERATIVE

tais-toi / taisons-nous / taisez-vous

PRESENT PARTICIPLE

se taisant

PRESENT SUBJUNCTIVE

je	me taise
tu	te taises
il/elle/on	se taise
nous	nous taisions
vous	vous taisiez
ils/elles	se taisent

IMPERFECT

je	me taisais
tu	te taisais
il/elle/on	se taisait
nous	nous taisions
vous	vous taisiez
ils/elles	se taisaient

CONDITIONAL

je	me tairais
tu	te tairais
il/elle/on	se tairait
nous	nous tairions
vous	vous tairiez
ils/elles	se tairaient

PAST PARTICIPLE

tu

EXAMPLE PHRASES

Il s'est tu. He stopped talking.
Taisez-vous! Be quiet!
Sophie, tais-toi! Be quiet Sophie!

---

je/j' = I   **tu** = you   **il** = he/it   **elle** = she/it   **on** = we/one   **nous** = we   **vous** = you   **ils/elles** = they

▶ tenir (to hold)

PRESENT

je	tiens
tu	tiens
il/elle/on	tient
nous	tenons
vous	tenez
ils/elles	tiennent

PRESENT SUBJUNCTIVE

je	tienne
tu	tiennes
il/elle/on	tienne
nous	tenions
vous	teniez
ils/elles	tiennent

PERFECT

j'	ai tenu
tu	as tenu
il/elle/on	a tenu
nous	avons tenu
vous	avez tenu
ils/elles	ont tenu

IMPERFECT

je	tenais
tu	tenais
il/elle/on	tenait
nous	tenions
vous	teniez
ils/elles	tenaient

FUTURE

je	tiendrai
tu	tiendras
il/elle/on	tiendra
nous	tiendrons
vous	tiendrez
ils/elles	tiendront

CONDITIONAL

je	tiendrais
tu	tiendrais
il/elle/on	tiendrait
nous	tiendrions
vous	tiendriez
ils/elles	tiendraient

IMPERATIVE

tiens / tenons / tenez

PAST PARTICIPLE

tenu

PRESENT PARTICIPLE

tenant

EXAMPLE PHRASES

Tiens-moi la main. Hold my hand.
*Elle **tenait** beaucoup à son chat.* She was really attached to her cat.
Tiens, prends mon stylo. Here, have my pen.
Tiens-toi droit! Sit up straight!

⇨ *See pages 88–91 for information on how to form the reflexive verb **se tenir**.*

je/j' = I tu = you il = he/it elle = she/it on = we/one nous = we vous = you ils/elles = they

▶ tomber (to fall)

PRESENT

je	tombe
tu	tombes
il/elle/on	tombe
nous	tombons
vous	tombez
ils/elles	tombent

PERFECT

je	suis tombé(e)
tu	es tombé(e)
il/elle/on	est tombé(e)
nous	sommes tombé(e)s
vous	êtes tombé(e)(s)
ils/elles	sont tombé(e)s

FUTURE

je	tomberai
tu	tomberas
il/elle/on	tombera
nous	tomberons
vous	tomberez
ils/elles	tomberont

IMPERATIVE

tombe / tombons / tombez

PRESENT PARTICIPLE

tombant

PRESENT SUBJUNCTIVE

je	tombe
tu	tombes
il/elle/on	tombe
nous	tombions
vous	tombiez
ils/elles	tombent

IMPERFECT

je	tombais
tu	tombais
il/elle/on	tombait
nous	tombions
vous	tombiez
ils/elles	tombaient

CONDITIONAL

je	tomberais
tu	tomberais
il/elle/on	tomberait
nous	tomberions
vous	tomberiez
ils/elles	tomberaient

PAST PARTICIPLE

tombé

EXAMPLE PHRASES

*Attention, tu vas **tomber**!* Be careful, you'll fall!
*Nicole **est tombée** de cheval.* Nicole fell off her horse.
*Elle s'est fait mal en **tombant** dans l'escalier.* She hurt herself falling down the stairs.

---

je/j' = I **tu** = you **il** = he/it **elle** = she/it **on** = we/one **nous** = we **vous** = you **ils/elles** = they

▶ **traire** (to milk)

PRESENT

je	trais
tu	trais
il/elle/on	trait
nous	trayons
vous	trayez
ils/elles	traient

PRESENT SUBJUNCTIVE

je	traie
tu	traies
il/elle/on	traie
nous	trayions
vous	trayiez
ils/elles	traient

PERFECT

j'	ai trait
tu	as trait
il/elle/on	a trait
nous	avons trait
vous	avez trait
ils/elles	ont trait

IMPERFECT

je	trayais
tu	trayais
il/elle/on	trayait
nous	trayions
vous	trayiez
ils/elles	trayaient

FUTURE

je	trairai
tu	trairas
il/elle/on	traira
nous	trairons
vous	trairez
ils/elles	trairont

CONDITIONAL

je	trairais
tu	trairais
il/elle/on	trairait
nous	trairions
vous	trairiez
ils/elles	trairaient

IMPERATIVE

trais / trayons / trayez

PAST PARTICIPLE

trait

PRESENT PARTICIPLE

trayant

EXAMPLE PHRASES

*À la ferme, on a appris à **traire** les vaches.* We learnt to milk cows on the farm.
*Elle **trait** les vaches à six heures du matin.* She milks the cows at 6 am.

---

je/j' = I **tu** = you **il** = he/it **elle** = she/it **on** = we/one **nous** = we **vous** = you **ils/elles** = they

▶ **vaincre** (to defeat)

PRESENT

je	vaincs
tu	vaincs
il/elle/on	vainc
nous	vainquons
vous	vainquez
ils/elles	vainquent

PRESENT SUBJUNCTIVE

je	vainque
tu	vainques
il/elle/on	vainque
nous	vainquions
vous	vainquiez
ils/elles	vainquent

PERFECT

j'	ai vaincu
tu	as vaincu
il/elle/on	a vaincu
nous	avons vaincu
vous	avez vaincu
ils/elles	ont vaincu

IMPERFECT

je	vainquais
tu	vainquais
il/elle/on	vainquait
nous	vainquions
vous	vainquiez
ils/elles	vainquaient

FUTURE

je	vaincrai
tu	vaincras
il/elle/on	vaincra
nous	vaincrons
vous	vaincrez
ils/elles	vaincront

CONDITIONAL

je	vaincrais
tu	vaincrais
il/elle/on	vaincrait
nous	vaincrions
vous	vaincriez
ils/elles	vaincraient

IMPERATIVE

vaincs / vainquons / vainquez

PAST PARTICIPLE

vaincu

PRESENT PARTICIPLE

vainquant

EXAMPLE PHRASES

*L'armée **a été vaincue**.* The army was defeated.
*La France **a vaincu** la Corée trois buts à deux.* France beat Korea 3 goals to 2.

je/j' = I **tu** = you **il** = he/it **elle** = she/it **on** = we/one **nous** = we **vous** = you **ils/elles** = they

▶ valoir (to be worth)

PRESENT

je	vaux
tu	vaux
il/elle/on	vaut
nous	valons
vous	valez
ils/elles	valent

PERFECT

j'	ai valu
tu	as valu
il/elle/on	a valu
nous	avons valu
vous	avez valu
ils/elles	ont valu

FUTURE

je	vaudrai
tu	vaudras
il/elle/on	vaudra
nous	vaudrons
vous	vaudrez
ils/elles	vaudront

IMPERATIVE

vaux / valons / valez

PRESENT PARTICIPLE

valant

PRESENT SUBJUNCTIVE

je	vaille
tu	vailles
il/elle/on	vaille
nous	valions
vous	valiez
ils/elles	vaillent

IMPERFECT

je	valais
tu	valais
il/elle/on	valait
nous	valions
vous	valiez
ils/elles	valaient

CONDITIONAL

je	vaudrais
tu	vaudrais
il/elle/on	vaudrait
nous	vaudrions
vous	vaudriez
ils/elles	vaudraient

PAST PARTICIPLE

valu

EXAMPLE PHRASES

Ça **vaut** combien? How much is it worth?
Ça **vaudrait** la peine d'essayer. It would be worth a try.
Il **vaut** mieux ne pas y penser. It's best not to think about it.

▶ vendre (to sell)

PRESENT

je	vends
tu	vends
il/elle/on	vend
nous	vendons
vous	vendez
ils/elles	vendent

PRESENT SUBJUNCTIVE

je	vende
tu	vendes
il/elle/on	vende
nous	vendions
vous	vendiez
ils/elles	vendent

PERFECT

j'	ai vendu
tu	as vendu
il/elle/on	a vendu
nous	avons vendu
vous	avez vendu
ils/elles	ont vendu

IMPERFECT

je	vendais
tu	vendais
il/elle/on	vendait
nous	vendions
vous	vendiez
ils/elles	vendaient

FUTURE

je	vendrai
tu	vendras
il/elle/on	vendra
nous	vendrons
vous	vendrez
ils/elles	vendront

CONDITIONAL

je	vendrais
tu	vendrais
il/elle/on	vendrait
nous	vendrions
vous	vendriez
ils/elles	vendraient

IMPERATIVE

vends / vendons / vendez

PAST PARTICIPLE

vendu

PRESENT PARTICIPLE

vendant

EXAMPLE PHRASES

Il m'a vendu son vélo pour 50 euros. He sold me his bike for 50 euros.
Est-ce que vous vendez des piles? Do you sell batteries?
Elle voudrait vendre sa voiture. She would like to sell her car.

je/j' = I **tu** = you **il** = he/it **elle** = she/it **on** = we/one **nous** = we **vous** = you **ils/elles** = they

▶ venir (to come)

PRESENT

je	viens
tu	viens
il/elle/on	vient
nous	venons
vous	venez
ils/elles	viennent

PERFECT

je	suis venu(e)
tu	es venu(e)
il/elle/on	est venu(e)
nous	sommes venu(e)s
vous	êtes venu(e)(s)
ils/elles	sont venu(e)s

FUTURE

je	viendrai
tu	viendras
il/elle/on	viendra
nous	viendrons
vous	viendrez
ils/elles	viendront

IMPERATIVE

viens / venons / venez

PRESENT PARTICIPLE

venant

PRESENT SUBJUNCTIVE

je	vienne
tu	viennes
il/elle/on	vienne
nous	venions
vous	veniez
ils/elles	viennent

IMPERFECT

je	venais
tu	venais
il/elle/on	venait
nous	venions
vous	veniez
ils/elles	venaient

CONDITIONAL

je	viendrais
tu	viendrais
il/elle/on	viendrait
nous	viendrions
vous	viendriez
ils/elles	viendraient

PAST PARTICIPLE

venu

EXAMPLE PHRASES

*Elle ne **viendra** pas cette année.* She won't be coming this year.
*Fatou et Malik **viennent** du Sénégal.* Fatou and Malik come from Senegal.
*Je **viens** de manger.* I've just eaten.

---

je/j' = I **tu** = you **il** = he/it **elle** = she/it **on** = we/one **nous** = we **vous** = you **ils/elles** = they

▶ vêtir (to dress)

PRESENT

je	vêts
tu	vêts
il/elle/on	vêt
nous	vêtons
vous	vêtez
ils/elles	vêtent

PERFECT

j'	ai vêtu
tu	as vêtu
il/elle/on	a vêtu
nous	avons vêtu
vous	avez vêtu
ils/elles	ont vêtu

FUTURE

je	vêtirai
tu	vêtiras
il/elle/on	vêtira
nous	vêtirons
vous	vêtirez
ils/elles	vêtiront

IMPERATIVE

vêts / vêtons / vêtez

PRESENT PARTICIPLE

vêtant

PRESENT SUBJUNCTIVE

je	vête
tu	vêtes
il/elle/on	vête
nous	vêtions
vous	vêtiez
ils/elles	vêtent

IMPERFECT

je	vêtais
tu	vêtais
il/elle/on	vêtait
nous	vêtions
vous	vêtiez
ils/elles	vêtaient

CONDITIONAL

je	vêtirais
tu	vêtirais
il/elle/on	vêtirait
nous	vêtirions
vous	vêtiriez
ils/elles	vêtiraient

PAST PARTICIPLE

vêtu

EXAMPLE PHRASES

Il *était vêtu* d'un pantalon et d'un pull. He was wearing trousers and a jumper.
Il faut se lever, se laver et *se vêtir* en 10 minutes. You have to get up, get washed and get dressed in 10 minutes.

▷ See pages 88–91 for information on how to form the reflexive verb *se vêtir*.

je/j' = I **tu** = you **il** = he/it **elle** = she/it **on** = we/one **nous** = we **vous** = you **ils/elles** = they

▶ **vivre** (to live)

PRESENT

je	vis
tu	vis
il/elle/on	vit
nous	vivons
vous	vivez
ils/elles	vivent

PRESENT SUBJUNCTIVE

je	vive
tu	vives
il/elle/on	vive
nous	vivions
vous	viviez
ils/elles	vivent

PERFECT

j'	ai vécu
tu	as vécu
il/elle/on	a vécu
nous	avons vécu
vous	avez vécu
ils/elles	ont vécu

IMPERFECT

je	vivais
tu	vivais
il/elle/on	vivait
nous	vivions
vous	viviez
ils/elles	vivaient

FUTURE

je	vivrai
tu	vivras
il/elle/on	vivra
nous	vivrons
vous	vivrez
ils/elles	vivront

CONDITIONAL

je	vivrais
tu	vivrais
il/elle/on	vivrait
nous	vivrions
vous	vivriez
ils/elles	vivraient

IMPERATIVE

vis / vivons / vivez

PAST PARTICIPLE

vécu

PRESENT PARTICIPLE

vivant

EXAMPLE PHRASES

Ma sœur vit en Espagne. My sister lives in Spain.
Il a vécu dix ans à Lyon. He lived in Lyons for 10 years.
Les gorilles vivent surtout dans la forêt. Gorillas mostly live in the forest.

---

je/j' = I   **tu** = you   **il** = he/it   **elle** = she/it   **on** = we/one   **nous** = we   **vous** = you   **ils/elles** = they

▶ **voir** (to see)

PRESENT

je	vois
tu	vois
il/elle/on	voit
nous	voyons
vous	voyez
ils/elles	voient

PRESENT SUBJUNCTIVE

je	voie
tu	voies
il/elle/on	voie
nous	voyions
vous	voyiez
ils/elles	voient

PERFECT

j'	ai vu
tu	as vu
il/elle/on	a vu
nous	avons vu
vous	avez vu
ils/elles	ont vu

IMPERFECT

je	voyais
tu	voyais
il/elle/on	voyait
nous	voyions
vous	voyiez
ils/elles	voyaient

FUTURE

je	verrai
tu	verras
il/elle/on	verra
nous	verrons
vous	verrez
ils/elles	verront

CONDITIONAL

je	verrais
tu	verrais
il/elle/on	verrait
nous	verrions
vous	verriez
ils/elles	verraient

IMPERATIVE

vois / voyons / voyez

PAST PARTICIPLE

vu

PRESENT PARTICIPLE

voyant

EXAMPLE PHRASES

*Venez me **voir** quand vous serez à Paris.* Come and see me when you're in Paris.
*Je ne **vois** rien sans mes lunettes.* I can't see anything without my glasses.
*Est-ce que tu l'**as vu**?* Did you see him? or Have you seen him?
*Est-ce que cette tache **se voit**?* Does that stain show?

⇨ *See pages 88–91 for information on how to form the reflexive verb **se voir**.*

---

je/j' = I **tu** = you **il** = he/it **elle** = she/it **on** = we/one **nous** = we **vous** = you **ils/elles** = they

▶ **vouloir** (to want)

PRESENT

je	veux
tu	veux
il/elle/on	veut
nous	voulons
vous	voulez
ils/elles	veulent

PRESENT SUBJUNCTIVE

je	veuille
tu	veuilles
il/elle/on	veuille
nous	voulions
vous	vouliez
ils/elles	veuillent

PERFECT

j'	ai voulu
tu	as voulu
il/elle/on	a voulu
nous	avons voulu
vous	avez voulu
ils/elles	ont voulu

IMPERFECT

je	voulais
tu	voulais
il/elle/on	voulait
nous	voulions
vous	vouliez
ils/elles	voulaient

FUTURE

je	voudrai
tu	voudras
il/elle/on	voudra
nous	voudrons
vous	voudrez
ils/elles	voudront

CONDITIONAL

je	voudrais
tu	voudrais
il/elle/on	voudrait
nous	voudrions
vous	voudriez
ils/elles	voudraient

IMPERATIVE

veuille / veuillons / veuillez

PAST PARTICIPLE

voulu

PRESENT PARTICIPLE

voulant

EXAMPLE PHRASES

*Elle **veut** un vélo pour Noël.* She wants a bike for Christmas.
*Ils **voulaient** aller au cinéma.* They wanted to go to the cinema.
*Tu **voudrais** une tasse de thé?* Would you like a cup of tea?

je/j' = I **tu** = you **il** = he/it **elle** = she/it **on** = we/one **nous** = we **vous** = you **ils/elles** = they

How to use the Verb Index

The verbs in bold are the model verbs which you will find in the Verb Tables. All the other verbs follow one of these patterns, so the number next to each verb indicates which pattern fits this particular verb. For example, **aider** (*to help*) follows the same pattern as **donner** (number 29 in the Verb Tables).

All the verbs are in alphabetical order. For reflexive verbs like **s'asseoir** (*to sit down*) or **se taire** (*to stop talking*), look under **asseoir** or **taire**, not under **s'** or **se**.

Superior numbers (¹, ² etc) refer you to notes on page 105. These notes explain any differences between the verbs and their model.

With the exception of reflexive verbs which *always* take être, all verbs have the same auxiliary (**être** or **avoir**) as their model verb. There are a few exceptions which are indicated by a superior number ¹ or ².

An asterisk (*) means that the verb takes **avoir** when it is used with a direct object, and **être** when it isn't.

⇨ For more information on verbs that take either **avoir** or **être**, see page 114.

abaisser	29	accomplir	39	adorer	29	aiguiser	29
abandonner	29	accorder	29	adosser	29	aimanter	29
abattre	10	accoter	29	adoucir	39	aimer	29
abêtir	39	accoucher	29	adresser	29	ajouter	29
abîmer	29	accouder (s')	29	advenir³	90	ajuster	29
abolir	39	accourir⁵	17	aérer	35	alarmer	29
abonder	29	accoutumer	29	affaiblir	39	alerter	29
abonner	29	accrocher	29	affairer (s')	29	alimenter	29
aborder	29	accroître⁶	22	affaisser (s')	29	allécher	35
aboutir	39	accroupir (s')	39	affamer	29	alléger	67
aboyer	54	accueillir	23	affermir	39	alléguer	35
abréger	67	accumuler	29	afficher	29	aller	4
abreuver	29	accuser	29	affirmer	29	allier	20
abriter	29	acharner (s')	29	affliger	46	allumer	29
abrutir	39	acheminer	29	affoler	29	altérer	35
absenter (s')	29	acheter	2	affranchir	39	alterner	29
absorber	29	achever	44	affréter	35	alunir	39
absoudre⁴	71	acquérir	3	affronter	29	amaigrir	39
abstenir (s')	84	actionner	29	agacer	13	ambitionner	29
abstraire	86	activer	29	agenouiller (s')	29	améliorer	29
abuser	29	adapter	29	agir	39	aménager	46
accabler	29	additionner	29	agiter	29	amener	44
accaparer	29	adhérer	35	agrandir	39	ameuter	29
accéder	35	adjoindre	43	agréer	19	amincir	39
accélérer	35	admettre	48	ahurir	39	amoindrir	39
accepter	29	admirer	29	aider	29	amollir	39
accompagner	29	adopter	29	aigrir	39	amonceler	5

amorcer	13	assembler	29	balader (se)	29	bouffir	39
amplifier	20	assener	44	balafrer	29	bouger	46
amputer	29	**asseoir** (s')	**7**	balancer	13	**bouillir**	**12**
amuser	29	asservir	39	balayer	60	bouleverser	29
analyser	29	assiéger	67	balbutier	20	boulonner	29
anéantir	39	assigner	29	baliser	29	bourdonner	29
angoisser	29	assimiler	29	bannir	39	bourrer	29
animer	29	assister	29	baptiser	29	boursoufler	29
annexer	29	associer	20	baratiner	29	bousculer	29
annoncer	13	assombrir	39	barbouiller	29	bousiller	29
annoter	29	assommer	29	barioler	29	boutonner	29
annuler	29	assortir	39	barrer	29	braconner	29
anoblir	39	assoupir	39	barricader	29	brailler	29
anticiper	29	assouplir	39	basculer	29	braire[7]	86
apaiser	29	assourdir	39	baser	29	brancher	29
apercevoir	68	assujettir	39	batailler	29	brandir	39
apitoyer	54	assumer	29	batifoler	29	branler	29
aplatir	39	assurer	29	bâtir	39	braquer	29
apparaître[2]	57	astiquer	29	**battre**	**10**	braver	29
appareiller	29	astreindre	61	bavarder	29	bredouiller	29
apparenter	29	atermoyer	54	baver	29	breveter	5
apparier	20	attabler (s')	29	bêcher	29	bricoler	29
appartenir	84	attacher	29	becqueter	42	brider	29
appauvrir	39	attaquer	29	bégayer	60	briguer	29
appeler	**5**	atteindre	61	bêler	29	briller	29
applaudir	39	atteler	5	bénéficier	20	brimer	29
appliquer	29	**attendre**	**8**	bénir	39	briser	29
apporter	29	attendrir	39	bercer	13	broder	29
apprécier	20	atterrir	39	berner	29	broncher	29
apprendre	66	attirer	29	beugler	29	brosser	29
apprêter	29	attraper	29	beurrer	29	brouiller	29
apprivoiser	29	attribuer	29	biaiser	29	broyer	54
approcher	29	augmenter	29	bichonner	29	brûler	29
approfondir	39	autoriser	29	biffer	29	brunir	39
approprier	20	avachir (s')	39	blaguer	29	buter	29
approuver	29	avaler	29	blâmer	29	cabrer (se)	29
appuyer	54	avancer	13	blanchir	39	cacher	29
arc-bouter	29	avantager	46	blaser	29	cadrer	29
argenter	29	aventurer	29	blêmir	39	cajoler	29
arguer	29	avertir	39	blesser	29	calculer	29
armer	29	aveugler	29	bloquer	29	caler	29
arpenter	29	avilir	39	blottir (se)	39	câliner	29
arracher	29	aviser	29	**boire**	**11**	calmer	29
arranger	46	aviver	29	boiter	29	calomnier	20
arrêter	29	**avoir**	**9**	bombarder	29	calquer	29
arriver	**6**	avouer	29	bondir	39	camper	29
arrondir	39	bâcler	29	bonifier	20	capituler	29
arroser	29	bafouer	29	border	29	capter	29
asphyxier	20	bagarrer (se)	29	borner	29	captiver	29
aspirer	29	baigner	29	boucher	29	capturer	29
assagir	39	bâiller	29	boucler	29	caractériser	29
assainir	39	baiser	29	bouder	29	caresser	29
assassiner	29	baisser	29	bouffer	29	caricaturer	29

caser	29	coincer	13	conseiller	29	crépir	39
casser	29	coïncider	29	consentir	78	creuser	29
cataloguer	29	collaborer	29	considérer	35	crever	44
catapulter	29	collectionner	29	consister	29	cribler	29
causer	29	coller	29	consoler	29	**crier**	**20**
céder	35	coloniser	29	consolider	29	critiquer	29
ceindre	61	colorer	29	consommer	29	crocheter	2
célébrer	35	colorier	20	conspirer	29	**croire**	**21**
celer	2	combattre	10	constater	29	croiser	29
censurer	29	combler	29	consterner	29	**croître**	**22**
cercler	29	commander	29	constituer	29	crouler	29
certifier	20	commémorer	29	construire	24	croupir	39
cesser	29	**commencer**	**13**	consulter	29	crucifier	20
chagriner	29	commettre	48	contacter	29	**cueillir**	**23**
chahuter	29	communier	20	contaminer	29	**cuire**	**24**
chamailler	29	communiquer	29	contempler	29	culbuter	29
chanceler	5	comparaître	57	contenir	84	cultiver	29
changer	46	comparer	29	contenter	29	cumuler	29
chanter	29	compenser	29	conter	29	curer	29
chantonner	29	complaire	63	contester	29	daigner	29
charger	46	compléter	35	continuer	29	damner	29
charmer	29	complimenter	29	contraindre	18	danser	29
charrier	20	compliquer	29	contrarier	20	dater	29
chasser	29	comporter	29	contraster	29	débarquer	29
châtier	20	composer	29	contredire	28	débarrasser	29
chatouiller	29	composter	29	contrefaire	37	débattre	10
chauffer	29	comprendre	66	contrevenir[1]	90	débaucher	29
chausser	29	compromettre	48	contribuer	29	débiliter	29
chercher	29	compter	29	contrôler	29	débiter	29
chérir	39	concéder	35	convaincre	87	déblatérer	35
chiffrer	29	concentrer	29	convenir[1]	90	débloquer	29
choisir	39	concerner	29	convertir	39	déboîter	29
chômer	29	concevoir	68	convier	20	déborder	29
choquer	29	concilier	20	convoquer	29	déboucher	29
choyer	54	**conclure**	**14**	coopérer	35	débourser	29
chuchoter	29	concourir	17	copier	20	déboutonner	29
circoncire[8]	81	concurrencer	13	correspondre	70	débrailler (se)	29
circonscrire	31	condamner	29	corriger	46	débrancher	29
circonvenir[1]	90	condenser	29	corrompre	76	débrayer	60
circuler	29	condescendre[1]	25	corroyer	54	débrouiller	29
cirer	29	conduire	24	côtoyer	54	débuter	29
ciseler	2	conférer	35	coucher	29	décaler	29
citer	29	confier	20	**coudre**	**16**	décanter	29
clarifier	20	confire[9]	81	couler	29	décaper	29
classer	29	confirmer	29	couper	29	décapoter	29
classifier	20	confisquer	29	courber	29	décéder[2]	35
cligner	29	confondre	70	**courir**	**17**	déceler	2
clignoter	29	conforter	29	coûter	29	décélérer	35
clouer	29	congédier	20	couvrir	56	décentraliser	29
coder	29	congeler	2	cracher	29	décerner	29
codifier	20	**connaître**	**15**	craindre	18	décevoir	68
cogner	29	conquérir	3	craquer	29	déchaîner	29
coiffer	29	consacrer	29	**créer**	**19**	décharger	46

disposer	29	effaroucher	29	endormir (s')	30	envoler (s')	29
disputer	29	effectuer	29	enduire	24	**envoyer**	**34**
dissocier	20	effeuiller	29	endurcir	39	épandre	89
dissoudre[12]	71	effondrer	29	énerver	29	épanouir	39
distendre	89	efforcer (s')	13	enfanter	29	épargner	29
distinguer	29	effrayer	60	enfermer	29	éparpiller	29
distordre	50	égaler	29	enfiler	29	épater	29
distraire	86	égarer	29	enflammer	29	épeler	5
distribuer	29	égayer	60	enfler	29	éplucher	29
diversifier	20	égorger	46	enfoncer	13	éponger	46
diviser	29	élaborer	29	enfouir	39	épouser	29
divorcer	13	élancer (s')	13	enfreindre	61	épouvanter	29
donner	**29**	élargir	39	enfuir (s')	40	épreindre	61
dormir	**30**	électrifier	20	engager	46	éprendre (s')	66
doubler	29	élever	44	engloutir	39	éprouver	29
douter	29	éliminer	29	engourdir	39	épuiser	29
dresser	29	élire	45	engraisser	29	équilibrer	29
durcir	39	éloigner	29	engueuler	29	équiper	29
durer	29	éluder	29	enivrer	29	équivaloir	88
ébahir (s')	39	émanciper	29	enjoliver	29	esclaffer (s')	29
ébattre (s')	10	émaner	29	enlacer	13	escorter	29
ébaucher	29	embarrasser	29	enlever	44	**espérer**	**35**
éblouir	39	embaucher	29	enneiger	46	esquisser	29
ébranler	29	embellir	39	ennuyer	54	esquiver	29
écarteler	2	emboîter	29	énoncer	13	essayer	60
écarter	29	embourgeoiser (s')	29	enquérir (s')	3	essorer	29
échanger	46	embrasser	29	enquêter	29	essouffler	29
échapper	29	émerger	46	enraciner	29	essuyer	54
échauder	29	émettre	48	enrager	46	estimer	29
échauffer	29	émigrer	29	enregistrer	29	estropier	20
échelonner	29	emménager	46	enrichir	39	établir	39
échouer	29	emmener	44	enrouler	29	étaler	29
éclabousser	29	**émouvoir**	**32**	enseigner	29	étayer	60
éclaircir	39	emparer (s')	29	ensevelir	39	éteindre	61
éclairer	29	empêcher	29	ensuivre (s')[3]	82	étendre	89
éclater	29	empiéter	35	entamer	29	éternuer	29
éclipser	29	empirer	29	entasser	29	étiqueter	42
écœurer	29	emplir	39	entendre	89	étirer	29
éconduire	24	employer	54	enterrer	29	étoffer	29
économiser	29	empoisonner	29	enthousiasmer	29	étonner	29
écorcher	29	emporter	29	entourer	29	étouffer	29
écouler	29	emprisonner	29	entraîner	29	étourdir	39
écouter	29	emprunter	29	entraver	29	étrangler	29
écraser	29	encadrer	29	entrelacer	13	**être**	**36**
écrémer	35	encaisser	29	entremettre (s')	48	étreindre	61
écrier (s')	20	enchaîner	29	entreprendre	66	étudier	20
écrire	**31**	enchanter	29	**entrer***	**33**	évader (s')	29
écrouler (s')	29	encombrer	29	entretenir	84	évaluer	29
édifier	20	encourager	46	entrevoir	93	évanouir (s')	39
éditer	29	encourir	17	énumérer	35	évaporer	29
éduquer	29	endetter	29	envahir	39	éveiller	29
effacer	13	endoctriner	29	envelopper	29	éventer	29
effarer	29	endommager	46	envisager	46	évertuer (s')	29

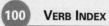

immoler	29	intituler	29	lubrifier	20	meurtrir	39
impatienter	29	intriguer	29	lutter	29	miauler	29
impliquer	29	introduire	24	mâcher	29	mijoter	29
implorer	29	inventer	29	machiner	29	mimer	29
importer	29	invertir	39	magnifier	20	miner	29
impressionner	29	investir	39	maigrir	39	minimiser	29
imprimer	29	inviter	29	maintenir	84	mobiliser	29
improviser	29	invoquer	29	maîtriser	29	modeler	2
inaugurer	29	irriter	29	majorer	29	modérer	35
inciter	29	isoler	29	malfaire	37	moderniser	29
incliner	29	jaillir	39	malmener	44	modifier	20
inclure[16]	14	jaser	29	maltraiter	29	moisir	39
incommoder	29	jaunir	39	**manger**	**46**	moissonner	29
incorporer	29	**jeter**	**42**	manier	20	mollir	39
incriminer	29	jeûner	29	manifester	29	monnayer	60
inculper	29	**joindre**	**43**	manigancer	13	monopoliser	29
indiquer	29	jouer	29	manipuler	29	**monter***	**49**
induire	24	jouir	39	manœuvrer	29	montrer	29
infecter	29	juger	46	manquer	29	moquer (se)	29
infester	29	jumeler	5	manufacturer	29	**mordre**	**50**
infirmer	29	jurer	29	manutentionner	29	morfondre (se)	70
infliger	46	justifier	20	marcher	29	mortifier	20
influencer	13	labourer	29	marier	20	motiver	29
informer	29	lacer	13	marquer	29	moucher	29
ingénier (s')	20	lâcher	29	marteler	2	**moudre**	**51**
inhaler	29	laisser	29	masquer	29	mouiller	29
initier	20	lamenter (se)	29	massacrer	29	**mourir**	**52**
injurier	20	lancer	13	masser	29	mouvoir[17]	32
innover	29	languir	39	matérialiser	29	muer	29
inoculer	29	larmoyer	54	**maudire**	**47**	multiplier	20
inonder	29	laver	29	maugréer	19	munir	39
inquiéter	35	lécher	35	mécaniser	29	mûrir	39
inscrire	31	légaliser	29	méconnaître	15	murmurer	29
insensibiliser	29	légiférer	35	mécontenter	29	museler	5
insérer	35	lésiner	29	médire	28	muter	29
insinuer	29	**lever**	**44**	méditer	29	mutiler	29
insister	29	libérer	35	méfaire	37	mystifier	20
inspecter	29	licencier	20	méfier (se)	20	nager	46
inspirer	29	lier	20	mélanger	46	**naître**	**53**
installer	29	ligoter	29	mêler	29	nantir	39
instituer	29	limer	29	menacer	13	narrer	29
instruire	24	limiter	29	ménager	46	naviguer	29
insulter	29	liquéfier	20	mendier	20	navrer	29
insurger (s')	46	liquider	29	mener	44	nécessiter	29
intégrer	35	**lire**	**45**	mentionner	29	négliger	46
intensifier	20	livrer	29	mentir	78	négocier	20
intercéder	35	loger	46	méprendre (se)	66	neiger	46
interdire	28	lorgner	29	mépriser	29	**nettoyer**	**54**
intéresser	29	lotir	39	mériter	29	nier	20
interloquer	29	loucher	29	mesurer	29	niveler	5
interroger	46	louer	29	**mettre**	**48**	noircir	39
interrompre	76	louper	29	meubler	29	nommer	29
intervenir	90	louvoyer	54	meugler	29	normaliser	29

Notes

1) Auxiliary = **avoir**.

2) Auxiliary = **être**.

3) Only infinitive and 3rd persons of each tense used.

4) Past participle: **absous, absoute**.

5) Conjugated with either **avoir** or **être**.

6) No circumflex on: **j'accrois, tu accrois**, and **accru**.

7) Hardly used except in the infinitive and the 3rd persons of the present, future and conditional.

8) Past participle: **circoncis**.

9) Past participle: **confit**.

10) No circumflex on: **je décrois, tu décrois**, and **décru**.

11) When **demeurer** means *to live*, the auxiliary is **avoir**; when it means *to remain*, the auxiliary is **être**.

12) Past participle: **dissous, dissoute**.

13) Present participle: **faillant**; past participle: **failli**; future: **je faillirai**, *etc*; conditional: **je faillirais**, *etc*. NB: **J'ai failli tomber** = I nearly fell.

14) When **fleurir** means *to prosper*, the present participle is **florissant**, and the imperfect is **florissait**.

15) Past participle: **frit**; used mainly in the present tense singular and in compound tenses.

16) Past participle: **inclus**.

17) Past participle: **mû, mue, mus, mues**.

18) Past participle: **nui**.

19) In questions, **je peux** can be replaced by **je puis**: **Puis-je vous aider?** May I help you?

20) Subjunctive: **je prévale**, *etc*.

21) Future: **je prévoirai**, *etc*; conditional: **je prévoirais**, *etc*.

22) Used only in the infinitive, present and past participles, and compound tenses.

23) Past participle: **relui**.

24) No past participle, no compound tenses.

MORE FANTASTIC TITLES IN THE
COLLINS EASY LEARNING FRENCH RANGE:

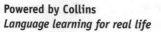

Easy Learning French Dictionary
ISBN 978-0-00-733149-9

Easy Learning French Grammar
ISBN 978-0-00-736782-5

Easy Learning French Verbs
ISBN 978-0-00-736974-4

Easy Learning French Idioms
ISBN 978-0-00-733735-4

Easy Learning French Conversation
ISBN 978-0-00-722974-1

Easy Learning French Words
ISBN 978-0-00-723159-1

Easy Learning Complete French
ISBN 978-0-00-729941-6

Brand new title, available from March 2011:
Easy Learning French Grammar & Practice
ISBN 978-0-00-739139-4

NEW

The bestselling Collins Easy Learning range also includes Spanish, Italian, German, Irish, Polish and Chinese titles. For further information visit **www.collinslanguage.com**

Want to see for yourself?
Go online to
www.livemocha.com/trial
and enter this code:
A2GQ-2T50-0PQC-Z5JE

About Livemocha
Livemocha redefines language learning by combining dynamic online courses in over 30 languages with the world's largest community of language learners. Livemocha has over 7 million members from over 190 countries.

FREE TRIAL OF
LIVEMOCHA ACTIVE FRENCH

Powered by Collins
Language learning for real life

Livemocha Active French is an innovative and effective online course that will teach you to speak French in real-life situations. The course combines world-class content from Collins with the world's largest community of language learners on Livemocha.

- Real French conversation videos, with subtitles in both English and French
- Grammar and vocabulary exercises to build your skills and measure your progress
- Speaking and writing practice and feedback from native French speakers

Collins and Livemocha reserve the right to withdraw this free trial offer at any time